The Millennials
on Film and
Television

The Millennials on Film and Television

Essays on the Politics of Popular Culture

Edited by
BETTY KAKLAMANIDOU *and*
MARGARET TALLY

McFarland & Company, Inc., Publishers
Jefferson, North Carolina

LIBRARY OF CONGRESS CATALOGUING-IN-PUBLICATION DATA

The Millennials on film and television : essays on the politics of popular culture / edited by Betty Kaklamanidou and Margaret Tally.
    p.   cm.

Includes bibliographical references and index.

ISBN 978-0-7864-7880-4 (softcover: acid free paper) ∞
ISBN 978-1-4766-1514-1 (ebook)

1. Generation Y—United States. 2. Popular culture—United States. I. Kaklamanidou, Betty, 1972– editor of compilation. II. Tally, Margaret, 1960– editor of compilation.

HQ799.7.M545 2014
305.2—dc23
                                            2014001995

BRITISH LIBRARY CATALOGUING DATA ARE AVAILABLE

© 2014 Betty Kaklamanidou and Margaret Tally. All rights reserved

No part of this book may be reproduced or transmitted in any form or by any means, electronic or mechanical, including photocopying or recording, or by any information storage and retrieval system, without permission in writing from the publisher.

On the cover: cast of *The Big Bang Theory*, 2012, shown from left: Melissa Rauch, Simon Helberg, Johnny Galecki, Kaley Cuoco, Jim Parsons, Mayim Bialik, Kunal Nayyar (CBS/Photofest)

Manufactured in the United States of America

McFarland & Company, Inc., Publishers
* Box 611, Jefferson, North Carolina 28640*
* www.mcfarlandpub.com*

To my Usual Suspects:
Petros, Eleni, Lia, Nick and little Dimitris!
—Betty

To my incredible and insightful daughters,
Lila and Serena, who embody the hope and
optimism of the millennial generation.
—Margaret

Table of Contents

Introduction: The Twenty-First Century Generation and the ABC Family Brand (Betty Kaklamanidou and Margaret Tally) — 1

Secrets and Lies: Gender and Generation in the ABC Family Brand (Caryn Murphy) — 15

Lavender Identity and Representation in the Media: The Portrayal of Gays and Lesbians in Popular Television (Sean Robinson and Bernice Alston) — 31

Exploring Discourses of Engagement in *2 Broke Girls* (Alison N. Novak) — 46

The Mindy Project: South Asians and Television Multiculturalism (Janani Subramanian) — 62

The Big Bang Theory: Nerds and Kidults (Janice Shaw) — 78

The Emotional Power of Technology, Community and Morality in *The Vampire Diaries* (Margo Collins) — 94

Generational Conflict, Twenty-First-Century Horror Films and *The Cabin in the Woods* (Karen J. Renner) — 110

The Scream of a Generation: "Generation Me" in *Scream 4* (Sotiris Petridis) — 126

"Comedy Natives": Generations, Humor and the Question of Why Smart + Funny Is the New Rock and Roll (Margaret Tally) — 140

The Romantico-Sexual Narrative and Intertextuality in *Friends with Benefits* and *No Strings Attached* (BETTY KAKLAMANIDOU) 155

Labor Narratives and *The Devil Wears Prada* (CHRISTOPH BÜETTNER) 169

Works Cited 185
About the Contributors 197
Index 199

Introduction

The Twenty-First Century Generation and the ABC Family Brand

BETTY KAKLAMANIDOU *and* MARGARET TALLY

While this collection was being prepared, we came across a couple of episodes of *Kate & Allie* (CBS, 1984–1989), a popular as well as critically acclaimed series that represented two divorced moms tackling their lives with their three children in a New York brownstone in the Village. Despite the almost 30 years between the broadcast of the episodes in question (both first aired in January 1986) and the time these lines are being written, what struck us most were the overwhelming similarities we found when it comes to popular culture representations of generational conflicts in U.S. culture. In episode 15 of season 3, entitled "Too Late the Rebel," there is a sit-in at Allie's (Jane Curtin) university instigated by a young Ben Stiller in his first appearance as an actor. The students oppose the university's investment in a chemical company which was indicted over pollution violations, as they consider the university's involvement unethical. Kate (Susan Saint James) enters the dean's office in search of Allie and urges the students to sit in based on what she did in the 1960s. Two generations confronted; the baby boomers, and more specifically, the hippies and radicals of the 1960s and 1970s and Generation X who had begun to establish themselves as the yuppies. Kate considers the kids less active, more afraid than they were in the 1960s, while the kids seem to respect both women.

In episode 12 of the same season, entitled "Dark Victory," Kate finds herself alone at the dentist's office during a blackout and arranges a "blind" date with a man she meets in the dark without knowing he is black. Both George (David L. King) and Kate feel awkward during their date and once they're back at Kate's, she asks him if they're both bigots. George is much calmer and self-composed and tells Kate that despite them being the "rebel" generation of the 1970s, they have now become "comfortable, middle-aged conservatives who don't break the rules."

Kate cannot fathom that it's been more than 20 years since she protested against what she believed was unjust and George comforts her by claiming that "they're "too old for certain things but [...] not exactly [their] own parents either." Kate realizes that their date was not a great idea and tells George that Jenny and Emma, Kate's and Allie's teenage daughters, "thought it was really fabulous that [they] were going out" and hopes that "their kids won't even notice" racial difference in the future.

Two major conclusions can be made. First, each generation usually perceives the younger generation as "different," and usually inferior in specific ways—Kate the radical and passionate 1960s rebel finds the younger generation "less active" and perhaps more obedient to authority. Second, each generation tends to stop "progressing" after a certain numbers of years have passed and its members have settled in their ways—regarding every sector of their life—although Kate believes in racial equality and has perhaps fought for it, she cannot bring herself to enter an interracial relationship and leaves this "obstacle" for hers and Allie's teenage daughter to overcome. Naturally, these conclusions are based on a fictional script which bears a mild conservatism, obeying the rules of U.S. network broadcasts, while promoting feminist issues at the same time.[1] On the other hand, these observations bear a striking resemblance to most research and critiques on both the generation of baby boomers and that of Generation X.[2]

According to most academic studies, each generation is characterized by specific, unique traits that are directly influenced by the sociopolitical climate of their time. Thus, the baby boomers enjoyed prosperity and influenced culture and politics while Generation Xers were initially viewed with skepticism and even hostility. To complicate matters further, the social sciences do not provide a binding definition for the term "generation," nor for the appropriate and/or exact year of birth for an individual to be part of this or that grouping, nor a single historical event that could mark the beginning or end of a given generational category. What is more, scholarly research on generations, whether it is conducted from an anthropological, sociological, and/or historical perspective, usually constitutes the outcome of the work of middle-class, middle-aged, Caucasian academics. This perspective can potentially limit the scope of the examination to their own subjective experience, which in turn could possibly end up excluding a more thorough examination, one which takes into account a generational analysis based on age, race, ethnicity, or class which might then reveal different attitudes, perspectives, and statistics. We make this point now as we both belong to this somewhat limiting category of individuals; as Caucasian, heterosexual, middle-class scholars (albeit one GenXer from Greece and one baby boomer from the United States), we can only observe or comment on racial, geographical or class issues of representation that involve heterosexual, white, middle-class individuals.

This collection does not presume to present any absolute definition or propose a definite theory. Instead, we aim to provide a specific examination of the representations of the millennial generation on U.S. film and television. Some of the questions that led us to this volume are: Who are the millennials? What, if anything, distinguishes them from previous generations? Is it their numbers, their common collective memory, their abilities? What unites them? Is it the internet and social media? Is it the economic recession spread all over the world? What are their likes and dislikes? Are the millennials more progressive or is their liberalism just a phase due to their young age? Are they bored and selfish, as they are sometimes accused of, or is it the economically insecure social context they find themselves in that drives them to indifference? Is money the only motive behind their professional choices or are they looking for a job that will satisfy their creative aspirations as well? Is the "hook-up" a new trend in romantic relationships or just a short-term fad? Are their representations in the media true or false, if we take into account that their overwhelming majority is constructed by GenXers and Baby Boomers? To what extent are they themselves a social construction of the media, a way to create a specific group who can then be marketed to, based on a certain set of assumptions about their likes and dislikes?

Sociopolitical Context and Major Characteristics

The new millennium has fascinated scholars, scientists and artists alike long before it became a reality. Although the year 2000 did not in fact signal the end of the world as neither did the year 2012, it is now more than evident that this new era, marked by crisis, uncertainty, and loss, can be paralleled to what precedes death and signifies a new beginning. What Jean Comaroff and John L. Comaroff (2000: 292) call "messianic, millennial capitalism" is often identified as the culprit behind the turbulent times millions of individuals find themselves trapped in. Neoliberal practices, such as the re-organization of economies so that the rich acquire more while the poor continue to lose what little they had, the weakening of labor power and unions as well as the delegitimization of "state interventionism" (Mark Blyth 122), led to a wide range of social impasses and/or conflicts in both Europe as well as the United States. As we move towards the middle of the millennium's second decade, most countries in the western world are struggling with long-term financial crises and/or recessions and their consequent societal conflicts. These conflicts revolve around the re-emergence of a clearly defined societal stratification that separates individuals on a whole host of levels, including those arising from ethnic and national differences; migrant workers versus legal citizens; minorities based on their sexual differences, and so on.

Nevertheless, there is another group of individuals who constitute a larger group and who, taken together, were significantly impacted by the policies put into place in the western world during the last two decades. This group of individuals for whom "the modernist ideal in which each generation does better than its predecessor" cannot become a reality is known as *Generation Y*, the *Net Generation* or simply *Millennials* (Comaroff and Comaroff 2000: 306).

The millennials, who are the largest generation in America's history, resist a simple definition. However, a number of general characteristics can be drawn: these 20-something young men and women (millennials are defined as those individuals who were born between 1984 and 1992 and who came of age after 2000) never knew a world without a wide array of technological devices at their disposal (internet connection, mobile phones, apps, etc.). This exposure to and comfort with technology has also translated into their being exposed to a steady diet of media. Perhaps because of this experience, or as Todd Gitlin has referred to it in the subtitle of his 2001 book, *Media Unlimited*, of "the torrent of images and sounds (that) overwhelms our lives," one of the effects of this saturation is to create a sense of irony about the very possibility for authentic communication. While most millennials can communicate instantaneously, then, through a multiplicity of technological devices, they no longer trust that these communicative acts have any real meaning attached to them.

The millennials also share the distinction of being the most educated generation in American history. Nevertheless, despite their education, they have delayed their careers, in no small part because the economy has eroded the sense that there are jobs available to match their intended careers. It's hard to launch a career, in other words, unless one sets out to be a service worker, such as a barista at a local Starbucks. This generation, who were born between the presidencies of Bush I and Clinton, and who came of age between Presidents Bush II and Obama, view politics and societal norms with skepticism;

they tend to marry later in life; stay at home well after their eighteenth birthdays, and are aware of the fact that the recent financial crisis and more general economic malaise of the last five years will deter them from reaching the middle class status that their parents were able to attain. Downward mobility is a defining feature of this group, which again is a first in recent American history (Pew 2010).

The cultural, social and political importance of this generation is evident in several new studies that attempt to delineate the twenties as a separate and unique period in an individual's psychosocial development. Just as adolescence was acknowledged as a key stage of physiological and psychological changes in a person's life, in the beginning of the twentieth century with the publication of Stanley G. Hall's groundbreaking study, *Adolescence: Its Psychology, and Its Relations to Physiology, Anthropology, Sociology, Sex, Crime, Religion, and Education* (Timothy Shary 1), millennials today are understood as being representative of a stage of life which has been newly coined "emergent adulthood." This stage, first described by psychologist Jeffrey Arnett in response to a similar pattern he saw emerging from his patients in this age group, is characterized by the following: exploration of identity; feelings of instability; a focus on the self; feeling in-between stages of life; and finally, a feeling of the possibilities of life, and a kind of optimism. These series of character traits translate into a prolonged dependence on parents and relatives as well as a kind of generalized vagueness and lack of clarity about their life goals and purposes in life.

Representing a New Type of Individual

As is often the case in contemporary popular culture, the U.S. film and television industries adapted their representations of twenty-something characters to fit the new social data. Our preliminary findings reveal that television shows that feature millennials as main characters abound, from the female centered *New Girl* (Fox, 2011–present), *The Mindy Project* (Fox, 2012–present), *Don't Trust the B---- in Apt. 23* (ABC, 2011–2012), *Girls* (HBO, 2012–present), and *2 Broke Girls* (CBS, 2011–present), to the ensemble *Happy Endings* (ABC, 2011–2013), *Rules of Engagement* (CBS, 2007–2013), *Underemployed* (MTV, 2012–present), *How I Met Your Mother* (CBS, 2005–present), and the short-lived *Partners* (ABC, 2012), and the family sitcoms *Raising Hope* (Fox, 2010–present), *Ben and Kate* (Fox, 2012–2013), all place twenty-something heroes and heroines at the center of their narratives. They portray millennials dealing with such myriad issues as the politics of personal development, work, gender, social class and race, among others. Similarly, films such as *Friends with Benefits* (2011), *No Strings Attached* (2011), *Confessions of a Shopaholic* (2009), *Knocked Up* (2007), *Just Like Heaven* (2005), and *The Devil Wears Prada* (2006) center on millennial characters and focus mainly on the female audience, addressing the ways millennials view romantic relationships.

These fictional narratives, taken together, lead to a number of preliminary characteristics shared by their millennial protagonists, which will constitute the basis of the ensuing essays' in-depth analysis. These characteristics include, among others: a shift in values toward seeing themselves as strongly tied to their use of technology; a generation that is the least religious and has had the least experience of exposure to wartime service of any generation in history; unlike the Boomers, they possess a high degree of comfort with their parents and a strong sense of self-esteem, based on parental support; they are more concerned with parenthood and marriage over work, even as they marry in fewer numbers than other generations. Romantically, they tend to prefer "hook-ups," that is, a casual and indeterminate connection to others sexually which is not so much about the inability to find intimacy with another person as it is about a kind of prolongation of "dating," with benefits. In terms of their outlook toward life, they possess a high degree of optimism (despite the largest number of unemployed people in their age cohort since the Great Depression), as well as a kind of openness to/acceptance of different ethnicities and sexualities, and a sense that there are endless possibilities (Pew). In short, representations of millennials on film and television are fascinating and complex, as they represent not so much a specific age group as a projection, in the realm of fiction, of how our culture has tried to construct this specific historical group.

Interestingly enough, despite the recent psychological and sociological studies on the millennials, as well as their coverage in recent news and popular presses, there is still no study which specifically examines the fictional representations of this generation. We argue that a detailed analysis and investigation of the narratives that center on millennials could result in significant observations regarding the characteristics, behaviors and attitudes of these young people. Are millennials unique? If not, do cycles repeat themselves? If they are, what distinguishes them from previous generations? Do the representations of millennials in films and TV shows, that mostly serve as sites of contestation for conversations about the generations and young people, end up recycling the same issues? Who owns the process of creation in the culture industries? Is it the elders who are trying to capture the younger market? If so, what does this mean in terms of the images that are produced?

In some sense, this collection is an extended conversation on the merits and drawbacks of the bifurcation of this group into a simple dichotomy of "Generation Me" or "Generation We," and most of the work being done in interpretation of the cultural texts is to show that these representations are themselves created or constructed. The true millennial, in this sense, is both/and, not either/or. And the best cultural artifacts capture this duality. So, our collection offers a way to interrogate the images, how they are constructed, as well as how they are participating in larger cultural and societal conversations about the world that the millennials are inheriting. This world has and will continue to be shaped by three oftentimes countervailing forces: the economy, technology and global climate change and the environment. Many of the stories we are reading about in popular culture on the millennials are shaped by these forces.

We believe that this collection is timely and arguably long overdue. Because there is a relatively thin bibliography regarding the representation of this vast age group in popular film and television, including its particular characteristics relative to the previous Generation X as well as the Boomers, we think that our scholarly contribution could fill a lacuna and could be of value to scholars as well as a more general audience. In sum, we think this demographic is fascinating and deserves serious attention, both for their choices as individuals and for the world they find themselves trying to navigate.

Theory, Methodology, Goals

Our collection draws on a multiplicity of theoretical frameworks, which taken together, might best be understood as a critical cultural studies approach to popular film and television. Each essay represents a different theoretical approach in this vein, and rather than make them conform into one unified whole, it is more helpful to understand them as attempting to grasp the meaning of the programs and films from a variety of perspectives. These different approaches, whether they focus on the audience; the text; the production and industry; the gender, racial or class politics or the literary and aesthetic meanings of the cultural "products," together help to reveal how theory can decipher how millennials are portrayed in contemporary popular culture (Jim Collins et al. 2–3).

We do not presume to be objective in our orientation, furthermore, or even celebratory of millennial representations, because they are somehow "popular," and therefore what the people want. Rather, we hope to explore the hegemonic underpinnings of these images and to take a position with respect to the practices involved in the creation of these representations. This being said, the essays do not try to force meanings onto some predetermined ideological framework but rather draw on these important theoretical traditions to help make sense of these contemporary depictions of the millennials.

In addition to thinking about the theoretical perspectives the essays draw on, it is also important to point out that we don't view these cultural images as occurring in isolation from other cultural practices and artifacts. If there is one thing that the millennials have taught us is that they themselves embed their viewing of cultural products within a steady stream of alternate media. In reading these essays, then, it immediately becomes apparent that whatever the theoretical approach they take, they help the reader place these narratives within the lived experience of the millennials themselves as avid consumers of multiple platforms. For example, most millennials have said that they use their computers to stream their favorite television programs. This small screen approach could usefully be taken into account when thinking about the intimate space that they are viewing shows on, and the perhaps individualized viewing that takes place when millennials watch a show with their earphones on from their computers. They may also be shifting back and forth from one screen to another during the commercials, checking Facebook or looking down at texts on their smartphone. All of these social acts complicate not only the reception of the films and programs, but may also reveal some really interesting perspectives concerning the ways in which the shows may be being produced with these distracted viewing habits in mind. It may be that critical theories of forms of production of cultural products could benefit from understanding these distractions and could help to explain why the programs contain a lot of exaggerated or over-the-top humor as a strategy to keep the millennials from switching to another platform.

In sum, what we are aiming for in this book is not one grand, unifying theory which could explain all of the programs and films which depict the millennials. We hope to show how these cultural products work at a number of levels, and through a variety of means, to shape our understanding of the millennials. In so doing, we can move toward a fuller conception of how cultural products work to create social meanings, which ultimately have very real political and social consequences.

The Essays

The essays are organized around two main mediums, television and film, between which there are many similarities as well as some striking differences. In the first essay, "Secrets and Lies: Gender and Generation in the ABC Family Brand," Caryn Murphy offers an analysis of the ways in which mainstream cable television channels try to market and brand their material to capture specific audiences. This kind of niche marketing is a departure from earlier practices of creating programs that would appeal to a mass audience. Murphy focuses specifically on the ABC Family channel and the ways in which it has tried to re-define its target audience to include millennials, with a special emphasis on millennial young women. By creating young female protagonists who are working through issues of identity, and in particular, white, middle-class young women, ABC Family has set out to create a brand that will attract this demographic group. At the same time, Murphy demonstrates how these television programs draw upon contemporary cultural discourses around young women as empowered subjects and in control of their own fate, thereby arguably tapping into other popular culture narratives of the neoliberal subject who can create their own identity and in fact, are responsible for their own fate.

Continuing the discussion of the ways in which television tries to draw on contemporary discourses to encourage brand identification with their programs, Sean Robinson and Bernice Alston explore the ways in which LGBTQ millennials are becoming more prominent in television shows directed towards millennials in "Lavender Identity and Representation in the Media: The Portrayal of Gays and Lesbians in Popular Television." Whereas some of the representations of LGBTQ characters border on stereotypes, there are also new pathways being opened up in terms of offering more realistic portrayals of the experience of being outside the dominant normative hetero universe of adolescence and young adulthood. Robinson and Alston also argue that these images have taken on new meanings not only for the heterosexual population who are being exposed to more diversity in the sexual orientation of characters, but for young people who are questioning their own sexuality, and are finding these narratives useful in identifying and coming to terms with their own complicated feelings about their sexual identities.

In "Exploring Discourses of Engagement in *2 Broke Girls*," Alison N. Novak explores more deeply the question of how millennials are framed in contemporary popular discourses as supposedly apathetic about politics and more generally, about their life prospects. Using the CBS situation comedy *2 Broke Girls* as a case study, Novak compares the two main characters and finds that the stereotype of millennials as somehow disengaged is tied to the class status of the two characters. Novak concludes that we need a much more nuanced understanding of the categories of engagement as opposed to apathy and that active disengagement is a useful distinction to understand how young millennial women, especially those who are working class, are trying to survive economically in a very depressed economy. Young millennial women who are from the middle and upper-middle class, by contrast, are far more optimistic that they could be the authors of their own fate, whatever their current economic reality is.

Questions around social identity can be found in Janani Subramanian's essay, "*The Mindy Project*: South Asians and Television Multiculturalism." The comedienne Mindy Kaling plays a South Asian gynecologist who is always in search of romance in one of the first television shows that predominantly features a woman of color. Subramanian examines the cultural assumptions within this portrayal and finds that the character embodies all of the tensions that millennials of color feel in this generation. From her analysis of the show, Subramanian finds that the main character's self-consciousness, as well as the supporting characters' reactions to her, reveal a kind of double consciousness, one that superficially acknowledges her differences while at the same time disavows this multiculturalsim. Subramanian traces this ambivalence to the larger American culture post–9/11 and explores how difficult it has been for people of South Asian identity to come to terms with their own ethnicity in the wake of the devastation wrought by 9/11.

The ways in which millennials occupy the popular imagination can also be seen in the recent television program *The Big Bang Theory*. Taking the conventional stereotype of the "nerd" in popular culture, Janice Shaw explores how the millennial nerd is represented in "*The Big Bang Theory*: Nerds and Kidults." Drawing on recent literature about "emerging adulthood," Shaw finds that the characters on the show embody all the qualities previously associated with childhood and adolescence. The four characters forego traditional social arrangements including marriage and children in favor of a communal life based on common interests and a consumer-based lifestyle. At the same time, they also embrace careers that are far from that of traditional work occupations and settings, so that their nerdiness can find expression in a non–9-to-5 lifestyle with jobs that are tied to their fascination with technology and science. The nerd stereotype signals for Shaw the adoption by millennials of a life where there is little attention paid to the traditional trappings of adulthood, and instead a kind of freedom from the kinds of responsibilities that earlier generations of twenty-somethings had to come to terms with.

Drawing on the notion that millennials are trying to construct their own identities in part through appropriating earlier characteristics, such as those embodied by the nerd, Margo Collins echoes this idea of self-transformation in "The Emotional Power of Technology, Community and Morality in *The Vampire Diaries*." Within the poles of characterizing the millennials as either "Generation Me" or "Generation We," Collins lands squarely in the "Generation We" camp, and notes the ways in which current televisions shows for millennials that have a vampire theme, such as *The Vampire Diaries*, portray millennials as committed to their peers and willing to sacrifice themselves for the good of the whole. At the same time, however, Collins finds that there is a kind of moral individualism demonstrated by these millennial characters, in the sense that they believe that they are not in a position to judge the actions of others and are morally relativistic. This is where she locates the idea that millennials are responding to actions and events from an emotional or subjective viewpoint and that the vampires in these programs adopt this kind of perspective as well. In a fascinating reversal, Collins finds that, unlike earlier narratives about vampires who change the world they enter, the millennials in these contemporary narratives change the vampire himself instead.

Continuing with this theme of how genres adapt to the prevailing cultural and historical moment they are in, Karen J. Renner applies this concept to a close reading of the slasher film in "Generational Conflict, Twenty-First-Century Horror Films and *The Cabin in the Woods*." The film, which is both an homage as well as an overturning of earlier slasher and horror films, offers a portrait of generational conflict where the older generation, who were once the victims in these films in the 1970s and 1980s, have now become the perpetrators, responsible for engineering the deaths of the millennials on behalf of "the Ancient Ones." Renner locates this victimization of the millennials in the film to a larger cultural stereotype of them as somehow selfish, lazy and focused on themselves to the exclusion of others, thereby fitting conveniently within the "Generation Me" camp. For Renner, however, the construction of millennials in popular culture as self-absorbed repeats earlier stereotypes of young people as egocentric, which each generation who came before them inevitably charges young people with. In this way, millennials end up being not so different than earlier generations, and the traits that we identify as being unique to them may in fact be part of a larger cultural pathologizing of young people. In this way, Renner offers the possibility that these slasher films which victimize millennials are ultimately a mirror of the current trend in society of demonizing them. Why our culture needs to engage in this kind of generation bashing becomes the central question which echoes through many of these chapters.

The theme of millennials as selfish, technologically oriented and obsessed with social media as a form of self-promotion continues in the next essay, by Sotiris Petridis, "The Scream of a Generation: 'Generation Me' in *Scream 4*." Petridis does a case study of the *Scream* franchise and finds that, interestingly enough, the first three films offered an incisive portrait of Generation X, the so-called generation that came before the millennials. However, by the time that *Scream 4* is made, the millennials are firmly in place in popular culture, and like Renner before him, Petridis finds that the millennial characters are portrayed in a negative light. Fifteen years (the fourth installment was made in 2011) and a generation later have reversed the portrait of the young people in the film from being focused on supporting one another to in fact critiquing them for their supposed selfishness and obsession with their own 15 minutes of fame. Like Renner, Petridis finds that these representations of millennials, repeated in *The Cabin in the Woods* as well as *Scream 4*, reveal something deeper about how contemporary culture views this younger generation and that the portrait of millennials in such a negative light ends up reproducing earlier representations of young people as not being up to the task of becoming adults.

Trying to trace the ways in which millennials have been defined in the larger culture, co-editor Margaret Tally's "'Comedy Natives': Generations, Humor and the Question of Why Smart + Funny Is the New Rock and Roll" focuses on recent narratives in popular culture that frame millennials as having a unique sense of humor. By exploring some cultural artifacts, such as television shows on the cable channel Comedy Central, which cater specifically to the male millennial market, to recent gross-out films such as *The Hangover* franchise, Tally finds that millennials are being aggressively marketed to through a process of deliberate branding of them as being humorous, first and foremost. Where the baby boomers were arguably targeted based on their love of rock and roll music, the millennials are branded as responding to their lives, and by extension, their consumer and aesthetic tastes, through the medium of humor. To the extent that millennial women are allowed to participate in this media landscape, through recent television shows such as *2 Broke Girls*, *Girls*, *The Mindy Project* and films such as *Bridesmaids*, Tally finds that they too are targeted through humor. This humor, in turn, which is raunchy and oftentimes vulgar, is assumed to be of a fundamentally different order from earlier forms of humor. In this way, the millennials are constructed in the larger culture as both distinct from earlier generations and as an identifiable market that can be branded through their use of humor as a way to define themselves.

The question of whether millennials are indeed unique or, as Renner and Petridis find, part of a larger cultural narrative that repeats over generations, is taken up in Betty Kaklamanidou's essay, "The Romantico-Sexual Narrative and Intertextuality in *Friends with Benefits* and *No Strings Attached*." Here, the focus shifts from the horror genre to that of romantic comedies, and the ways in which millennials are portrayed as having sexual encounters that can be seen as more casual than earlier generations. The question Kaklamanidou poses, through a careful reading of two contemporary romantic comedies, *Friends with Benefits* and *No Strings Attached*, is whether these kinds of new relationships, where the sex is supposedly unmoored from any form of romantic attachment, constitutes a new evolution of the romantic comedy genre. By deploying both genre and contemporary gender theories and finding that they are lacking in terms of grasping the full complexity of the contemporary male/female entanglements, Kaklamanidou instead maps out the new gender terrain that is being explored in these millennial narratives.

In addition to relationships, the problem of how millennials will come to terms with their identity as laboring subjects is also being interrogated, and the ways in which they attempt to make sense of their working lives in relation to the rest of their lives is also an open question for this generation. Christoph Büettner covers this terrain in "Labor Narratives and *The Devil Wears Prada*." Whereas the young women of *Girls* are portrayed as eschewing the traditional 9-to-5 workday, and the young women in *2 Broke Girls* are similarly trying to survive in a service economy with fragmented hours and unstable pay, the character of Andy in *The Devil Wears Prada* finds herself confronting an altogether different dilemma in relation to her worklife. The requirements of her job mirror what Büettner finds transpiring in the larger culture, where individuals are asked to give up not only their hours in their private lives to be a good worker, but indeed, must become identified with the work itself. This loss of the self to the job, where one's very personality is appropriated in order to do the job well, is for Büettner part of a larger discourse happening in society around the idea of the neoliberal subject in late capitalism.

Taken together, these essays offer us a rich and complex portrait of not only the representations of millennials in contemporary popular discourses, but more broadly, an exploration into the ways that our culture engages in these kinds of generational conversations as a vehicle for making sense of their lived realities. That is why, though seemingly superficial or light-hearted, popular narratives can help us to understand how the stories we tell ourselves through these cultural artifacts reveal our own anxieties, ambivalences, but ultimately, hopes for the possibility of social transformation. In this way, these stories, and the characters who make them come alive, offer us a crucial vantage point from which to observe the links between our hopes for the future and the present-day realities that may be preventing us from realizing those dreams.

Notes

1. For more on *Kate & Allie*, see Lynn C. Spangler (151–156).
2. For more information on the baby boomers see, among others, Doug Owram and Marty Gitlin. For more information on Generation X, see, among others, Christina Lee and Stephen C. Craig, and Stephen Earl Bennett.

Secrets and Lies

Gender and Generation in the ABC Family Brand

CARYN MURPHY

In a 1965 episode of the ABC sitcom *Gidget* (1965–1966), the fifteen-year-old heroine invests in a car and enrolls in an auto mechanics course so that she can learn to take care of it. This plot is framed by the character's frustration with young men her age, and her socially proscribed role as a dependent. Gidget's (Sally Field) attempt to learn auto maintenance is read as a threat to the appropriate gender order. As the only young woman in the class, Gidget becomes an easy target for the disapprobation of her male peers. They collude to make her "more equal than equal," demonstrating that she is physically incapable of performing tasks that they complete with ease, while socially reliant on the codes of chivalry. The conflict resolves when Gidget spots her salvation in the form of a soft drink advertisement that depicts a beautiful woman, elevated and admired by a crowd of young men. The scene quickly cuts away to Gidget twirling in a dress, having showered away the residue of her experiment with independence. In the final moments, Gidget explains her revelation directly to the camera, and thus the home audience: "Life sure is simple when you quit trying to complicate it. No woman is ever really helpless as long as there's a man around ... and she remembers she's a woman" (1.06, "A Hearse, A Hearse, My Kingdom for a Hearse"). The thread that runs through the episode's narrative is the objective fact of a gendered social order that benefits everyone; this is not far afield from other representations of gender anxieties in broadcast network sitcoms of the 1960s.

What is interesting is that this plot was effectively repeated in the ABC Family channel's sitcom *10 Things I Hate About You* (2009–2010),[1] almost 45 years later. The series' heroine Kat (Lindsey Shaw), a strident feminist, decides to convert her car to one with a biodiesel engine. She joins the all-male milieu of her high school's auto shop class, where her peers bet against her probability of success (1.05, "Don't Give Up").

There are similarities in these narratives and the industrial imperatives that produced them. In the 1960s, the ABC network aired *Gidget* as part of a larger strategy to target a younger group of viewers than CBS and NBC were reaching out to (Bill Osgerby 73); in the 2000s, the ABC Family channel designed its brand around targeting young women, employing programming and marketing strategies that were honed at the WB and the CW in the broadcast arena. Both *Gidget* and *10 Things* feature a teen girl heroine who marks the series' specific address to female viewers. Television executives assume that programs with female protagonists will be more likely to resonate with female viewers, and thus the narrative design of these shows indicates a desire to connect with this audience. In each half hour sitcom, the teen girl heroine is being raised by a caring and attentive single father, which helps to characterize her autonomy and relative independence; she is an adolescent, but she is also the "woman of the house."[2] And in episodes airing nearly 45 years apart, each series participated in the discourse of feminism—albeit in different ways.

Kat, the millennial heroine of *10 Things*, is physically and mentally capable. The concept of feminism has informed her life for as long as she can remember. Kat is independent, but driven by a desire to prove not just something about herself, but about women in general. She is encouraged by her best friend Mandella, who is portrayed by an Asian-American actress of size, Jolene Purdy. Kat is also an environmentalist, and committed to converting to biodiesel because she has come to view driving a gas guzzling car as a hypocritical practice. In order to undertake her mission, she goes online and downloads instructions; the accessibility of information is a key aspect of the character's independence and capability. Working alone, Kat grows frustrated and consults her father, but the narrative avoids easy answers here. Although Kat's father is an educated person, his expertise is in medicine and not mechanics; he offers to help her, but she has to guide him in interpreting the instructions. When she completes the conversion, the young men who bet against her do not hold a grudge. One young man tells the triumphant Kat, "Now I'm even more in love with you," and the entire group of boys applauds her as she drives out of the garage. Kat's expression of activism wins her the respect of her male peers, rather than their derision.

The ABC Family channel targets millennial women as a desirable niche audience, and their programming demonstrates a specific conception of this demographic. Millennials, born between approximately 1980 and 2000, are conceptualized by the network as diverse, engaged with global concerns, particularly environmentalism, and technologically adept, shaped by the influence of the internet and new media ("Getting to Know" A1–A4). Each of these aspects are in play in the aforementioned episode of *10 Things*, in addition to an unabashed commitment to gender equity that the narrative shores up through the heroine's triumph in a quest that is clearly framed as a "battle of the sexes." In contrast to the 1960s narrative, *10 Things* does not offer viewers an admonition or a cautionary tale in which the heroine's success in one arena is tempered by failure in another; here, the heroine wins and everyone celebrates. This essay argues that ABC Family has employed demographic research on millennials to establish its brand identity, reflecting their dominant ideology back at this generation in order to sell them products. I examine the industrial strategies that ABC Family has employed to target young women, and the correlation between this approach and the channel's representations of millennial women as empowered subjects.

"Identifying Gaps in the Marketplace": Cable Follows a Broadcast Model

Throughout its brief history, the ABC Family channel has been closely tied to the programming and target market strategies that were honed at the WB, a U.S. broadcast network that operated from 1995 to 2006. The WB had a smaller reach than the major broadcasters in the national market (NBC, CBS, ABC, Fox) and so it worked to establish itself by serving small segments of the overall audience who were desirable targets for advertisers. The WB emerged during the time period that Amanda Lotz has identified as the "multi-channel transition," in which the development of broadcast and cable alternatives were drawing viewers away from the major networks (12–13). As a broadcaster, The WB aired more hours of original prime-time programming and attracted larger audiences than advertiser-supported cable channels. Although cable channels targeted niche audiences at this time, they typically used a small amount of original programming to complement schedules of off-network syndicated series and Hollywood movies. The trends of the "neo-network era" have been examined by media scholar Michael Curtin, who argues that conglomerates have responded to the threat of competition and decreased productivity by shifting their business practices towards flexibility in production and distribution (186). The culture industries have employed two major strategies to maximize performance within these economic conditions; they offer mass media for global or national markets and they target niche audiences with media designed to encourage intense identification and devotion (Curtin 197).[3]

Although the WB network was not profitable, it was considered successful in its efforts to target 12-to-34-year-old women, a demographic that was both attractive to advertisers and difficult to reach through other broadcast networks. The WB served this specific audience in the interests of its conglomerate parent, Time Warner; similarly, ABC Family targets this niche in support of the overall market strategies employed by its corporate parent, Disney. In this section, I discuss the origins of ABC Family and the evolution of its millennial branding strategy in relation to the programming and practices of the WB.

The cable channel that is now called ABC Family has been held by multiple owners and attempted multiple audience targeting strategies since its inception as the Christian Broadcasting Network (CBN) in 1977. CBN, the first basic-cable network to be disseminated via satellite, was founded by Christian conservative Marion "Pat" Robertson. In the 1960s, Robertson had purchased a number of UHF stations that he used to establish a television ministry. His signature program, *The 700 Club,* offers a conservative Christian response to issues of the day; it premiered in 1966 and still airs on the ABC Family channel through contractual agreement, although Robertson's ministry is no longer involved in the channel's ownership (Michael Schneider 16). The channel's identity began to evolve when Pat Robertson's son took over management responsibilities in 1987, the result of his father's presidential campaign. Tim Robertson felt The Family Channel communicated a brand identity more effectively, and enacted this name change as a way of reaching an audience seeking programming that parents and children could watch together. The Family Channel separated from the Christian Broadcasting Network, but remained under Tim Robertson's leadership, becoming a regular part of cable line-ups nationwide in the early 1990s. In 1993, the company expanded its production capabilities through the acquisition of MTM studios. Though the channel relied heavily on syndicated programming, by the mid–1990s, it also produced a notable amount of original programming, including movies (Joe Flint 24).

The next major identity transformation occurred in 1997, when Fox Family Worldwide, a partnership between Rupert Murdoch's News Corp and Saban Entertainment, purchased the International Family Company as a joint venture. The new owners renamed the cable channel Fox Family, and sought to develop it as an outlet that would target children and operate as a competitor to Nickelodeon and The Disney Channel. They launched the retooled channel in 1998, offering syndicated children's programming during the day and family-oriented programming at night (Greg Braxton F1). Ratings plummeted as the older viewers who had been the channel's core audience left and the brand strategy attracted few new viewers. After three years of low ratings and management turmoil, Fox Family Worldwide was acquired by the Walt Disney Company in 2001 for a reported purchase price of $5.2 billion (Brooks Barnes B1). Disney had purchased Capital Cities/ABC in 1996, and envisioned this cable acquisition as a complementary asset.

The conglomerate interest behind the ABC Family Channel initially viewed it as a distribution outlet for off-network syndicated programming. There were early concerns about re-branding the channel, and the highest-rated programming during its first year included repurposed ABC programming such as *8 Simple Rules for Dating My Teenage Daughter* (2002–2004), *The Bachelor* (2002–present), and the strip *Whose Line Is It Anyway?* (1998–2004) (John Dempsey, "Alphabet Spells" 17). This strategy characterized the early years of the ABC Family identity, and some of the successes that the channel found in syndicated programming pointed the way toward the millennial branding strategy that the channel began to adopt in 2004.

During these early years, the ABC Family channel produced a minimal amount of original programming; it primarily utilized syndicated series that had originated on the WB broadcast network to develop a millennial-focused branding strategy. This programming included *7th Heaven* (WB, 1996–2006, CW, 2006–2007), the longest-running and highest-rated drama that the WB had ever aired, in addition to *Gilmore Girls* (WB, 2000–2006, CW, 2006–2007) and *Smallville* (2001–2006, CW, 2006–2011).[4] The cable channel also purchased off-network syndication rights to former WB sitcoms including *Sister, Sister* (ABC, 1994–1995; WB, 1995–1999) and *Sabrina, the Teenage Witch* (ABC, 1996–2000; WB, 2000–2003). Notably, these series had originally aired as part of the "TGIF" block that ABC used to target younger viewers on Friday nights in the 1990s.[5] When they were cancelled due to low ratings, the WB had picked them up and produced additional seasons because they appealed to the niche broadcaster's target audience. When *Variety* reported on the trend of cable channels purchasing syndication rights to the WB's dramas in order to draw young women, ABC Family's VP of acquisitions and scheduling told the trade paper, "Our audience composition is compatible with The WB's. These shows make a nice fit for the 12–34-year-olds we try to reach on a regular basis" (qtd. in Dempsey, "Frog Leaps" 24).

At the time that ABC Family began to focus on this audience target, the channel may have effectively served a supportive role for the WB's programming. For example, in the fall of 2004, ABC Family was airing a block of WB series in syndication from 5–8 p.m. EST, and all three of those dramas were still in production, airing new episodes on the "rival" broadcast network. Over the next few years, however, ABC Family would emerge as the programmer that targeted millennials most effectively, yielding higher ratings for programming.

Two major factors related to industrial structure played a key role in this victory. First, the WB television network, which had increasingly moved away from the teen girl audience, shut down in 2006, when Warner Bros. Television partnered with CBS for the joint venture, The CW. This new broadcast network carried over some of the WB's more successful programming, but has had little success with developing new series, and has generally been viewed as a branding and ratings failure. In 2008, Disney/ABC Television Group president Anne Sweeney claimed, "What has always served us well here has been identifying gaps in the marketplace," in reference to the cable channel's strategy of targeting millennial women, "A group that we found were fast becoming important in the media landscape" (qtd. in Schneider 16). Second, it makes more sense for a basic cable network to establish millennial women as a demographic target. Broadcast networks like The WB and The CW are made up of affiliate stations that sell local ads within their markets, and the specificity of the 12-to-34-year-old female audience is actually a hindrance in their efforts to generate revenues from local businesses. In contrast, basic cable networks receive revenues from national advertising and cable operators. By 2010, ABC Family was ranked among the top ten advertiser-supported cable networks (Barnes B1).

Original programming has evolved on ABC Family over time. Although the cable channel currently produces fewer hours of original programming per week than any broadcaster, as of this writing its ratings are higher than that of the CW (and sometimes other broadcast networks), and it has proven its ability to successfully launch new programs. The cable channel's success with millennial women is built on a multi-part strategy that utilizes and mimics the tactics employed by the WB, and later the CW, to target a similar audience. In addition to the series mentioned above, ABC Family purchased syndicated programming from the WB including the family drama *Everwood* (2002–2006) and the sitcom *What I Like About You* (2002–2006).

Although the success of syndicated programming helped to establish the direction that ABC Family would take, the channel's viewership growth has primarily been fueled by original series and made-for-television movies. In the arena of original series, ABC Family has taken a page from the niche broadcast playbook by literally working with the same show creators who previously had successes at the WB. Brenda Hampton, who created and executive produced *7th Heaven*, sold *The Secret Life of the American Teenager* (2008–2013) to

ABC Family in 2008. *Variety* reported that *Secret Life* was the highest-rated scripted program among viewers aged 12-to-34 in summer 2008, including broadcast and cable programming (Dempsey "ABC Family" 16). Over the course of five seasons, *Secret Life* maintained a large audience, and its success was used to promote the launch of a number of other original series.

When ABC Family began to develop its millennial brand in earnest in 2004, Kate Juergens was hired as an executive vice president of programming and development. Juergens had been the senior vice president of development at the WB, overseeing *Gilmore Girls* and *Smallville*, among others. At ABC Family, Juergens sought to develop a new series with Amy Sherman-Palladino, the *Gilmore Girls* creator who parted on bad terms with the CW in 2006. Sherman-Palladino's ABC Family series *Bunheads* premiered in 2012, alongside the channel's syndicated reruns of her prior broadcast series. The series attempts to replicate the tone of *Gilmore Girls*, and incorporates a number of the cast members who appeared in that series' seven-season run (Christina Radish).

Although the CW has failed to distinguish itself as a broadcaster, the longest running series the network has originated is *Gossip Girl* (2007–2012). The teen drama was perhaps the lowest rated and most written about new series during its first year on air. *Gossip Girl* was produced by 17th Street and Alloy, a company that had evolved from direct marketing clothing and consumer goods to teens to developing serial novels, and with *Gossip Girl*, serial television. Since 2010, ABC Family has worked continuously and profitably with Alloy; the company produces *Pretty Little Liars* (2010–present) and *The Lying Game* (2011–present) for ABC Family, while also producing *The Vampire Diaries* (2009–present) for the CW. Alloy also developed *Huge* (2011) and *The Nine Lives of Chloe King* (2011) for ABC Family; these series were similarly based in book properties, and each lasted only one season. As a program supplier, Alloy worked primarily with the CW and ABC Family, which offers further evidence of the similarity in the broadcast and cable channel's identities. In the summer of 2012, Alloy Entertainment was acquired by Warner Bros. Television. The company is continuing to develop properties for ABC Family, however; *Ravenswood*, a spin-off of *Pretty Little Liars*, premiered on ABC Family in 2013 (Sandra Gonzalez 23).

ABC Family has also successfully exploited its capabilities as a cable channel. It has typically launched new series during the summer months, when competition from broadcast network scripted programming is minimal. Most of their shows air with a mid-season "break" that begins in August or September. Mid-season premieres typically occur just after the new year, another time period when major broadcast networks depend on reruns. On the ABC Family channel, seasons include anywhere from 22 to 30 original episodes, but are spread out over two major portions of the year when they air in consecutive weeks in the manner of shorter series cable programming on HBO or FX. ABC Family works with much smaller budgets than broadcast networks do, and as mentioned above, produces fewer hours of original programming. As a result of these factors and a solid conception of brand identity, the cable channel is less risk averse than broadcasters and slower to cancel series with low ratings. In the next section, I discuss ABC Family's specific conception of millennials and the role this has played in the channel's branding and program development.

ABC Family's Millennial Turn

In the summer of 2007, ABC Family published a four-page advertising section in *Advertising Age*, discussing the channel's rebranding toward the millennial audience. "Getting to Know the Millennials" served to stake the cable channel's claim on this youth demographic, and it outlined the major generational characteristics that ABC Family took into account in its branding. For instance, the channel defined the generation as "83 million Americans born between 1977 and 1996," which does not literally match any demographers' estimates on millennials, but did serve to identify ABC Family's primary target as 12-to-30-year-olds in 2007 (A1).[6] Further, the advertorial broke out demographic facts including: "Millennials spend almost 15 hours a day interacting with various media and communications technologies," and "45 percent of Millennials refer to themselves as non-white" (A1). The advertorial also notes that ABC Family hired Frank N. Magid Associates to conduct research on young viewers, which resulted in the firm's Millennial Strategy Program (Julie Liesse A2). This research informed the cable channel's conception of the most important aspects of millennial identity, and informed its overall strategy; for example, the channel worked to encourage second-screen engagement with their programming from a very early point and their original programming reflects greater diversity in race, ethnicity and sexual orientation than broadcast prime-time programming as a whole during this time. The episode of *10 Things I Hate About You* described in the introduction incorporates nearly every aspect of ABC Family's market research about millennials, organizing it around the focal point of feminism, which the advertorial does not address.

Paul Lee, the network's then-president, summed up the findings of ABC

Family's strategic research on millennials, stating, "We have discovered that this is an audience that is very social, passionate about their families and passionate about media." He continued, "They are very happy to follow their stories onto all platforms. Over the past three years, we have written for them on all platforms" (qtd. A4). Lee referenced cable, the ABC Family website, and program delivery services like iTunes as specific platforms that the channel utilized to engage the target audience. The detailed discussion of ABC Family's branding and target market strategy is particularly notable because it ran before the channel made a significant investment in original programming. The "past three years" that Paul Lee refers to were a time period, beginning in 2004, when the channel determined that millennials would be their target, and they supported this strategy with off-network syndication purchases of programs that had previously been used to target a 12-to-24-year-old audience by The WB network.

ABC Family's limited experiments with original programming that targeted millennials had significantly yielded results for the cable channel as of 2007; *Wildfire* (2005–2008), a drama about a young female horse jockey aired for four seasons. Sci-fi drama *Kyle XY*'s (2006–2009) ratings set a record for original programming at the channel (Schneider 19). *Lincoln Heights* (2007–2009), a black cast drama about family life in a Los Angeles neighborhood premiered to critical acclaim. The 2007 *Advertising Age* piece was timed to coincide with the premiere of *Greek* (2007–2011), a comedy/drama about campus life that launched alongside an immersive internet campaign designed to engage viewers. By this point, ABC Family was defining millennials as tech-savvy, second-screen focused, and longing for connectivity. The website that accompanied *Greek*, virtualrush.com, embodied these ideas by offering users opportunities to engage with cast members and enter contests to win roles as extras on the show.

The channel's efforts to characterize millennials as tech-savvy and yearning for connection are evident in the way it promotes its programs through social media. SocialGuide has ranked *Pretty Little Liars* among the top five most-tweeted series consistently since 2011 (Tanner Stransky 33). The series' stars live tweet during east coast airings of episodes, an effective practice that encourages the target audience to watch the episodes as they premiere. ABC Family further encourages second-screen engagement by including onscreen hashtags in episodes, so that viewers are prompted to respond to specific plot points and character revelations. The practice of using Twitter to engage with television is becoming more common, particularly among millennial users. ABC Family has exploited this growth in support of its overall millennial branding; the strategy addresses viewers with the expectation of second-screen engagement, and it invites them to engage in a virtual simulation of a viewing community. In practice, the strategy serves to manage audience response. Although ABC Family makes their programming available via multiple platforms (full episodes are available online, for example), the value of Twitter engagement is that it encourages live viewing. ABC Family is therefore guiding their millennial audience to consume the programming in a particular way, and to make their presence (as potential consumers) evident to advertisers by responding to the programming through relatively structured channels.

In keeping with ABC Family's research on millennials, each of these shows feature diverse casts. For example, the cast of *Secret Life* includes actors who are white, Asian-American, Latino, and African-American. *The Lying Game* features a Native American actor, Blair Redford, who plays a native character, Ethan Whitehorse. Beyond racial and ethnic diversity, the majority of the channel's series engage with representations of diverse sexualities and physical and intellectual abilities. Emily (Shay Mitchell), a lead character in *Pretty Little Liars*, is a Latina who comes to terms with her same-sex orientation over the objections of her conservative family. One of her love interests was portrayed by an African American actress. In *Switched at Birth*, two teen girl protagonists confront questions of nature vs. nurture as they come to terms with the fact that they were not raised by their biological parents. Bay (Vanessa Marano) realizes that although the family who raised her is white and upper middle-class, her birth mother is Puerto Rican and working-class. Daphne (Katie Leclerc), who was raised by Bay's biological mother in a working-class neighborhood, contracted meningitis and lost her hearing at age three. Each episode incorporates scenes in which characters communicate in American Sign Language, and an ASL-only episode aired in March 2013. Bay and Daphne consider the roles that class, ethnicity, and ability have played in their lives as they get to know each other and their biological families. Diversity serves a narrative purpose in each of these series, but it also fits into the channel's larger strategy of targeting millennials by acknowledging the wide spectrum of human identities. In Osgerby's study of teen television programming in the 1960s, he writes, "The teenage market that emerged in America after World War II was pre-eminently white and middle-class" (77). Working-class and non-white identities were rendered invisible in the mass culture emergence of the baby boom teenager. In contrast, ABC Family represents millennial teens in a milieu that is marked and shaped by diverse identities and perspectives.[7]

Often, racial and ethnic representations in ABC Family dramas are consistent with contemporary representational strategies that have been categorized as "colorblind" diversity (Herman Gray 186), in which difference is visible, but the significance of difference and its meaningful operation in society is rarely, if ever, acknowledged. On the one hand, it's possible to examine how an array of distinct identities are refracted through the lens of white middle-class experience in ABC Family programming, but the channel's representational strategies are not solely derived from ethnocentrism. Instead, it results from the effort to conceptualize millennials as a market, and the characteristics (derived from research efforts) that best support an identifiable consumerist identity. Market research on millennials consistently indicates a central, inherent contradiction: this generation is conventional, they make decisions by consensus, and they are more reliant on their parents than previous generations, a reliance that continues well into adulthood. Simultaneously, members of this generation maintain a self-conception characterized by rugged individualism. The channel's diverse narrative universe is largely uncomplicated by institutionalized racism and social stratification related to prejudice and discrimination, as it is by overwhelming, if not insurmountable, structuring obstacles of contemporary life. This representational strategy operates in the service of flattering millennials as a diverse but interconnected generation of achievers; programming is optimistic rather than confrontational, relegating problems to the individual, and therefore, addressable level.

ABC Family's Girl-Powered Dramas

The discussion of millennials in the popular and trade presses has been marked by an emphasis on femininity. Although the generation as a whole is considered to be a desirable consumer group, owing to its size, millennial women in particular have been identified as more reliable consumers. The Geppetto Group, a market research firm, estimated that millennials were spending eight billion dollars a year in the feminine sectors of cosmetics and personal care products (Melanie Marchie 64). At the time that ABC Family moved to develop a millennial brand, American Demographics estimated that teen girls were spending "a healthy portion of the $170 billion" that millennials contributed to the economy each year (Pamela Paul 6). Jessica K. Taft has examined the contemporary discourse of Girl Power, arguing that one of its central significations in the 1990s was based in consumerism (74–75). However, when ABC Family pitched its millennial brand identity to advertisers in 2007, the channel did not include specific data on gender. "Getting to Know the Millennials" offers statistical information and trends related to the generation as a whole, and it frames this with an introductory anecdote about Kristen, "A bubbly 18-year-old who loves performing in musicals, collecting vintage jewelry and working with kids" (A1). ABC Family did not claim young women as a specific audience target in 2007, but here, as in their programming, young women are configured as centrally important to the identity of their generation. In discussions of their millennial brand identity, the channel's executives emphasize optimism, connectivity, and a sense of responsibility. As this market research informed the development of a slate of programming with female protagonists, it has translated into representations of young women as active and empowered subjects.

The majority of the series developed for ABC Family have featured female protagonists, including *Wildfire, The Secret Life of the American Teenager, Make It or Break It* (2009–2012), *10 Things I Hate About You, Pretty Little Liars, Huge, The Nine Lives of Chloe King, Switched at Birth, The Lying Game,* and *Jane by Design* (2012).[8] Each of these series features at least one teen girl protagonist, and some of them feature ensemble casts of teen girl characters, as in *Pretty Little Liars*. The protagonist in *Bunheads* is an adult woman, but she teaches dance to a core group of four teen girls (the "bunheads" referred to in the show's title). In each of these series, the goals and drives of young women move the story forward. They are the heroines who the audience is meant to root for, and as a result of this consistent narrative design, these programs do not reproduce traditional ideologies of passive femininity. The young women at the center of ABC Family dramas and dramedies are independent, assertive, and in keeping with the channel's conception of millennials; they are closely connected with their families, their friends, and involved to varying degrees in social activism.

ABC Family series further promote close identification with a young female audience through heavy serialization in scripted series that adhere to the traits of the soap opera genre. Michael Z. Newman and Elana Levine describe the "widely held cultural assumption that soaps feature never-ending stories, with complications spinning off from even the resolutions that do occur, and that this kind of narrative trajectory reads as feminine" (90). The kind of continuing drama is evident in ABC Family series including *Pretty Little Liars, The Lying Game, Secret Life* and *Switched at Birth*. The former two titles, produced by Alloy, are so heavily serialized that the plotting becomes convoluted over the course of just a few episodes due to the lack of narrative resolution and webs of character interrelationships. Both of these series place teenage girls in the midst of suspenseful plots, counterbalancing their typical teenage concerns with larger narratives of crime investigation. In *Pretty Little*

Liars, a group of four friends are being tormented by a seemingly omniscient presence identified as "A." While they approach the messages they receive from "A" as a mystery that they can solve, it is clear that they are often in physical danger. Although each of the main characters is involved in a romantic relationship, their friendship is the central focus of the series. Again and again, the narrative emphasizes that although these young women are uncertain about their ability to rely on parents, siblings, or romantic partners, their friendship is impervious to threat.

In *The Lying Game*, twin sisters who were separated at birth share one identity in order to investigate not only the circumstances that have kept them apart, but a murder that may be related. Alexandra Chando plays both Sutton, who was raised by a wealthy family, and Emma, her twin who was raised in foster care. The narrative is invested in the nature of identity and interpersonal relationships; as Emma pretends to be Sutton, her disparate background informs her entirely different relationship to the people in Sutton's life. Both of these series characterize their young female protagonists as simultaneously under threat and confident about their ability to investigate and overcome it. They not only encourage close identification with the characters through social media promotions, but on a narrative level, they use plot twists and cliffhangers to encourage audience engagement.

Secret Life and *Switched at Birth* are slightly more conventional primetime serials than *Pretty Little Liars* and *The Lying Game*. Although storylines continue from episode to episode, they feature fewer plot twists over time, and are thus more straightforward. The narrative universe of *Secret Life* revolves around a young woman who got pregnant at age fifteen and decided to keep the baby. The series is less moralistic in tone than creator Brenda Hampton's WB series, *7th Heaven*; *Secret Life* mixes comedy and drama to present Amy (Shailene Woodley) as a teen girl faced with difficult choices and challenges. She has a supportive group of friends and family, and although each of these characters has their own particular set of concerns, the narrative presents them as a community with a shared investment in seeing Amy succeed. Early on, critics took issue with Amy's brief consideration and quick rejection of abortion as an option (Alessandra Stanley E1). Throughout the series' five-season run, however, teen characters engaged in discussions of sexual health, birth control, sexual orientation, and relationships in ways that were engaging and relatable for a sizable millennial audience. *Switched at Birth*, described briefly above, explores some of the same territory as *The Lying Game*, but is not framed as a thriller. Bay and Daphne discover that they were not raised by their biological parents, and the narrative consistently explores questions related to the nature of family and individual identity. Although the protagonists are not literally related, they become as close as sisters as they adjust to the changes in their lives. *Secret Life* and *Switched at Birth* are melodramatic, with plot lines concerning alcoholism, adultery, and divorce that unfold as long-term story arcs. In these series, young women's lives do not revolve around young men. The teen girl protagonists are involved in romance plotlines, but more narrative emphasis is placed on stories about their relationships with family and friends.

ABC Family has developed a slate of series that represent young women as central actors in their own lives. These representations of teen girls as confident, assertive, and goal-driven are a product of the channel's desire to target this audience and sell them to advertisers. ABC Family's series are shaped by the conception of millennials derived by market researchers. A number of these series feature female friendship ensembles, which narrativizes the research finding that millennials "make decisions by consensus" (Liesse A2). The programming continually equates friendship with kinship, and ABC Family further emphasizes this with their channel's tagline, "A new kind of family." Anne Sweeney has noted that Disney-ABC Television views "optimism and positivity" as "very much in the spirit of our brands" (qtd. in Denise Martin 24). The ABC Family brand in particular, employs these qualities to represent young women as capable agents of change in the environments they inhabit.

Conclusion

In considering ABC Family's millennial branding through original programming, I want to emphasize that the channel has demonstrated a high degree of intentionality and concerted effort to minimize risk. It is possible to examine how the channel's programming serves a unified brand identity because of the industrial conditions in which it was produced. The channel has developed original programming slowly, beginning with one series and adding hours from year to year, offering an average of five hours of programming a week. ABC Family produces the majority of its programming in-house, at ABC Family Original productions. These series maintain exceptionally low budgets, and new shows are heavily promoted through existing ones as an attempt to generate audience interest and guarantee success. In dramatic programming, ABC Family has only cultivated relationships with outside production companies who have had proven successes with the WB and the CW broadcast networks. ABC Family, as a subsidiary of Disney, mimicked the development of Warner Bros. WB network in order to target a similar audience, which resulted in industrial practices that were initially supportive of the broadcast network's programming.

Overall, the strategy attempts to capitalize on the millennial branding developed by a niche market broadcaster, making it cost effective by operating according to the logics of cable as a distribution outlet. It is not my intention to argue that ABC Family programming offers a literal representation of millennial identity. The channel's market research indicates major trends related to this generation's view of its ability to affect change, its multiculturalism, and its social and technological connectivity. It targets this generation of viewers, young women in particular, by offering representations of themselves as smart, capable, and powerful, and this strategy has been consistently successful since 2007. The channel's focus on this demographic imbues millennial women with a kind of cultural importance, as ABC's focus on teenagers similarly functioned in the 1960s. Millennial women live in a society that has been and continues to be characterized by inequities, but social, political, and economic factors related to gender do not play a role in ABC Family programming. As a result, its series operate on the level of wish-fulfillment, imagining a world in which young women are only inhibited by their own ambition.

Notes

1. The television series was based on the popular 1999 film of the same title.
2. Gidget and Kat are both negotiating maturation without an adult female role model in their homes. There is a long storytelling tradition of motherless heroines in western storytelling, but these two examples coincide with larger social movements engaged with women's roles in society. *Gidget* aired early in the second wave feminist era, and Kat's character first appeared in a 1999 film, in the midst of the third wave of feminism. Although this essay is not specifically focused on how these series engage with feminist movements, these characters were certainly crafted with the expectation that they would resonate with female viewers during time periods in which women's social roles were shifting.
3. See also: Michael Curtin's "From Network to Neo-Network Audiences," in *The Television History Book*, for a more detailed discussion on the changes in the television industry that have resulted from conglomeration.
4. ABC Family aired *7th Heaven* as of 2002, and added *Gilmore Girls* and *Smallville* in 2004.
5. The acronym "TGIF" is widely used as a shorthand to indicate "Thank God, it's Friday." However, ABC trademarked these initials in association with its Friday night block of sitcoms, claiming the initials stood for "Thank Goodness It's Funny."
6. Neil Howe and William Strauss are cited in the advertorial. Their book-length overview, *Millennials Rising*, defines Millennials as the generation "born in or after 1982" (4).
7. This commitment to representing diversity is not unique in contemporary American television. For example, *Glee* (Fox, 2008–present) incorporates diversity related to race, eth-

nicity, sexual orientation, and ability. This representational strategy is pervasive in ABC Family original programming, however, to a larger degree than any other broadcast or cable channel.

 8. It is a common strategy for U.S. cable channels to rely on reality series for original programming, because the format can attract large audiences and is typically produced for lower costs than scripted series. The ABC Family channel, however, has not developed a significant presence in reality television. In 2013, for example, *The Vineyard* (2013–present) and *Dancing Fools* (2013–present), were the only reality originals on the channel's schedule.

Lavender Identity and Representation in the Media

The Portrayal of Gays and Lesbians in Popular Television

SEAN ROBINSON AND BERNICE ALSTON

It is axiomatic to say that today's millennial generation is growing up in a media-centric world, influenced by many forms of popular culture. As new research (e.g., Corey Johnson & Rudy Dunlap; Gilad Padva) suggests, this new world order has implications for the identity development of current generations. According to Victoria Rideout, Ulla Foehr, and Donald Roberts, who conducted a national survey of 8- to 18-year-olds, youth today on average use some form of media more than 7.5 hours a day, much more time than they spend in school or with parents.

In contemporary society, popular media culture is the dominant culture. Yet what about those individuals who are part of specific subcultures and go underrepresented in mass media, such as LGBTQ individuals? How does the mass media represent and portray their lives? Likewise, how do LGBTQ individuals interpret what they see and hear, as well as what they don't see or hear in popular culture and mass media? What are LGBTQ millennials in the twenty-first century learning about who they ought to be, and how they ought to behave? What are these youth and young adults discovering about family, love, intimacy, sex, and sexuality?

Drawing from both cultural studies and queer theory perspectives, the purpose of this essay is to explore the ways that gay and lesbian millennials are portrayed in contemporary television programs and what gay and lesbian individuals are being taught within such media. Using textual analysis, we reviewed key episodes of several recurring television shows in the United States with gay or lesbian characters who represent second wave millennials,[1] including

Glee (Fox, 2009–present), *90210* (The CW, 2008–2013), *The Secret Life of the American Teenager* (ABC Family, 2009–2013), and *Pretty Little Liars* (ABC Family, 2010–2013). The episodes discussed below were chosen because they contained explicit scenes or plot lines about issues related to sexual orientation and identity. We watched these shows and episodes with the following broad, conceptual questions in mind:

- How does the show reinforce or disrupt traditional dichotomies of what it means to be heterosexual/homosexual?
- How does the show give voice to certain characters while marginalizing, silencing, or stigmatizing other characters? [Alexander Doty 7].

From this complex and situated reading of popular television shows, both represented and consumed by millennials, a more pluralistic account of media can be constructed, one that emphasizes tensions and contradictions. In our analysis, we take to heart Jason Mittell's call to examine media texts as "sites for discursive practice" (9). Instead of focusing on the aesthetic codes or features of new media, we apply Mittell's practice of analyzing sets of themes and patterns that surface across media texts.

The Millennial Generation and Gay Issues

We primarily relied on shows that had gay or lesbian characters who were born between 1990 and 2000, thus appearing as high school teens or college aged young adults. Recent research on the millennials by Paul Taylor and Scott Ketter reveals a number of characteristics that are important to understand and keep in mind when discussing this generation, especially around issues relevant to the LGBTQ community. Millennials are different from members of other generations when it comes to their experience with and exposure to LGBTQ individuals who are out and open. More than half of millennials (54 percent) say they have a close friend or family member who is gay. This compares with 46 percent of Gen Xers, 44 percent of Boomers and 26 percent of members of the Silent generation. Millennials are more likely to favor gay marriage than are members of other generations. Fully half favor legalization of gay marriage, while just 36 percent oppose it, making millennials the only living generation in the United States that tilts positively on this question. Furthermore, only 36 percent of millennials say gay couples raising children is an unwelcome trend in society; the rest don't think it makes a difference.

These statistics on millennials are important to keep in mind given the issues we observed in the shows we watched, such as coming out, dating/intimacy, dealing with support by family and friends, gay marriage and adoption.

Because millennials are immersed in consumer culture, popular culture and entertainment media play a prominent role in their daily lives. As an out gay man who had few positive gay role models in either real life or in the mass media, a college educator, and member of Gen X, it has been the experience of the lead author that popular culture today can indeed provide a resourceful entry point into the world by offering youth and young adults material to understand or create their own appropriations of mass-produced culture. The perspectives of the second author, a female, heterosexual graduate student and a member of the millennial generation, offer a unique juxtaposition into those very entry points of interpretation and key insights of television media. It is our hope that this analysis of what millennials are consuming will lay the groundwork for future explorations of LGBTQ individuals in popular culture.

Gay and Lesbian Characterizations and Representations

Consuming media that represent gay and lesbian youth offers a powerful means of socialization for young people who are coming to terms with their sexuality, as they serve as a template for their own negotiations about whether and how to come out to family and friends, managing relationships in school or the work place, as well as dealing with issues related to dating, sex, and forming intimate relationships. Amber B. Raley and Jennifer L. Lucas suggest that because many LGBTQ youth do not have adult LGBTQ role models, they may turn to the media for assistance with their identity formation (22). Moreover, Padva argues that the media may be young people's first contact with the LGBTQ community (106). If these youth look to the media, do they in fact see themselves reflected, and if so, how? A recent study by Annemarie Vaccaro exploring the intergenerational differences between Baby Boomers, Gen Xers, and Millennials reveals that the most striking difference between the generations is identity management (116). Wrestling with multiple, fluid, and intersecting identities is commonplace for millennials. Indeed, one of Vaccaro's participants seemed to struggle with being gay because many parts of his identity never seemed to fit in with what was portrayed by the media, including television, about what it meant to be a gay man (126). The experiences of this participant, which mirrored that of many others in Vaccaro's research, is precisely why understanding media representations of LGBTQ individuals is important. As Richard Dyer contends, "Because, as gays, we grew up isolated not only from our heterosexual peers but also from each other, we turned to the mass media for information and ideas about ourselves" (1).

In the following sections, we first offer highlights of specific episodes and scenes from each of the television shows we reviewed. The scenes illustrate some of the different ways sexuality and sexual identity are revealed and portrayed by various characters. We then offer an overall textual analysis of what we view as some of those key patterns and themes across the shows as they relate to sexual identity and orientation.

90210

In the fall of 2008, a group of friends from West Beverly High School hit the primetime line up with the television show *90210* (The CW, 2008–2013), set in Los Angeles, California. Although this group of high school students were similar to the original *Beverly Hills 90210* (Fox, 1990–2000) protagonists, this cast appeared to parallel a much more intense reflection of the internal and external conflicts that adolescents and young adults of the current millennial generation face. It was during the bulk of the third season and into the beginning of the fourth that sexual orientation became a predominant theme, heavily explored via two of the primary characters, Teddy (Trevor Donovan) and Ian (Kyle Riabko). During the third season, Teddy, a popular student and a star tennis player, begins to come to terms with his feelings for Ian, an openly gay male student.

After the two have an intimate encounter, Teddy tries to avoid his feelings and acts as if nothing happened. However, once he realizes that his feelings for Ian will not go away and that he still has to face him, Teddy becomes hostile and physically aggressive. As the season progresses, Teddy begins to become more accepting of his own sexuality and of Ian. Midway into the season, Teddy tells Ian that he likes him and wants to continue seeing him but is not ready for anyone to know about their relationship. Ian replies, "I came out of the closet in the 9th grade, and am not ready to go back." The two continue spending time with each other and Teddy appears to be comfortable with Ian as long as his feelings for him are not exposed. Eventually, Teddy comes out about his relationship with Ian to his friends.

After Teddy has come out as gay, he walks in on his friends as they were in the midst of talking about going to see "hot girls" playing volleyball after school. When Teddy enters the room, the discussion stops and everyone looks uncomfortable; he does not get invited to join his friends. Teddy later reveals to Silver (Jessica Stroup) that his friends are "being weird" and "blowing" him off. After Silver reveals Teddy's feelings to Dixon (Tristan Wilds), Liam (Matt Lanter), and Navid (Michael Steger), they decide to take him to a gay club. However, once they are there, they all appear uncomfortable again. Teddy and his friends seem to believe that certain social behaviors are associated with being gay and "acting" in a certain way are part of being gay. This assumption creates the need for Teddy to disavow his interest in gay bars, and in socializing with other gay individuals, as a way to fit into a more heterocentric milieu.

By the start of season four, however, Teddy is becoming more comfortable with his own sexuality but still has not told his father that he is gay. Throughout the show, there seems to be one person who Teddy is able to confide in, his ex-girlfriend, Silver. During a conversation about why he has not revealed his sexual orientation to his father yet, Silver tells him, "Telling people you are gay is not about being easy... it's about not apologizing for who you are. You aren't doing this for your dad... you are doing this for you." After this conversation, Teddy calls and leaves his father a voicemail telling him that he is gay. Near the end of season three, Teddy and Ian break up, and at the beginning of season four, we are introduced to Teddy's new college boyfriend.

Glee

Glee (FOX, 2009–present) is an American musical comedy-drama television series that focuses on the failures and successes of the William McKinley High School glee club, while its members deal with relationships, sexuality and social issues. Most of the television shows' characters have faced challenges related to their own sexuality and gender identity and appear to gain a better understanding about their own identity over time. The characters Kurt (Chris Colfer), Santana (Naya Rivera), and Karofsky (Max Adler) clearly illustrate the struggles and dilemmas that individuals might go through in coming to terms with identifying as gay or lesbian.

In season two, Santana, a female member of the Glee club, accuses a male student, Karofsky, of being gay. Santana confronts him and says that he is a "late in life gay," who will probably hide his sexuality and be exposed later in life. She reveals that she is "playing on the same team," and suggests that they become "beards," explaining that the term refers to a scenario in which two individuals pretend to date, when at least one of them is gay or lesbian, in an effort to hide their true sexuality from others. Santana sees this ruse as a way for her to be able to run for prom queen. When Santana walks out of the room after another prom queen has been announced, Brittany (Heather Morris), Santana's bi-curious love interest, attempts to console her. Trying to make sense of why she did not win, Santana says, "They must have sensed that I was a lesbian. Do I smell like a golf course?" Brittany replies, "They don't know what you're hiding. They just know that you're not being yourself. If you were to embrace all of the awesomeness that you are, you would have won." This exchange clearly indicates the danger of staying in the closet for some; yet for many gays and lesbians, they feel damned if they come out, damned if they stay in (Kristin Griffith and Michelle Hebl). It is also during this season that Kurt struggles to find a way to come out to his father. With the aid of his peers, he soon finds his voice, and through a tearful exchange with his father, his sexuality is revealed.

In season two, episode 20, another poignant scene takes place when Kurt is preparing for the prom. His father Burt (Mike O'Malley), boyfriend Blaine (Darren Criss), and stepbrother Finn (Cory Monteith) are sitting in the living room discussing tuxedos for the prom when Kurt enters the room, in what he has decided to wear. While showing off the kilt and blazer he has chosen, he tells them that he plans to also add a sash and beads to his attire. His father tells him that he thinks that he is trying to "stir the pot" a little, because he believes Kurt wants attention. Blaine agrees, adding that they all just don't want to give anyone a reason to start trouble.

Later, Kurt and Blaine appear to be enjoying themselves at the prom, until the principal announces that Kurt has been chosen as the prom queen. Saddened and embarrassed, Kurt runs out of the prom, and Blaine runs out behind him. Kurt exclaims, "Don't you get how stupid we were! We thought that just because no one was teasing or beating us up that no one cared, like some sort of progress had been made. But it's still the same." Blaine tries to console him by telling him, "It's just some stupid joke." Kurt replies, "No it's not! All of that hate, they were just afraid to say it out loud so they did it by secret ballot."

Although Kurt appears to be comfortable and proud of his sexual identity, he has to deal with the challenges of the discomfort of others. He is challenged when heterosexuals use his own sexuality as a weapon against him. The message to viewers is clear; although a person may be gay, they should not "act" like it, as in Kurt's case, or they can be punished and ridiculed. But a contradictory message is sent in this same scenario when Santana does not get voted prom queen: if you are not honest and open, and try to hide who you are, you will be punished by not getting what you really want—to be "just like everyone else"—because you are in fact *not* like everyone else.

During *Glee*'s third season, both Santana and Karofsky begin to come to terms with their individual sexual identities. Santana is open about her relationship with Brittany and although Karofsky does not come out, he starts to gain a better understanding about his feelings. During this season, Kurt begins to receive Valentine's Day gifts from a secret admirer. After the secret admirer asks him out on a blind date, Kurt learns it is Karofsky, who has since transferred to a different high school. Karofsky tells Kurt, "When I was at McKinley, I hated who I was. I took that out on you because there you were so proud... it has taken me a while, but for the first time in my life I'm trying to be honest about how I feel." Kurt tells Karofsky that he views him as a friend and suggests that he try to come out to others. Although Karofsky is able to reveal his feelings to Kurt, he makes it clear that he is still not ready for others to know that he is gay. For Karofsky, the closet is still the safest place to be, at least for the time being.

The Secret Life of the American Teenager

The Secret Life of the American Teenager (ABC Family, 2008–2013) chronicles the lives of a group of six high school students and their families in Glen Valley, California. Originally created around issues related to teen-pregnancy, *Secret Life* chronicles a number of challenges and struggles facing these younger millennials trying to find their way through life and love, amid the tensions related to sex, gender issues, drug abuse and family break-ups.

It is not until the end of season four, in episode 24, that viewers are directly presented with issues connected to sexual identity, when we see Grace (Megan Park), a high school senior, begin to question her own sexuality. She admits to her best friend Adrian (Francia Raisa) that she is curious about what it would be like to kiss a girl, and she invites Adrian to kiss her. Soon after, unable to deal with her emerging feelings and confusion, she confides in her mother, Kathleen (Josie Bissett). Grace's mother attempts to console her and says, "It's no one's fault if you're gay." Kathleen tells Grace that she would prefer that she be straight because being straight is easier than being gay, especially in high school. Later on in the conversation, Kathleen actually encourages Grace to keep on "questioning" her sexuality, and to take time to think about how she feels. At the same time, she admonishes her to do her exploration without sex or intimacy for a change. This advice only works for a short while, after which Grace seeks out her former boyfriend for sex, as a way to dispel her confusion and anxiety around her sexuality. She eventually realizes this tactic does not work.

Later, in this same episode, Grace begins to literally try on her lesbian identity and goes to school dressed in a fedora, loose pants, and a jean vest. In the hallway, she is confronted by Adrian, who is the school's known, out lesbian. Grace tells Adrian that she dressed this way because she is gay. Adrian tells Grace that there is "no uniform for people being gay," while the other girl simply gives Grace a very disapproving look while shaking her head in disbelief. In season five, Grace is still unable to deal with her confusion about Adrian, and tells her that she doesn't think that it would be a good idea for them to be friends anymore because of their kiss.

Pretty Little Liars

Pretty Little Liars (ABC Family, 2010–present) is an American teen drama mystery-thriller television series, loosely based on the popular series of novels written by Sara Shepard. Set in the fictional town of Rosewood, Pennsylvania, the series follows the lives of four high school girls—Spencer (Troian Bellisario), Emily (Shay Mitchell), Hanna (Ashley Benson), and Aria (Lucy Hale)—whose clique falls apart after the disappearance of their queen bee, Alison (Sasha Pieterse). One year later, they begin receiving messages from a mysterious figure using the name "A," who threatens to expose their secrets. Early on in season one, one of the secrets that "A" reveals is the fact that Emily is a lesbian. Her friends are all shocked, but eventually are very supportive, especially when Emily begins to date a new student at school.

In the same season, Emily's father Wayne (Eric Steinberg) believes that someone or something is bothering her and erroneously believes it is related to "boy troubles" at school. Fearful that "A" will out her first, Emily tells him that "she isn't who they think she is" and blurts out a tearful "I'm gay." Her father ends up telling her mother, who completely breaks down. During this conversation, Emily's mom asks her father, "How are we going to fix this?" Her dad responds, "Fix this? This is not like buying a bracelet. This is who she is." Emily's mother cannot accept her sexual identity and accuses Maya (Bianca Lawson), Emily's girlfriend, of "turning" her into something she isn't.

Emily's parents appear to have conflicting feelings about her relationship. Her father wants to be supportive but her mother's feelings are hindering their ability to support their daughter in the way she needs. Emily's mother Pam (Nia Peeples) views her daughter's sexuality as a problem that they need to fix, lest it ruin her life. Although Emily seems to be relieved to be honest with her parents about her sexuality, she is concerned about the future. She tells her friends, "I don't know what it will be, but it's going to be different." The conflict between Emily's mother and father continues over several episodes, with her mother never fully understanding or accepting Emily's identity as a lesbian.

In season's one episode 12, Emily's parents invite her girlfriend Maya to dinner so they can meet her, and they seem to be accepting of her, especially her father. After dinner, Emily thanks her mother for "being okay" with her relationship with Maya. However, her mother tells her "[t]he whole thing makes me sick to my stomach," and walks out of the room. Emily stands alone looking both hurt and shocked, and we later see her mother sobbing alone in the pantry, unable to deal with her daughter's sexuality and her emerging identity as a lesbian.

Discussion

As Suzanna D. Walters states, "TV has become our national cultural meeting place, a site of profound social meaning and effect" (27). Television audiences are often exposed to many of the societal and cultural issues and topics that are currently represented throughout our vastly fragmented media. Compared to movies, television is evolving more quickly and is often seen as a more accurate depiction of real life (Matthew Gilbert). However, Walters contends the study of LGBT issues on television is seen as complex and scholars and television critics (e.g., Steven Capsuto; Linda Holtzman; Andy Mangels; Stephen Tropiano) disagree over whether television is particularly reflective of the cultural realities of its represented audience. Indeed, cultural representations do not simply mirror reality. They also construct and fabricate it. Visibility/invisibility and social exclusion/inclusion of groups, such as LGBTQ persons, can be produced, maintained, and shored up by representations within the mass media. According to Judith Butler, television representations cannot be read as merely cultural and detached from the processes of social construction and power dynamics of society (35). Given the ubiquity of television as a form of mass media, it is important to consider the ways in which inclusion/exclusion and visibility/invisibility shows up within these shows. Likewise, it is important to appreciate the contributions of these shows in bringing LGBTQ issues and representations to the masses.

The scenes we reviewed are but a snapshot of some of the larger themes and plot lines that gay and lesbian characters are confronted with in these specific television shows, and the ways in which LGBTQ millennials might view themselves as portrayed in popular culture. In most of the shows, many scenes involving a gay or lesbian character center on issues related to that individual's sexual orientation and identity, whereas sexual orientation and identity is rarely the issue or focus when heterosexual characters are portrayed or interact with one another. This may lead to the assumption and stereotype that lesbians, and especially gay men, are highly "sexual" beings, and that every action, interaction, feeling, or thought revolves around their sexual orientation. Making one's sexuality the center of attention when gay or lesbian characters are on the screen may in turn cause LGBTQ individuals to remain silent and hide their identity for fear of being seen in this one-dimensional light. Yet, a gay man or a lesbian cannot be represented as just making observations about his or her life without either challenging the heterosexual norms, or blending in and assimilating (Richard Goldstein 47). There is, in essence, a catch–22 in how the gay or lesbian individual can be portrayed—inclusion within heterosexual circles yet invisible as gay or lesbian (i.e., closeted), versus exclusion from heterosexual circles yet visible as gay or lesbian.

Furthermore, although there is an increase in the number of LGBTQ writers (David Kirby), it is more likely than not that many producers, directors and writers are heterosexual, which means that the narratives portrayed are more likely to represent a heterosexual understanding of the gay/lesbian character's sexual identity and corresponding thoughts, feelings, and actions. The danger in this is that viewers may begin to recognize and understand homosexuals from that heterosexist viewpoint (Helene A. Shugart 73), in which heterocentric behaviors and appearances are expected, but within certain parameters.[2] For instance, in *90210*, after Teddy comes out as gay, his friends are all suddenly portrayed as hyper-masculine, and yet anxious around him. They shut Teddy out of their conversation about girls on the beach, and later they take him to a gay bar to show they support him. Clearly, Teddy's heterosexual friends try to understand his world, but only from their heteronormative experience and perspective.

Although the coming-out experiences seen within these television narratives might present contradictory messages, the current visibility of this particular and crucial life moment in these portrayals in popular culture has been a strong force in shaping gay life and identity. It provides a space where audiences can witness and understand these experiences, and serve as a model for LGBTQ audiences, particularly youth and young adults, of the process and emotions one might encounter. On the other hand, for most fictional coming-out stories on television, the focus still remains on the reactions and feelings of the heterosexual characters and not the celebration of the homosexual character's true identity. The plot line is centered on how the parents or friends come to terms with this new discovery and their process of acceptance towards the homosexual's sexuality and lifestyle.

This is certainly the case with Grace's parents in *The Secret Life* and with Teddy's friends in *90210*. While these narratives have the intention of normalizing the coming-out experiences of LGBTQ individuals, they can instead emphasize the anguish and grief experienced by both the gay/lesbian and heterosexual characters that can happen when young people try to come out to their family and friends. This particular "coming-of-age" phase for the gay/lesbian character differs from a heterosexual's "coming-of-age" moment, because the homosexual needs to explain his/her lifestyle and yearns for acceptance, whereas heterosexuality is already understood and taken for granted by a majority of society; heterosexuals never have to discuss when or how they knew they were straight; heterosexuals rarely have to explain their general attractions to the opposite sex; heterosexuals rarely have to fight to be accepted (Walters). The portrayals of the coming-out experience on contemporary television also differ between gays and lesbians. Once gay male characters discover their identity and become part of the gay community, it becomes a social experience as they are often seen as socializing with other gays, like Ian, Kurt, Blaine, and others. Lesbian sexual identity is depicted, on the other hand, as a more personal, romantic experience, as the characters happen to "fall in love with a woman," like Emily in *Pretty Little Liars*, or involves a "free-spirit's" sexual experimentation, like Grace (Walters 208). Absent in most portrayals of the lesbians we profiled is the social aspect often seen with male characters, in which gay men socialized more openly with other gay men or were seen in public places, like bars, where they congregated.

Nonetheless, television does provide a cultural space for gay and lesbian youth to understand sexuality. A number of Mary Gray's research subjects acknowledged that their exposure to gay and lesbian characters and subjects on television was how they first knew homosexuality existed (1164). Adrianne Holz Ivory, Rhonda Gibson, and James Ivory reported that even gays and lesbians are more influenced by less stereotypical depictions and more realistic situations on television, in terms of self-discovery and exploration, and that these depictions helped them to feel more comfortable accepting who they were. So, in this sense, in terms of an accurate representation of the full range and diversity of LGBTQ individuals that exist in real life, these shows are somewhat less than accurate, but at least they are able to raise awareness of the existence of gays and lesbians in the world. This visibility also pertains to the ways in which they can portray some of the experiences that gays and lesbians have, including instances of bullying and intimidation, because of their sexual orientation. These depictions of discrimination and violence also help to raise awareness of the possible places where people can go to get support for dealing with these experiences. For example, in episode 14 during season three of *Glee*, the subject on bullying and suicide associated with homosexuality led to a 300 percent increase in Web and hotline traffic for the sponsoring organization, The Trevor Project[3] (Curtis Wong).

Sara B. Netzley's research also suggests that the increase of gay characters has provided more role models for gay youth and has helped to foster some feelings of acceptance by the larger community. Thus, Netzley argues that television could teach gay and lesbian individuals about different gay-related issues, or establish role models that might be difficult to find in heterosexual communities. Many gay, lesbian or bisexuals may not discover their sexuality or "come out" until late adolescence, and due to the lack of knowledge or interaction with homosexuals, these youth oftentimes look to the media to understand how they might be viewed by others or how they should behave. They can form their identities based upon these representations, and if the characters are unrealistic, then they may be modeling themselves after more stereotyped images of gays and lesbians in the larger culture. Television depictions may spark homosexual youth's self-discovery, especially among those young individuals who are not as exposed to homosexuality, but the inauthenticity of the characters may do more harm than good.

The earlier age of coming-out for contemporary youth is thought to be more common than older generations of homosexuals because of the more prevalent images of gays and lesbians in recent popular culture (Walters 199). Recent research in the United Kingdom found that the coming-out age for teenagers has drastically decreased. The average age of coming out for individuals currently in their 30s was 21 (Ritch Savin-Williams), but now it is common for individuals as young as 10, 12, or 14 to come out (Wong). Unfortunately, the questioning and coming-out process for millennials can still be just as challenging and troubling as it was for Grace, Teddy, Kris, Santana, Karofsky and Emily. Additional research by Ritch Savin-Williams and Lisa Diamond highlight the dynamic, fluid nature of sexual identity development among young men and women which does not follow an easy or clear path, as exemplified in all of the shows discussed.

Nonetheless, these narratives can also depict a celebration of gay life, and provide homosexual audiences with the confidence and power to accept their identity, as is the case for Teddy, Kurt, and Blaine. Many of these depictions have also validated or shaped the way LGBTQ individuals and the greater mainstream community view homosexuality. Therefore, even though sometimes inaccurate, negative or partial representations exist, there are still glimpses of positive experiences that might be valuable to both LGBTQ viewers and heterosexuals' attitudes towards LGBTQ self-confidence and acceptance.

Walters argues that this is not to say the process and experience of coming out for the individual is noticeably easier; but through mass media, like television shows and film, the individual's friends and family are exposed to more cultural representations of homosexuals, making homosexuality seem less abnormal or unnatural, as it was once commonly perceived (10–11). Walters discovered that the visibility within the media has both aided and hindered the coming-out experience for many individuals; media representations have both generated heterocentric and stereotypical attitudes, as well as provided resources or helped to develop a sense of empowerment. Larry Gross contends that sexual minorities are depicted differently in the media, compared to their majority heterosexual counterparts, and these depictions often effect the group represented (19). Gross further believes that the media representations of fictionalized homosexuals as different from heterosexuals or as outsiders causes gays and lesbians to experience isolation, exclusion or marginalization in their everyday lives.

This is especially true if there is little or no visible LGBTQ portrayals in popular media, as this can further the LGBTQ individual's sense of isolation from the rest of society (Netzley 982). But when these characters are viewed in realistic social encounters with friends, families, and partners, it reinforces their similarity to heterosexuals and legitimizes their right to their sexuality. There is a fine line, however, between assimilating and being just like everyone else for the purpose of inclusion, and being excluded because you are not *really* just like everyone else. The characters we examined in these shows straddled that fine line, and oftentimes found themselves unable to cope with the reality of the situation. Kurt wanted to be himself, but was distraught when he was made fun of. Santana wanted to fit in, but was dismissed because she was not being authentic and honest about who she really was. Teddy acknowledged his sexuality, but distanced himself from that side of himself socially, lest he be ostracized. Karofsky tried to commit suicide because of the constant bullying related to his sexuality. The path is not an easy one. But how these fictionalized characters confront, negotiate and deal with their sexuality can have a potentially positive impact on how those LGBTQ viewers navigate their own identities.

Conclusion

The Gay & Lesbian Alliance Against Defamation (GLAAD) is a leading organization that lobbies the media and entertainment industries to depict accurate images and represent the diversity of the LGBT American community. Since 2005, GLAAD has compiled an annual report, "Where Are We in TV?" to present recent trends of LGBTQ characters and issues in the current television season. In the 2012–2013 television season, GLAAD estimates that LGBTQ scripted characters represent 4.4 percent of all scripted series regular characters on the five broadcast networks: ABC, CBS, The CW, Fox, and NBC. This is an increase from last year, with 31 series regular characters identified as gay, lesbian, bisexual or transgendered. The shows we watched were strategically drawn from among these networks and their affiliates since they are more likely to be seen by a wider audience. Nonetheless, there is still a large discrepancy in LGBTQ characters on television when compared to the heterosexual characters in terms of diversity along race, ethnicity, social class, or gender.

GLAAD's research highlights how lead characters on prime-time television shows do not represent the sexual—and even racial and ethnic—make-up of the general public. But, GLAAD both applauds and criticizes television's growing efforts in creating diversity in people and situations. Gay men (67 percent) are seen as more prevalent characters than lesbian women (33 percent), but only one bisexual and one transgender character are seen on prime-time television. Cable television has depicted greater diversity that is reflective of the general public, with more people of color and sexualities than prime-time television (GLAAD, 2012). Given the increasing number of LGBTQ individuals being scripted into shows across network and cable channels, it is important to understand both the way LGBTQ characters are being portrayed, and the impact of such characterizations on viewers across the board.

Extensive research has been conducted regarding groundbreaking television shows for LGBTQ visibility, including studies on *Will and Grace* (NBC, 1998–2006) and *Ellen* (ABC, 1994–1998) during the 1990s and into the 2000s, and contemporary teens shows like *Buffy the Vampire Slayer* (The WB, 1997–2003) and *Dawson's Creek* (The WB, 1998–2003). However, little research exists in the past couple of years regarding more recent television shows, especially as general attitudes are gradually shifting towards greater acceptance of gay rights.

American television has witnessed a significant increase in LGBTQ characters and issues, but there still remains a relative dearth of research centered on the ways that LGBTQ characters are portrayed and the impact of such LGBTQ representations on various audiences. In order to cultivate positive attitudes, further advocacy for equal rights, and eliminate the social and legal marginalization of the LGBTQ community, the media should continue to offer more diverse sexual and personal experiences of this community, and play a more formative role in sexuality education. This form of edutainment, as it is sometimes called, would create and improve accurate character depictions and further impact young adult LGBTQ individual's self-perceptions and acceptance of the community. Without this level of understanding, popular culture is consigned to reproducing increasingly out of date narratives that no longer hold true, and that may ultimately be counterproductive.

Notes

1. According to sociologists (e.g., Neil Howe and William Strauss; Jean Twenge), the millennial generation encompasses those born between 1982 and 2000. Some researchers (e.g., Jennifer Zapatka) have actually broken this group into two, the early millennials, those born 1980 to 1994, and the later, second wave millennials, who are born after 1994.

2. Interestingly, the opposite can also happen when gay writers create heterosexual characters who have certain mannerisms or characteristics stereotypically associated with gays and lesbians. One popular example is the brothers Niles (David Hyde-Pierce) and Frasier (Kelsey Grammer) Crane, from *Frasier* (NBC, 1993–2004); they are two straight men, created by a team of writers that at one point included up to five gay writers, who exhibit some stereotypical traits and behaviors associated with gay men (David Kirby).

3. Founded in 1998, the Trevor Project is the leading national organization providing crisis intervention and suicide prevention services to lesbian, gay, bisexual, transgender, and questioning youth. For more information: http://www.thetrevorproject.org/.

Exploring Discourses of Engagement in *2 Broke Girls*

ALISON N. NOVAK

In a 2011 feature in *New York Magazine* titled "The Kids Are Actually Sort of Alright," Noreen Malone reflected on the widespread illusion that the millennial generation was "metaphysically ill-equipped" to take on the real world (par. 6). Malone suggested "we're done with that kind of engagement, for now," offering a position that the millennial generation was becoming disengaged and apathetic with almost every facet of life, including political influence, career, love, financial independence, and material possessions (par. 16). However, since the article's publication, it seems that the millennial generation's engagement may be far from completely lost.

Consider the 2012 United States presidential election. In the months before the election, media were boisterous in their evaluation of eligible youth voters as uninterested, unmotivated, and apathetic. Publications as large as *The New York Times*, and as local as *The Berkshire Eagle* from Pittsfield, Massachusetts, lamented that youth were largely absent from campaigns, especially compared to the efforts and presence of the millennial generation in the previous 2008 presidential election. "Amid what could be called an undeclared war on the hopes and dreams of young people, many of the potential victims appear content to hibernate through the election" wrote Michael Paul Williams of the *Richmond Times Dispatch* (par. 13). He continued, "regardless of your politics, there's too much at stake to be passive," insinuating the group was misinformed and unaware of the importance of voting (Williams par. 19).

Despite such grim diagnoses of the group's apathetic disposition, Election Day 2012 came with a surprising twist. Millennial voter turnout in the 2012 election neared 50 percent, having a much larger impact than predicted by the news media (CIRCLE; James Rainey). However, the appearance of millennials on Election Day did not come as a surprise to all. In fact, many academics such as William Howe and Neil Strauss predicted the power and fervent enthusiasm of the millennial generation's political and civic participation well before Election Day.

An important question arises from this discrepancy: where do media perceptions of millennial apathy come from? If not from the actions and behaviors of the millennial's themselves, what other sources of millennial representation lent the news media to make such dramatic and inaccurate predictions? These types of predictions are far from an anomaly when it comes to the millennial generation. As noted in *Slouching Toward Adulthood*, Sally Kaslow observes, outside of political predictions, millennials are often portrayed in the news media as disengaged and apathetic on a number of topics, ranging from personal finances to relationships to career goals (30).

And, to further complicate the matter, John Clarke et al. have observed that "the subject (of millennials' perceived apathy), has, of course, been massively treated, above all in the mass media. Yet, many of these surveys and analyses seem mainly to have multiplied the confusions and extended the mythologies surrounding the topic" (3). To understand where the news media's false predictions and representations of millennial apathy develop from, it is necessary to examine other media sources of millennial representation. Clarke et al. continue, "We cannot afford to be blind to such a development [the developing representations of youth culture in the media]... any more than we can afford to be blinded by them" (4).

These observations point to the need to construct some kind of framework for understanding where these perceptions of millennials as relatively disengaged from politics is coming from. While many scholars have begun to theorize these phenomena, very few studies have focused on identifying these engagement practices in mediated discourses, particularly as they relate to class distinctions (Evan Resnick; Debra S. Vidali; Lloyd L. Sederer; Erica Weintraub Austin, & Bruce E. Pinkleton). Therefore, this essay will also provide a case study of a framework that can be used to identify engagement discourses in the media.

More specifically, the essay investigates the mass media representations of apathy and engagement in the millennial generation through a discourse analysis case study of the CBS sitcom *2 Broke Girls* (2011–present). Drawing from Stuart Hall and Tony Jefferson's representation framework, as well as work on engagement and apathy, this study looks for depictions of the millennial generation's engagement and apathy on the popular television show.

Engagement, Apathy and Active Disengagement

The term *engagement* is defined in many contexts; however, perhaps the most well recognized definition comes from Sidney Verba and Norman H. Nies, who link engagement with political participation (2). Engagement is "those activities by private citizens more or less directly aimed at influencing the selection of government personnel and/or the actions they take" (2). From this definition, the emphasis on influence and action are important to understanding what engagement is and how it is displayed. Engaged individuals are those who intentionally act in an effort to enact change or influence outcomes. Evan Resnick agrees with this action and influence definition and reflects that the challenge in defining engagement lies in the multitude of contexts that it is used in (555). Resnick defines engagement as "a quintessential exchange relationship," where engagement leads to a relationship (potentially a cause and effect relationship) between an individual and object (561). Here, "object" refers to what the individual is engaging with, which could be another individual, a culture, or an inanimate item. Resnick also identifies three forms of engagement behavior (561). First, the individual can directly modify the object. Second, the individual can manipulate or reinforce the object (560). Third, the individual can modify preferences and opinions of others engaging with the object (560). These three forms of engagement can be used to identify the phenomenon. When an individual is displaying one of these three behaviors, they can be identified as taking part in an engaged relationship. When an individual is not displaying one of these three behaviors, they can be identified in a non-relationship, where apathy lies between the individual and object.

Lloyd L. Sederer writes that "apathy is the enemy," a problem that affects not just the individual, but the whole American nation (3). "Those who are apathetic have lost the capacity to feel and act; they are disconnected and numb" (3). In his critique of national gun-control efforts post the 2011 shooting of Representative Gabrielle Giffords, Sederer argues that "apathy drains the suffering we could feel from doing nothing, from staying the same (3). It dulls the pain needed to motivate change." (4). Further, Erica Weintraub Austin and Bruce E. Pinkleton argue that apathy is the absence of engagement (216). Apathy is the lack of engagement, interest, and participation in a facet of life. Other scholars, such as Stephen Craig et al. argue that apathy is not an active reluctance to be uninvolved or disengaged, but rather a disinterest in a topic, issue, action, or object (290). Outside of research on apathetic behaviors during emergency situations, very few studies have examined how apathy is represented in the mass media.

In her 2010 article, Debra S. Vidali argues for the importance of understanding the range of engagement and the forms of active disengagement in the millennial generation. Vidali asserts the conceptualization of youth engagement with all facets of life (career, finances, relationships, media consumption...) is often falsely defined as a binary of *total engagement* (youth as completely passionate, committed, and driven) and *total disengagement* or *apathy* (youth as totally impassionate, uncommitted, and not driven). Vidali critiques these mediated representations of youth and instead proposes the concept of *active disengagement*. She theorizes that millennials have reasons behind moments of disengagement, which is often falsely interpreted as apathy, in mainstream television. Whereas total disengagement and apathy imply that the individual is not engaged because he or she does not care, active disengagement implies that the individual is not engaged for a reason. Vidali found that individuals who were actively disengaged (in this case with media) provided five distinct reasons for such behavior. These include: identifying oneself as lazy and or topically indifferent on specific (not all) issues; social pressures dictate what they should and should not be engaged with; rather than actively becoming engaged, they wait for others around them to motivate their interests. Other reasons given include that they do not have enough time to be fully engaged. And finally, there are some who blame the media's bias, story overkill, manipulation, and misplaced priorities as a reason to avoid engagement (376).

Vidali argues apathy is actually quite rare among youth and in particular the millennial generation (371). Much more common is the sophisticated phenomenon of active disengagement, which is often misinterpreted as apathy by media producers and even the millennials themselves. Vidali writes that millennials often interpret their own active disengagement as apathy or total disengagement as a result of media narratives that falsely interpret them. Despite this, her study still concludes that apathy and disengagement are vastly different from active disengagement.

Vidali's work suggests that the binary of engagement and apathy is steadfast in mediated representations of the millennial generation, despite its inaccuracy. In her view, it is the much rarer mediated appearance of actively disengaged youth that is a more accurate representation of millennials. Combining Resnick's three forms of engagement, Vidali's conceptualization of active disengagement, and Sederer's, and Austin and Pinkleton's definition of apathy, this study provides an analysis of the discourses surrounding millennial representations on the sitcom *2 Broke Girls*.

Relevant to this television show are social class distinctions that predict or contribute to individual engagement. Very few studies have thoroughly examined the relationship of social class to engagement practices. In their development of an engagement typography, Gene Rowe and Lynn J. Frewer argue that the challenge in identifying engagement causes and effects lies in the difficulty researchers face in defining engagement. In their own work, the authors found that social class is a contributing factor (although they could not conclude to what degree) to public participation, in the form of voting, volunteering, and donations to charity. This is supported by Laura Wray-Lake and Daniel Hart, who found that the differences between the opportunities of poor youth and upper-class youth accounts for some of the differences between those who display high amounts of civic engagement and those who display low amounts. Youth who were raised in the upper-class tend to show more civic engagement in the form of volunteering and voting. While the authors could not conclude a singular reason for this, they did offer that the difference could be potentially explained by the educational opportunities accepted by youth when they have financial security (456). As this demonstrates, it is important to consider social class as a related representation in the mass media. In the analysis, examples of engagement, apathy, and active disengagement will be identified, as well as the characters' representations of social class, allowing for a reflection on the depiction of millennial engagement in popular television.

2 Broke Girls

Premiering in September 2011, the CBS sitcom *2 Broke Girls* traces the antics and adventures of roommates Max Black (Kat Dennings) and Caroline Channing (Beth Behrs). The two girls are from dramatically different upbringings, Max from a poor working-class family, and Caroline from a wealthy upper-class lifestyle. However, because Caroline's father was arrested and charged with a Ponzi scheme, Caroline now finds herself broke and working as a waitress at the same diner as Max. Despite Caroline's plight, she still identifies as upper-class, considering her current financial situation only temporary, and never shedding her love of expensive clothes, foods, and furniture. Max and Caroline become friends and roommates by forging a bond over the dream of one day opening their own cupcake shop. The show is written by Michael Patrick King, the director of the two *Sex and the City* films (2008 and 2010) and a regular writer for *Sex and the City* (HBO 1998–2006) and many other successful TV shows, and stand-up comedian Whitney Cummings, creator and star of the NBC sitcom *Whitney* (2011–present). *2 Broke Girls* features a cast including the girls' neighbor and part time boss Sophie (Jennifer Coolidge), diner boss Han Lee (Matthew Moy), diner cook Oleg (Jonathan Kite), and elderly cashier Earl (Garrett Morris) (Nellie Andreeva par. 5).

Upon its premiere, the show received a variety of reviews, ranging from positive, encouraging the use of post-feminist language and humor, to lamenting the show's use of racial humor and offensive language. Mary McNamara, *Los Angeles Times* television critic, wrote, "Despite a diversionary opening salvo of post-feminist raunch and unfortunate racial stereotyping, '2 Broke Girls' is a solid, old-fashioned sitcom about two mismatched girls taking on the big city and making' their dreams come true" (par. 1). In the aftermath of the first two episodes, critics attacked the show for its use of racial humor centered on the diner boss, Han Lee, a shorter Asian character who is made fun of for his poor driving skills (Alyssa Rosenberg par. 2).

However, it was not just the racial stereotypes critics reflected on; the depiction of the two 20-something main characters also garnered attention. Aly Semigran of PopWatch.com titled her review "'2 Broke Girls': Promising Series Nailed Twenty-Something Poverty; NYC, Not So Much," reflecting on the perceived accuracy of the show's representation of the millennial generation (par. 1). Relating *2 Broke Girls* to other new shows such as *New Girl* and *Whitney*, Alessandra Stanley of *The New York Times* suggests:

> The networks obviously hope that R-rated humor will draw younger viewers who were raised on "South Park." And it is a sign of change that women on television can be as provocative—almost—as men. But change isn't always progress, and youth is overrated. A lot of the bluer jokes are labored; all three shows are at their best when they dig deeper and come up with fresher, more organic comic material [par. 9].

The article goes on to suggest that the focus on young twenty-something characters who struggle to fully adapt to adulthood is a trend. Perhaps more startling is the perception in these reviews that the shows are accurate and truthful in their representations of millennials. While other facets of *2 Broke Girls* are critiqued, the depiction of the millennial generation is applauded. If one of the trends in television sitcoms is to cast youthful main characters struggling to make their transition to adulthood, it is useful to study these shows for the way youth is represented, especially when the news media views these representations as accurate. What also makes the sitcom even more important is its popularity. The Nielsen Company reports that the show was the sixth highest premier in Fall 2011, maintaining its appeal across both the 18–49 and 50–75 age demographics (Robert Seidman par. 2).

Discourse Analysis

As a way to begin to understand how the show offers up specific representations of the millennials, it is helpful to draw on the ways in which the dialogue is constructed in the show. More generally, discourse analysis methods are used to explore the language, themes, patterns, and structures exhibited within a set of texts. To fully explore the discourses present in *2 Broke Girls*, James Paul Gee's critical discourse analysis methods will be used. A critical discourse analysis looks at one related text or unit of discourse and relates it to a situated meaning. It allows for the examination of language as an indicator of opinion, identity, and larger societal place. Discourse analysis assumes "language in use is always part and parcel of and partially constitutive of, specific social practices and that social practices always have implications for inherently political things like status, solidarity and the distribution of social goods, power" (Gee 68).

For this study, the set of texts examined will include the entire first season of *2 Broke Girls*, or 24 twenty-minute episodes. Centered on the representation of millennial engagement, this discourse analysis will specifically look for instances where the show's characters are engaged, apathetic, or actively disengaged. While most millennial engagement research has been conducted on political engagement, by expanding the definition of engagement using Resnick's three relationship behaviors, Vidali's five active disengagement expressions, and Sederer's, and Austin and Pinkleton's definition of apathy, we can expand the search for engagement beyond political borders. The chart below summarizes the indicators of engagement, active disengagement, and disengagement/apathy, which will be used to analyze the television show. The findings section will report and critique the appearance of each type of engagement, as well as provide an overall analysis of the show's representation of the millennial generation.

Table 1: Engagement Indicators

Engagement Type	*Engaged*	*Actively Disengaged*	*Disengaged or Apathetic*
Indicators	Resnick's relationship behaviors: 1. Directly modifying the object 2. Manipulating or reinforcing the object 3. Modifying others	Vidali's active disengagement expressions: 1. Lazy or indifferent 2. Social Pressures 3. Don't seek out information, but recognize its value 4. Not enough time 5. Blame media bias	Sederer's apathy definition: Those who are apathetic have "lost the capacity to feel and act; they are disconnected and numb" Austin and Pinkleton's apathy definition:

Engagement Type	Engaged	Actively Disengaged	Disengaged or Apathetic
	who engage with the object	6. Self-reflection and explanation of behavior	Lack of engagement, interest, and participation

Because this is a qualitative discourse analysis of the television show, it will rely on the connection of examples to support conclusions. Throughout the analysis, quotes will be used to connect the findings to the dataset and improve the reliability of the results. Further, through saturation or the finding of the same result repeatedly throughout the cases in the dataset, the study's validity will also be improved.

Findings

Although both Max and Caroline find themselves in similar financial conditions in the show's first episode they display different orientations towards their economic plight. Caroline is determined to regain her wealth, success, and social standing in Manhattan, which provides her with the incentive to start her own cupcake business, save money, and network for potential job opportunities. However, Max is content with her current financial situation, calling it "adequate" and "the best she'll ever do." Representing the girls as opposites depicts two very different millennial identities to the audience. The first representation, most prominently displayed through Caroline, is highly engaged, providing examples of Resnick's relationship behaviors. The second representation, often characterized through the dialogue and behavior of Max, is a bit more complicated, displaying engagement as a mix of active disengagement and apathy.

Caroline's language and actions situate a discourse of engagement within the television show. From the first episode, Caroline is shown taking control of her own life as well as the life of her new roommate. For example, as Caroline is attempting to carry four plates of food at once, Max offers to help.

While Caroline clearly needs the assistance of the well-seasoned Max, she proceeds to try to work things out on her own, finding her own place to sleep overnight (the subway), earning her own income, and even performing tasks at the diner without knowing the language (ex: marrying the ketchup). Fitting with Resnick's relationship behaviors, Caroline's actions are examples of "directly modify the object" or in this case her financial situation. Rather than accept her change in finances and social status, she devises a plan to make a comeback without anyone's help.

Later, Caroline agrees to move in with Max, bringing her full-size horse to live on their small patio. During the last scene of the first episode, Caroline describes her comeback plans to Max, which now rely on their joint venture to create a successful cupcake business.

> MAX: When did you put this whole horse in my yard thing together?
> CAROLINE: I can't help it. I see an opportunity and I make it happen. Like with your cupcakes.
> MAX: Like what with my cupcakes?
> CAROLINE: Ready? To open a bake shop, all we need is 250 grand startup money to get the real estate, basic equipment...
> MAX: Yeah, oh? (sarcastic) 250 grand, that's all?
> CAROLINE: Yeah (nodding enthusiastically)
> MAX: Did Chestnut here (referring to the horse) kick you in the head while I was in Starbucks?
> CAROLINE: Hear me out. If we both work two jobs and make $2,000 a week, we could open a cupcake business in little over a year. In the past two days, we've made $387, and that's a good start. We can make extra money at other jobs, like publicists, advertising executives...
> MAX: Janitors, drug mules...
> CAROLINE: We really need to work on your self-esteem. So, you cupcakes; me business background; us success. What do you think?
> MAX: I think you have a horse.
> CAROLINE: I think *we* have a horse.
> MAX: Don't get attached.

Here, Caroline is not only attempting to directly modify the object (the current financial situation of both girls), but is also attempting to "modify others who engage with the object," Resnick's third relationship behavior. Caroline is reliant on Max's baking skills, and while Max is less optimistic about the new business venture, Caroline attempts to motivate Max and get her engaged in the new project so that they both can change their financial situations. Caroline's character is not only engaged in the new business and career because of her own actions, but it is through her interactions and attempts to get Max interested that she truly displays her engagement.

Caroline's engagement is also echoed in other aspects of her new life. When Caroline decides it is time to stop sleeping on Max's couch and purchase her own bed, she creates a vision board for what she wants the new bed (and the sleep she is expecting to get from it) to help her accomplish. When describing it to Max, Caroline must convince Max to allow the installation of a bed in the living room.

Again, Caroline's success relies on modifying the behavior of others, one of Resnick's indicators of engagement. Further, the creation of the vision board is a sign that she is attempting to directly modify the object—in this case, her life. By creating a visual reminder of the things that she wants to accomplish (a tactic that has worked for her in the past), she attempts to change her status.

Caroline's dedication to her vision for a successful life is challenged greatly during the first season, particularly when she is asked to apartment-sit for a dog. She decides to take some time off work and take the opportunity to "go on spring break" at the nearby apartment. Caroline repeatedly tells Max that she won't be working on the cupcake business while she is on "spring break" because she feels like she is overworked and needs time off. However, when an opportunity to network at a cookbook release party presents itself, Caroline cannot help herself but to hand out business cards and network with food bloggers. Once again, Caroline is attempting to directly modify the object, in this case, the cupcake business's reputation.

Max also arguably demonstrates engagement when she describes that she has never gone on spring break. She tells Caroline, "I don't take time off. I can't afford it." In this revelation, Max begins to show dedication to the cupcake business, particularly when she stays up all night to make cupcakes for an interested food blogger, despite also committing to the spring break lifestyle of Caroline. Max, like her roommate, attempts to directly modify her life, by committing to create and distribute the cupcakes.

Toward the end of the season, Caroline tries to get Max to show more enthusiasm and optimism for the cupcake business. Feeling disheartened after the two fail to save as much money as Caroline hoped, she encourages Max to quit her babysitting job and to instead put all of her energy into the cupcake business.[1]

Caroline again attempts to modify Max's position and engagement with the cupcake business, hoping that Max's full attention will encourage more sales and networking. Later, Max quits her babysitting job, but only after she gets into a fight with her employer, Peach. While Max eventually does leave her job and become more engaged in the cupcake business, it is not for the reasons Caroline initially described, but rather because of the time that Max gains when her schedule is not overextended with two jobs.

While Caroline is almost always depicted as an engaged individual in many activities, Max frequently supports the active disengagement and apathy discourses present in the show. Active disengagement differentiates itself from apathy through characters who are self-reflecting and explaining why they do not get involved or become engaged. The series begins with Max differentiating herself from two millennial hipster customers, by reflecting on her lifestyle choices and how they oppose millennial hipster stereotypes. The scene begins with Max harassing one of the customers who snapped his fingers to gain her attention.

Max provides a lot of explanations for why her lifestyle is what it is, further differentiating herself from other people her age. This self-reflection at the heart of active-disengagement is again displayed when she explains her own actions. For example, when reflecting on a fight she got into at the Goodwill, she and Caroline describe why they reacted to another girl's threats the way that they did.

Self-reflection like this comes at moments when Max must face the differences between her and Caroline, particularly in their joint cupcake business. In these instances, self-reflection often comes at the end of the episode, after the differences between Max and Caroline's engagement put the business at risk. During an episode where Max must make kosher cupcakes for a Jewish family, Max decides to make regular cupcakes and tell the family that they are kosher. Max explains to Caroline (who protests the lie) by saying "I don't respect anyone's tradition, that's kinda my tradition." Her initial reflection on her disengagement with the proper kosher ingredients fits with Vidali's "lazy or indifferent" active disengagement indicator (376). While this offers some explanation for Max's disengagement in the kosher cupcake project, it is not until the end of the episode, after Max was taken care of by the Jewish family, that she openly reflected the real reason for her kosher apathy. Having never been exposed to Jewish culture or felt the pressures of religious tradition, she admits that she did not previously understand the need for kosher products. Again, although Max's realization came too late for the Jewish celebration, her self-reflection and articulated understanding suggests that she is actively disengaged.

However, Max's disengagement is not always coupled with subsequent explanations and self-reflection that are at the heart of Vidali's active disengagement framework. There are many instances where Max's disengagement is apathetic, such as when she and Caroline get into a fight over the future of the cupcake business. During one fight, Caroline quits the business and says she is done with Max. Max replies that she does not have a future.

Statements like this one lend themselves to the view that Max is disengaged with her future as a whole, and not just the cupcake business. This is reaffirmed through her ongoing criticism of Caroline's networking and business attempts. When Caroline decides to go to a coffee shop to try to find a new vendor for the cupcakes, Max sarcastically retorts "that's exactly what I was going to do." It is not just that Max makes these comments; she also follows through by not going with Caroline to networking opportunities, and mocks their outcome. Fitting with Austin and Pinkleton apathy definition, these comments represent Max's general disinterest with the cupcake business.

Outside of Max's lack of engagement and enthusiasm towards hers and Caroline's joint venture, there are other representations of apathy. Throughout the first season, Caroline is depicted as disinterested in forming romantic relationships. When Max tries to instigate a relationship between Caroline and their business web developer, Caroline protests, saying "I don't want a one night stand, and I don't want a relationship right now." Caroline repeatedly fends off Max's comments regarding her single status by saying she's just not ready to date and doesn't want to just "hit it and quit it." These responses to Max's inquiries often come without explanation, left as statements rather than invitations for debate or conversation. Caroline's apathy towards establishing a romantic relationship, then, is conveyed through her disinterest towards initiating a relationship as well as her lack of self-reflection on why she doesn't want to begin a relationship in the first place.

Max is further depicted as apathetic to organization in her personal, financial, and material life. Max routinely protests Caroline cleaning the apartment, sarcastically saying "I like the clutter, it hides the bugs."

When Caroline comes across Max's disorganized purse, Max again rejects Caroline's help, supporting her mess by saying that it mirrors the rest of her life. Caroline responds by asking, "So what you are telling me, your finances are as messy as your purse?" Max sarcastically responds, "yup!" Again, despite an entire episode being devoted to Max's messy purse and tax record, Max never provides a reason for the mess or even self-reflects on it. Rather it is the concern and comments of friends such as Caroline and Sophie that get Max to comment. Here, Sederer's definition of apathy is fully articulated in Max's lack of action when it becomes clear her mess is responsible for causing her to lose important tax documents.

Finally, both girls are represented as disengaged in an episode revolving around new customer comment cards at the diner. As the boss, Han, reads the mostly negative comments, Max and Caroline talk over him, and lead Oleg the cook and Earl the cashier to speak over him at the same time. The lack of interest in the customer comment cards, and the outright ignoring of the feedback, lead the audience to view Max and Caroline's behavior as apathetic. Not only do they not adapt their behavior to the feedback of the comment cards, they fail to even listen to what their boss has to say. Sederer's apathy definition is again fulfilled.

Discussion

This reading of millennials' apathy and engagement on *2 Broke Girls* reveals that there is no singular discourse surrounding millennial engagement. There is limited variety in the topics that the girls display engagement with. Caroline's engagement is almost exclusively focused on the cupcake business and her economic plight. Alternatively, there is much more variety in the topics that feature active disengagement and apathy. These include forming romantic relationships, organization, taxes, and customer comment cards. Further, while only one character (Caroline) regularly features engaged behaviors, both main characters have moments of active disengagement and apathy. These topics are described in the previous sections, but it is the overall meaning of this discrepancy that will be addressed here.

Beyond the topical differences, there is variance in the way the two characters present their forms of engagement. As the girl's neighbor, Sophie states, "You two are like these cupcakes. One is dark and heavy, one is light and fluffy." Max, who has dark hair, average weight, and a sarcastic personality is contrasted with the skinny, blonde, and Wharton-educated Caroline. The contrast between the visual aesthetic of the two main characters assists viewers in perceiving the differences in their forms of engagement and general outlook on life. Importantly, the contrast drawn between Max and Caroline's socio-economic levels draws an interesting parallel between the engagement practices of the poor versus the wealthy. Although broke now, Caroline repeatedly cites being raised in a wealthy household as the reason why she is so engaged with the business.

Caroline regularly cites that her Wharton education, working on Wall Street, and upper-class lifestyle as factors that will help with the launching of the cupcake business. It is her past financial security that drives and educates her current business plans. Importantly, interactions like this one indicate a significant relationship between social class and the capability of being fully engaged. Perhaps what allows Caroline to be engaged is her class privilege, which gave her the financial and social confidence to pursue her dreams and never give up on her goals. Caroline's class background grants her agency to focus on a Wharton education.

Alternatively, Max cites her own impoverished upbringing to explain why she doesn't "care about life." In the second episode, Max explains, "Listen, everybody is broke in their twenties, and everybody hides from stuff. You run into freezers. I practice ignorance and blackout drinking." Max's poorer social class limited her ability to focus on anything other than earing enough money to survive. Thus, unlike Caroline, she did not have the same agency or affordances, thus limiting her idealism. Again, the juxtaposition of the characters cements the identity of those who are engaged and those who are apathetic. It is the wealthy, blonde, Ivy League educated girl who is most engaged, and the poor, school-dropout who is most apathetic.

It appears that *2 Broke Girls* significantly represents engagement, active disengagement and apathy as connected to social class. Playing off of stereotypes of the poor versus the wealthy, the two main characters suggest that it is money that is a primary indicator of engagement. Max, who represents the long-term working class, is shown as disengaged. She spends the majority of the first season attempting to teach Caroline the realist personality needed to financially survive as working-class in New York City. However, it is Caroline who was born wealthy and is determined to be wealthy again, who tries to convince Max to dream big and never give up on your dream, even when it may cost her in the short term. Also of importance are that Caroline and Max represent female members of their social class. Traditionally, working class women are hardened by their need to manage a job, family, and self (Anne Orloff 52). Upper class women develop a sense of agency, a desire to have-it-all, and accept every opportunity presented to them (Orloff 53). More research on the display of gender, social class, and engagement needs to be done to fully explore the relationship between the three.

In analyzing the engagement behaviors on *2 Broke Girls*, the indicators first identified by Resnick, Vidali, Sederer, and Austin and Pinkleton are useful to take into account. While there were limited examples of engagement beyond Caroline's behaviors regarding the cupcake business, it is clear that two of Resnick's three behavioral indicators of engagement worked well. First, directly modifying the object was the most prevalent of the three indicators represented in the show. Caroline regularly refers to her networking passion and business skills as having the potential to modify the success of the cupcake business and ultimately modify her current financial and social disgrace. As Caroline continues to try to convince Max that the cupcake business can be a success, she argues, "Just keep making those amazing cupcakes and I'll do the rest, till you believe." This example demonstrates that in her attempts to modify the object, Caroline must also modify others who engage with the object. It is not enough that Caroline believes in the project, she must also convince Max that it is possible. She needs Max's baking skills to ultimately make the business a success. Therefore, Resnick's first and third behavioral indicators of engagement work well in this analysis.

It is Resnick's second indicator, "manipulating or reinforcing the object," that is missing from the discourse of the show. This can be explained by the show's premise that the girls are attempting to grow out of their broke status, and become successful entrepreneurs. While this theme is challenged by Max's apathetic disposition to the business, it does explain why the girls would not demonstrate a desire to actively maintain the status quo.

In considering Vidali's five active disengagement indicators, easily the most common behavior demonstrated in this form of engagement is the first, that of laziness or indifference. What separates this from the indifference as an indicator of apathy as described by Sederer, and Austin and Pinkleton, is that Max regularly reflects and explains her indifference. It is the role of active-reflection that is critically important to active disengagement. For example, when Max tries to calm down Caroline who is excited over attending a Metropolitan Gala, Max states, "Can you take it down a notch? Hipsters are starting to look at us like we are trying too hard." Statements like this one explain why Max tries to appear indifferent. She fears being judged or grouped with others her age, especially the hipsters. Again, while not all of Vidali's five behavior indicators are used to represent engagement in the show, her framework of self-reflexivity and explanation does help in the analysis and differentiation of active disengagement and apathetic discourses.

Finally, the apathetic definitions of Sederer, and Austin and Pinkleton, while broad, were also useful in identifying apathetic behaviors and discourses in *2 Broke Girls*. Importantly, discourses of apathy are often identified by their lack of inclusion in the other two categories of active disengagement. For example, behavior was identified as apathetic because it lacked clear self-reflection on the behavior, as would be needed to fit with Vidali's active disengagement framework. This is visible when Max critiques Caroline's testimony about her father's involvement in the Ponzi scheme as boring.

Examples such as this appear regularly throughout the first season, helping to demarcate the moments of apathy and active disengagement. These moments also reinforce Sederer's argument that apathy is identified based on a lack of engagement (3). Apathy can only be identified by absence of engagement behaviors and the self-reflection of active disengagement. Further, Vidali's argument that apathy and active disengagement are only separated by subtle differences rarely acknowledged by audiences is also critically important in analyzing the representation of these behaviors (376). If apathy and active disengagement are only a few self-reflective lines of conversation apart, it is likely that a non-critical viewer would have difficulty differentiating the nuances of each discourse. This is a topic that needs much more research to understand if and how these differences have an effect on the perception of the millennial generation by audiences.

Also important to future research is the consideration of the representation of social class, gender, and the millennial generation in media. As demonstrated in *2 Broke Girls*, closely related to engagement and apathy are the upper class and working class distinctions between Max and Caroline. Perhaps another way to differentiate engagement, active disengagement, and apathy are looking at the social class distinctions between characters. The series promotes that potential for engagement is strongly related to the affordances (both social and financial) offered by an individual's social class. Using this as a model, it may be possible to add social class representations to the three typologies offered by Vidali, Resnick, Sederer, and Austin and Pinkleton.

Conclusion

Reflecting back on Malone's 2011 feature in *New York Magazine*, it is clear that the general perception of the millennial generation is that of apathy and total disengagement. This discourse was reflected throughout the coverage of the 2012 presidential election, despite its inaccuracy as demonstrated by the impressive millennial voter turnout. But, the truth is, that concerns like Malone's are far more multi-faceted than simple intergenerational misunderstandings. There are many mediated and popular discourses surrounding millennial apathy that support the news media's predictions, such as those found in *2 Broke Girls*. Further, because engagement and social class are firmly related in this sitcom, further research must investigate the full relationship between the two, particularly in a generation that is living through one of the greatest economic recessions in history. The question following this analysis, then, is why doesn't the news media also pick up on, integrate, or adopt the other discourses of active disengagement and engagement? If Vidali's findings are correct, and engagement and active disengagement truly define millennial behaviors more than apathy (reinforced by the presence of all three on popular television sitcoms like *2 Broke Girls*), why are discourses of apathy found regularly in mainstream news?

Note

1. Max also holds a part-time babysitting job in Manhattan for a new socialite mother.

The Mindy Project
South Asians and Television Multiculturalism

Janani Subramanian

In the "Diwali" episode of the third season of *The Office* (NBC, 2005–2013), Kelly Kapoor, played by Mindy Kaling, says upon being asked about the origins of the Indian holiday, "Oh, um... I don't know. It's really old, I think." Kaling's character, a South Asian American like the actor herself, was superficial and self-absorbed on the show, and her comment represents the character's general ignorance of all things unrelated to celebrity gossip or her love life. *The Office* marked two facets of television produced after the millennium; a faux-vérité style that parodies the continuing popularity of reality television and a pervasive self-awareness that addresses a culturally savvy 20- to 30-something audience. Kaling's tongue-in-cheek performance of Kapoor as a millennial character obsessed with popular culture fit perfectly into this milieu. In addition, Kapoor's tenuous relationship to her ethnic identity represented the calculatedly minimal cultural awareness that often characterizes the millennial of color on network television; Kaling, as a member of Generation Y herself, continues this oscillation between awareness and ironic ignorance as creator, writer and star of her new show *The Mindy Project* (FOX, 2012–present). Network shows of the new millennium such as *Lost* (ABC, 2004–2010), *Grey's Anatomy* (ABC, 2005–present), *The Big Bang Theory* (CBS, 2007–present), *Parks and Recreation* (NBC, 2009–present), *New Girl* (FOX, 2011–present), *Scandal* (ABC, 2012–present), and more have made a concerted effort to add Black, Latino, Asian and South Asian characters to their casts; the shows, however, rarely address racial issues within their narrative arcs and treat their diversity matter-of-factly. This lack of attention to racial and ethnic identity reflects one of the paradoxes of race on millennial television—visible proof of racial diversity without any in-depth acknowledgement of that diversity.

Representations of gender and sexual identity also suffer from a paradoxical acknowledgement and disavowal of politics in what scholars have hesitantly deemed the "postfeminist" moment in popular culture. Shonda Rhimes, producer and show-runner of *Grey's Anatomy* and *Scandal*, two influential primetime dramas with diverse casts, was quoted in a 2008 *New York Times* article, stating: "I'm in my early 30's, and my friends and I don't sit around and discuss race... We're post-civil rights, post-feminist babies, and we take it for granted we live in a diverse world" (Matthew Fogel). Rhimes claims that she and her Generation Y characters were raised in a post-civil rights moment where explicit racial concerns are rarely voiced and a postfeminist moment where gender is not an impediment to professional or personal success.

Yet Rhimes's shows themselves manifest the contradictions inherent in her post–civil rights, post-feminist world, particularly *Scandal*, where her black female protagonist, involved in a heated affair with a white sitting president, rarely engages with racial or gender politics within the show's narrative, much to the consternation of fans and scholars.[1] Olivia Pope (Kerry Washington) has a successful and powerful career (that has seemingly little to do with her identity as a black woman), but her personal life is in shambles, highlighting the obsession with work-life balance that has pervaded postfeminist consciousness in the new millennium. The leading ladies of millennial television do grapple with the issue of how to define female success, yet they do so by way of a seemingly color- and gender-blind consumer-oriented ethos that emphasizes individual choice over the more political demands of second- and third-wave feminism.[2]

It is in this landscape of post-race, post-feminist millennial television that Mindy Kaling, another lead actress of color, crafted a name for herself in television comedy, first with her character Kelly Kapoor in *The Office* and then with her own situation comedy *The Mindy Project* (*TMP*). In this essay, I examine *TMP* and its star as representations of millennial multiculturalism—a carefully managed popular and consumer-oriented multiculturalism that acknowledges and disavows race and ethnicity at the same time. The first part of this essay contextualizes *TMP* within the conflicted place of multiculturalism in contemporary American culture, focusing specifically on South Asian identity in the wake of the millennium's defining event—9/11. I then discuss the role of South Asians in American situation comedies and of Kaling's character Kelly Kapoor on *The Office*, a show that heralded the thematic and stylistic changes of early millennial television comedy. Finally, I look closely at *TMP* as a show that brings together multiple facets of more recent millennial popular culture—postfeminism and multiculturalism—highlighting the way that Kaling, as a writer-comedienne of color in network television, manages both her ethnic identity and body image on network television and reveals the contradictions of racial formation and its representations. Tracing Kaling's development from *The Office* to *TMP* not only reveals a shift in sitcom form and themes from the beginning of the millennium, but also the ways recent television engages with the growing trend of Generation Y comediennes who are independent, self-aware, and exert increasing creative control both on and behind the screens of popular media.

South Asians, 9/11 and Consumer Citizenship

In both *The Office* and *TMP*, Kaling plays a second-generation Indian American, and in both programs her ethnic identity marks her as "sort of" different. Similar to her public persona, developed through her presence on Twitter and her 2011 memoir, *Is Everyone Hanging Out Without Me*, her characters acknowledge their parents' South Indian immigrant roots but situate themselves as fully assimilated young American women. Kaling and her engagement with cultural identity reflect the conflicted place of South Asians in general within the U.S.'s historically black-white racial formations. Shilpa Davé explains:

> The ability to fit in and depict South Asian racial difference (i.e. Apu) as "not too different" as opposed to the contrast emphasized in the black-white racial paradigm in the United States, offers an opportunity for the "not too different" to qualify for citizenship and, hence, gain access to political, economic and social power [3].

As Davé points out, India's colonization by the British Empire as well as Indian citizens' brown skin led to historically ambiguous categorizations for Indians living in the United States, creating complex and constantly changing criteria for American citizenship. Davé and scholars such as Vijay Prashad identify the 1965 Immigration and Nationality Act as the law that dramatically increased the number of highly educated and professional South Asians in America, consequently establishing "South Asian" as both a recognized Census category and, more problematically, a so-called "model minority," or a nonwhite population that has managed to attain financial and educational success within American society. The effect of this ethnically different, white-collar professional population in American popular culture, as Davé analyzes, is the association of what she calls the performance of "brown voice" or "brown face" with both "difference and privilege," which "disrupts cultural conversations about race and citizenship beyond the conventional binaries of black versus white *and* foreign versus domestic in American popular culture" (7). Kaling, as a South Asian writer, producer and actor in Hollywood who embodies a "different" and "privileged" romantic comedy heroine in *TMP*, moves this disruption into the realm of network television.

The 9/11 attacks further emphasized questions of race and citizenship for both the millennial generation and South Asian Americans. 9/11 was not only a formative experience of millennials' middle, high school or college years, but it also shaped their ideas of national security, foreign policy, terrorism, and America's relationship to the Middle East. Various scholars, including Morley Winograd and Michael Hais, claim that 9/11 and America's response to it shaped millennials' political views in two ways: millennials tend to be more liberal-minded than older generations and, at the same time, more patriotic, pointing to the often paradoxical, neoliberal aspects of millennial politics.[3] As mentioned, South Asians' brown skin has historically been difficult to categorize in American legal and political history, but 9/11 offered a new visibility to and different kinds of narratives for brown skin and its national and religious connotations, including both large-scale racial profiling and civil rights violations as well as a simultaneous reinforcement of an all-inclusive notion of "American-ness" (Inderpal Grewal 546).

Subsequent national and international political events, including the strategic use of black conservative figures such as Condoleeza Rice and Colin Powell in the service of U.S. aggression in Iraq and both elections of Barack Obama (2008 and 2012), point to the ways that racial diversity and multiculturalism can be held up as evidence of a strong American state but can also obscure more troubling divisions and inequalities. Television, as Lynn Spigel argues, played a crucial role in returning Americans to a sense of normalcy after 9/11, participating in the paradoxical thrust of multicultural millennial politics mentioned above. On the one hand, news and primetime programs like *The West Wing* (NBC 1999–2006) acknowledged the complexity of politics in the Middle East, but on the other hand, American television used a predominantly liberal humanist rhetoric, often infused with melodrama, that created a "through-line for the American past that flattered a despairing public by making them the moral victims of a pure outside evil" (Spigel 245).

The calculated multiculturalism of recent television programs reflects this ongoing oscillation between acknowledging cultural specificity and trying to forget it, and I argue that this is part of what Spigel calls the "fragmentation and centralization" of "postindustrial modes of capitalism" (260). Spigel refers to the fact that after 9/11, television programming and industrial practices were organized around a seemingly unified, nationalist, consumer-oriented vision as well as "niche politics of style" (256); representations of race and ethnicity reflected a similar preoccupation with acknowledging minorities while incorporating them into a larger vision of American citizenship. While 9/11 is never directly addressed in *TMP*, the show's use of a South Asian protagonist raises the specter of the ways brown skin has been both marginalized and assimilated in the American imaginary, particularly in the new millennium. As Grewal points out, part of the American government's response to 9/11 was to appeal to American citizens' consumer identity, "a consumer citizenship, untethered from, but also supported by the nation-state" (541).

I am interested in this notion of consumer citizenship—or the emphasis on the purchasing power of both viewers and characters—as it relates to American network television, which at its foundation constantly ties together representations of national culture and identity with consumption of products and raced/gendered identities. *TMP*, as a re-tooling of the romantic comedy in a sitcom format, with a curvy, South Asian, Generation Y female protagonist, represents the kinds of negotiations millennial television performs to create subtly raced, post-gender consumer-citizens. Grewal explains that post–9/11 pleas for national solidarity encouraged a move away from the hyphen that accompanies Asian-American or South Asian-American identities—Americans were "just Americans"—and shows like *TMP* can illuminate how that hyphen flickers in and out in American society. Kaling's performance as Mindy Lahiri not only defies conventional representations of South Asians, but it also highlights the way Generation Y negotiates with race and ethnicity across millennial popular culture.

South Asians and Situation Comedy

Before Kaling's stint on *The Office*, South Asian characters on American television were limited to either small, comedic guest roles in sitcoms (Babu in "The Café" episode of *Seinfeld* (NBC, 1990–1998)) or generic "terrorist" roles in dramas such as *24* (FOX, 2001–2010). Beginning with *The Office*, South Asians started to appear as recurring characters in network programs such as *Parks and Recreation*, *The Big Bang Theory*, *The Good Wife* (CBS, 2009–present), *Smash* (NBC, 2012–2013), and *Revenge* (ABC, 2011–present). The only program in that list that explicitly and consistently engages with a character's South Asian identity is *The Big Bang Theory*, where Raj Koothrappali's (Kunal Nayyar) thick Indian accent and social anxiety around women recalls tired representational clichés of Asian and South Asian men as emasculated nerds. Raj's characterization in *The Big Bang Theory* points to some of the pitfalls of post-racial multiculturalism on television, particularly the way the exaggerated nature of television comedy can rely on ethnic or cultural gags deemed safe because they do not violate the predominantly black-white rules of political correctness. Perhaps the most egregious recent example of exploiting South Asian culture on primetime network television is *Outsourced* (NBC, 2010–2011), an American sitcom about Indian call center workers in Mumbai, which highlighted fundamental tensions between the representational practices of American television and the omnipresence of global and multicultural forces in American society. As David Oh and Omotayo Banjo argue, *Outsourced*, with a white male protagonist at its center, surrounded by seemingly clueless Indian workers, embodies what Jodi Melamed has called "neoliberal multiculturalism"; on the surface the show generates humor by making fun of both American and Indian cultures, yet it ultimately uses its Indian context to reify American capitalism (Oh and Banjo 452).

How *The Big Bang Theory* and *Outsourced* represent multiculturalism raises questions about the format of the situation comedy in general in relation to representation. *The Big Bang Theory* is a traditional sitcom, filmed in multi-camera setups and limited to a few sets, which conveys both a sense of artificiality and the kind of closed-world feeling that the various narratives depend on. *Outsourced* and *TMP*, on the other hand, are examples of single-camera sitcoms, which are filmed in a more cinematic style, provide the illusion of shooting on location, and, in the current TV landscape, embody the cultural cache of "quality." Single-camera and "comedy vérité" sitcoms, as explored below, are variations on the traditional sitcom that update its style, yet in many ways retain its conservative representations of race, ethnicity and gender due to the short time frames (between 20 and 22 minutes content, and 8 to 10 minutes commercial breaks) and joke and gag-oriented narrative structures.

Patricia Mellencamp and George Lipsitz have shown that situation comedies from the 1950s, such as *I Love Lucy* (CBS, 1951–1957), *Burns and Allen* (CBS, 1950–1953), *The Goldbergs* (NBC, 1949–1956), *The Honeymooners* (CBS, 1955–1956), and *Life with Luigi* (CBS, 1952–1953) highlighted the limitations and possibilities of the form, simplifying the complicated experiences of the female and ethnic characters into humorous and consumer-oriented episodes. In the comedies that Lipsitz addresses, such as *Life with Luigi* and *Mama* (CBS, 1949–1957), for example, ethnic characters oscillated between being subjects and objects within the program, voicing their subjective experiences as ethnic Americans as long as those experiences remained commodity-centric and fit into television's overriding capitalist drive. From the 1960s onward, the television family expanded to include friends, neighbors, and colleagues, and with the changing definition of family came a shift in the politics of representation as well, where both women and minorities were given more exposure behind and in front of the cameras. Yet, as Herman Gray says, identity became a "minor if not incidental theme" in situation comedies such as *The Cosby Show* (CBS, 1984–1992) (76); sitcoms included more minority characters as long as storylines and themes confirmed television's predominantly consumer-oriented white, upper-middle class address.

The updates to the sitcom format of the new millennium, pioneered by shows such as *Malcolm in the Middle* (FOX, 2000–2006), *Arrested Development* (FOX, 2003–2006; Netflix, 2013–present), and *The Office*, featured a shift from multi-camera shooting to either a single-camera or vérité aesthetic and an on-location sensibility seemingly unfettered by artificial sets. Brett Mills, Ethan Thompson and Trisha Dunleavy have shown that the "comedy vérité" format, in particular, updates the situation comedy style in a way that distinguishes it in a saturated entertainment market and responds to trends such as reality television: "Exploiting the new outlets for humour facilitated by its hybridity, comedy verité [sic] has upgraded the live action sitcom for a popular culture now steeped in the aesthetics, concerns and even the jargon of 'reality' TV" (Dunleavy). The move away from set-based multi-camera sitcoms also seemingly led to less reliance on token minority characters for racial gags; shows such as *The Office* embodied a nonchalant, matter-of-fact attitude towards diversity that spoke to the post-racial ethos of millennial culture. As I explore below with *The Office*, though, these stylistic shifts did not change the marginalization of minority characters within white-centered milieus, instead highlighting the ways some of the specific styles of millennial television are implicated in its conflicted representations of multiculturalism. The "Diwali" episode of *The Office* mentioned in the beginning of the essay, for example, illuminates the ways a comedy vérité sitcom acknowledges the cultural specificity of Kelly Kapoor, Kaling's first television role, but at the same time uses her South Asian heritage as a backdrop for the romantic troubles of the show's white male protagonist.

The Office is not only a prime example of what is known as comedy vérité, marked by the use of a shaky documentary style aesthetic, but it also embodies the tongue-in-cheek irony and self-awareness of millennial cultural production. The use of a shaky camera, talking-head interviews and a plethora of straight-faced reaction shots create an ironic distance between the "documentary as a sober discourse of interrogation" and the "hilarious ineptitude of the subjects," bumbling middle management office workers and city employees (Thompson 68). *The Office* posits itself as an equal-opportunity offender—a common trope in post-racial comedy—yet the "Diwali" episode reveals the way its vérité aesthetic belies a deeper racial logic. The hook before the episode's credits jumps right into the episode's primary narrative, a group office outing to a nearby Diwali celebration. A slightly shaky camera captures the main office room, where Kelly is adjusting an Indian garment on her boyfriend Ryan (B.J. Novak); the camera then zooms quickly in on the boss Michael (Steve Carrell), smirking and saying, "Nice dress, Ryan." We cut back to Kelly, who corrects him and says it is a kurta, making Michael look foolish and locating her as the resident expert on Indian culture within a very white office environment.

Yet, the very next scene reveals Michael doing a talking head confessional—a one on one interview in his office—where he mocks Kelly's assumed ignorance of Diwali as a Hindu festival; in one small scene change, the viewer's assumption that Kelly is aware of her own cultural identity is immediately debunked. The quick oscillation in terms of character identification and style (from behind the scenes to talking head) highlights the way comedy vérité narratives in general move quickly and reveals the questionable place of cultural authenticity within the show, also pointing to a broader nonchalance towards political correctness that marks millennial culture in general. Kelly's information about the kurta is correct—we assume that Mindy Kaling, as the episode's writer, is lending her own expertise as a South Asian American to the storyline—yet she and her identity are quickly rendered as jokes by the show's white patriarchal presence.

The rest of the episode continues to oscillate between cultural specificity and debunking the importance of that cultural specificity. For example, at some point Michael brings the employees into the conference room, which is decorated with pictures of Hindu deities, and asks Kelly to explain the holiday. Kelly responds, "Um, Diwali is awesome. And there's food, and there's gonna be dancing. And, oh, I got the raddest outfit. It has, um, sparkles." When Dwight (Rainn Wilson), resident madman and nerd, begins to explain Diwali's true significance in Hindu mythology, Michael cuts him off with "all right, all right, this isn't *Lord of the Rings*." The humor in this scene relies on the interplay between the posters on the wall of actual Hindu deities, Kelly's superficiality and ignorance of her own culture in light of Dwight's knowledge, and the fact that Michael conflates Hindu mythology with fantasy literature. Adding to that, the quick cuts between Kelly, Michael and Dwight, the shaky camera, and the use of straight-faced reaction shots add to the humor by suggesting that a seemingly earnest attempt at cultural education is impossible in an office full of morons. On the one hand, Kelly's ignorance challenges the assumption that her South Asian heritage makes her an expert, but on the other hand, we only hear a fragment about Diwali's significance before Michael makes a culturally insensitive remark; moments of cultural specificity become lost in the fragmented nature of the comedy vérité style.

At the Diwali celebration itself, the use of Indian extras, authentic food and dancing lend an aura of verisimilitude, but they mostly work to highlight Michael's ignorance, and the episode's primary storyline ultimately focuses on him and his relationship problems in this milieu. Mindy's performance of ditzy Kelly bucks model minority stereotypes of South Asians as serious and hard-working, but at the same time, the fleeting and fragmented moments of South Asian culture in the "Diwali" episode act as a backdrop for the emotional development of the show's white male protagonist, exemplifying *The Office*'s tendency to marginalize its minority characters in favor of more narratively complex white male characters. The vérité style and jokes about ethnicity and race highlight identity's ironic treatment in millennial comedies such as *The Office*, but, to return to Spigel's terminology, this surface "fragmentation" belies television's more "centralized" focus on white male subjectivity (260).

Mindy Kaling's *Project*

Kelly Kapoor is positioned within *The Office* world as a spectacle of superficiality and of non-whiteness, and we read her character as both a performance of a South Asian female comic and as a marginal ethnic character on a predominantly white sitcom. With the creation of *TMP* in 2012, Kaling placed herself front and center in the show's narrative as Mindy Lahiri, a 30-something South Asian gynecologist living in New York City, as well as behind the camera as executive producer, writer, and sometimes director. Mindy's experiences are not rendered fleeting and fractured by a vérité style; she is instead the protagonist of a serialized romantic comedy, complete with a cinematic single-camera shooting style and glamorous New York City settings. Kaling is part of a cadre of Generation Y women in television comedy, including actor Zooey Deschanel and producer Liz Meriweather from *TMP*'s lead-in show *New Girl*, comedienne Whitney Cummings on *Whitney* (NBC, 2011–2013), Kat Dennings and Beth Behrs on *2 Broke Girls* (CBS, 2011–present) and actor/writer Lena Dunham on *Girls* (HBO, 2012–present). The female protagonists on these shows embody the postfeminist, millennial zeitgeist—they are intelligent and educated, yet often "lost" in terms of romantic relationships and/or professional goals. The humor of millennial female-centered television comedy stems from these women's often disastrous attempts at "having it all," and the offbeat performances of comic female stars, such as Deschanel, Cummings, Dennings and Dunham, are also guided by sharp self-awareness and irony; the shows themselves are carefully targeted to similarly hip, culturally savvy millennial audiences.

TMP and Kaling fit into this comedy mold, save for the fact that Kaling, unlike her peers, is not white. On the one hand, *TMP* is a somewhat radical endeavor in a millennial television landscape as the conventions of romantic comedies are adapted to a single-camera sitcom format with a curvy South Asian protagonist, revealing the underlying whiteness of postfeminist fantasies constructed through contemporary romcoms.[4] On the other hand, reflecting the conflicted place of multiculturalism in millennial politics and television, *TMP* makes little reference to Mindy's South Asian background, except for the odd joke, and constructs her as an ideal American consumer-citizen; she only has white male love interests, she is extremely fashionable, and she buys heavily into the romantic and consumer fantasies that American romcoms offer.

TMP represents a variation on the "hyperpostmodernism"—extensive use of self-awareness and irony—of millennial film and television (Valerie Wee). While the show self-consciously references the conventions of romantic comedy, it combines an ironic take on the genre with a more earnest approach to Mindy's search for love. The single-camera aesthetic, natural lighting, and seemingly on-location shooting makes the show look like a cinematic romantic comedy, one where a woman's desire is central to the narrative as she encounters a parade of potential love interests. For example, the opening sequence of the pilot episode features Mindy at different stages of her life—young girl, high school, and college—watching romantic comedies (*When Harry Met Sally...* [1989], *You've Got Mail* [1998], and *Notting Hill* [1999]). These romantic comedies not only act as a set-up for the show, where Mindy can live her own version of the aforementioned films, but they also emphasize the way that Mindy, as a millennial heroine, has internalized the conventions of these films to the extent that they guide her romantic expectations. The single-camera style—the camera floating through the room and focusing on Mindy's face as she watches her TV screen—foregrounds her subjectivity, which sets her up as the center of the world we are about to enter. Watching Mindy watch these films also emphasizes her difference—as a seemingly frumpy Indian girl with big glasses, she stands in stark contrast to the polished whiteness of Meg Ryan and Julia Roberts; in the first shot, we even see Mindy's mother sitting in a corner, dressed in a sari, a distinct marker of Mindy's second-generation status.

At the end of this opening sequence, the pilot continues and Mindy meets another doctor at her hospital, has a romantic elevator encounter, falls in love with the doctor, and at this point the sitcom grinds to a halt as a security guard suddenly appears on screen and says, "What does this have to do with the circumstances of your arrest?" We have jumped in time to the present day, where Mindy, frazzled and dressed in cocktail attire, tries to explain her actions on the day her former boyfriend gets married. In her recollection, she gets drunk, makes an inappropriate speech, rides home on her bicycle yelling "I'm Sandra Bullock," falls into a pool, and finally gets arrested for drunken and disorderly conduct. When she falls into the pool, Mindy has an encounter with a Barbie doll who tells her that she needs to get her life together and that, at least, *she* (the doll) has a boyfriend. The alternation between flashbacks and the present day, along with tracking shots, underwater shooting and special effects (a Barbie doll with a moving mouth), immediately distinguish the program as a different kind of situation comedy—one where the situations are not limited by linear narratives and interior sets and are instead motivated by our millennial heroine's absurd and offbeat mode of comedy.

Mindy's disheveled appearance and her clumsy, drunken antics set her up as an unruly screwball comedy heroine who literally breaks the spatial and temporal norms of the traditional sitcom. That said, the fact that the Barbie doll brings up a relationship as Mindy's key to getting her life back together— and the fact that this becomes the show's central conceit—point to the ways Mindy's unruliness and the show's self-awareness are contained within the bounds of heterosexual partnership. Her ethnic difference from the romantic comedy heroines of her childhood and the Barbie doll are not mentioned within the opening sequence (except for Mindy screaming "Racist" to a car that sideswipes her), also signaling to the viewer that race, while sometimes on display, is not a factor in Mindy's search for love. Kaling-as-writer and Lahiri-as-character both employ the "self-scrutiny" and "cool" of the millennial generation to re-think the romantic comedies of their youth (Christy Wampole); as millennial women of color, they also a-politically and nonchalantly add race and ethnicity to the romcom formula.

In many ways, Mindy writing herself as a romantic comedy heroine with a string of white, male love interests is a radical act, a feat also attempted by the writers of ABC's dramedy *Ugly Betty* (2006–2010), about a curvy, Hispanic recent college graduate (America Ferrara) trying to make it in the glossy world of magazine publishing. Mindy's and Betty's respective brown skins and unstarlet sizes recall Linda Mizejewski's analysis of Queen Latifah in the comedy *Bringing Down the House* (2003): "the excessiveness of this heroine is proscribed by the cultural ideals of white femininity, which in turn is pictured through very select bodies" ("Queen Latifah"). Mizejewski references Kathleen Rowe's use of the "unruly woman" paradigm, which suggests that excess of body and behavior is one way that "woman as subject" can lay "claim to her own desire," and Mindy's unruliness manifests itself not only in her ethnicity and body, but also in her aggressive and often disastrous pursuit of romance (Rowe 410).

In "Pretty Man" (1.20), for example, Mindy goes out by herself for a night on the town and ends up back in her apartment with a good-looking man (Josh Meyers); she finds out he is a prostitute, though, and for the rest of the episode attempts to "Pretty Woman" him, or convert him into a suitable romantic prospect as happens in the 1990 film of the same name. While the parameters of Mindy's sexuality are clearly outlined—she stops short of having sex with him, and it is clear that his occupation falls far below Mindy's and her friends' bourgeois standards—she still takes ownership of the romantic comedy conventions and turns them on their head. She assumes the patriarchal Richard Gere role of "fixing" the prostitute, including outfitting him with a new wardrobe, but she also tries on the Julia Roberts role when she tries to lounge sexily on the piano while he plays it. She ends up falling off the piano twice, and the element of slapstick excess just emphasizes the degree to which Mindy-as-performer slides easily between multiple gender roles, including sexual subject, male caretaker, love interest and screwball spectacle; her oscillation between gender roles and use of physical comedy reinforce Mindy's agency as an unruly yet assertive female protagonist, a combination of traits she shares with her millennial television peers such as *New Girl*'s Jess and *Girls*'s Hannah.

While Mindy-as-character is emotionally and physically unbalanced in refreshing and humorous ways, her unruliness is often contained in the show through its polished aesthetic, which points back to the consumerist ethos at its heart and raises doubts about its ability to truly deconstruct the Hollywood narratives that came before it. "Pretty Man," for example, transitions smoothly between various spaces, including the nightclub, Mindy's office, her home, a clothing store and the cocktail party of her co-worker Danny (Chris Messina). The use of multiple spaces, including outside street scenes of Mindy's apartment and office, not only emphasizes the on-location feel of the single-camera sitcom but Mindy's privileged existence as well. She sees the Skid Row apartment that the prostitute lives in (with an African roommate named DiKimbe

[Abdoulaye N'Gom]) and is shocked; the scenes that do take place in less sophisticated neighborhoods such as Staten Island, in episodes such as "Danny's Friend" (1.18), work to emphasize their difference from Mindy's comfortable lifestyle.

The notion of privilege, as Angela McRobbie argues, guides the postfeminist heroine's existence, for she is educated, professional and possesses the means to lead an independent life full of exciting choices, and these choices are negotiated along predominantly heterosexual, upper class and consumer-oriented lines. On the one hand, Mindy's white-collar occupation and comfortable lifestyle are believable because, to return to Davé's argument, South Asians are associated with privilege and success within American racial paradigms. On the other hand, Mindy's privilege as a postfeminist heroine mitigates her brown-ness, as her clothing, her apartment, and her similarly-privileged friends and coworkers construct her as "the right kind of subject who can make the right choices" and appeal to a hip and savvy millennial audience (McRobbie 10).[5]

One of the ways that Mindy attempts to be the "right" kind of subject for heterosexual coupling is through what McRobbie calls the "self-monitoring" facet of postfeminist subjectivity, where women "must become more reflexive in regard to every aspect of their lives" (9). In *Bridget Jones's Diary* (2001), which *TMP* borrows heavily from, McRobbie argues that Bridget's confessions to her friends, her diary, and her calorie-counting exemplify the "regime of personal responsibility" (10). *TMP* not only features a voice-over much like the one in *Bridget Jones*, a cinematic aural addition to the show's single-camera style that literally lets us hear the protagonist's self-monitoring, but it also constantly references Mindy's appearance, particularly her weight, as a limiting factor to being the "ideal" romcom protagonist. Mindy says in the pilot, "My body mass index isn't great, but I'm not like Precious or anything," and she continues to mention her "non-stick-figure-size an average of once every 7 minutes" thereafter (Sarah T.). While the frequency lessens over the course of the season, Mindy does regularly and matter-of-factly mention her body image in the show, her memoir and her off-screen interviews.

On the one hand, we are granted insight into the protagonist's (and actress's) subjectivity—her worry about being unruly—but on the other hand, the self-monitoring marks Mindy as a work in progress who can and will perfect herself, crafting the show's marketability to a 20- and 30-something, educated, savvy millennial female audience who is similarly molded by the anxieties of postfeminist society. Mindy's clothing also calls attention to her appearance; she wears bright pops of color and clashing patterns, which, along with her office and apartment décor, form an eye-catching and visually appealing color palette. The fact that Mindy is curvy, brown and dresses distinctively rightfully calls attention to a different kind of body as desirable on network television, but at the same time her body-consciousness and designer clothing package her as the Everywoman romantic comedy heroine who self-monitors to appeal to both male love interests and female viewers.

Mindy's suitors often call attention to her appearance, which not only emphasizes the show's problematic reliance on male affirmation but also the ways Mindy's appearance is linked to her ethnic identity; her most recent boyfriend Casey (Anders Holm), for example, says she looks like a "rapper's publicist" when they first meet. Mindy's allusion in the pilot to the independent and critically acclaimed drama *Precious* (2009) and its central heroine obliquely references race—she is "not Precious" in terms of both body weight *and* racial identity, pointing to the ways Mindy negotiates the opportunities and limitations of being a non-white comic performer on network television. Bringing up *Precious* and its poor, obese, troubled black protagonist raises the idea of unruly blackness within the narrative of *TMP* and highlights Mindy's privilege to be able to wear the clothes she does, move in the spaces she inhabits, and pursue her generally white, slim, wealthy love interests.

To return to what Prashad, Sunaina Marr Maira, and Davé have argued, South Asian identity has a varied and somewhat triangulated relationship to the American black-white racial paradigm, and in the case of *TMP*, Mindy often aligns and distances herself from blackness in ways that underline that she is not "too black" to be a viable romantic comedy heroine. In "In the Club," (1.3), Mindy attends a hip club with her colleagues, and she gets excited when she finds out NBA players will be there because "it's a scientific fact that black guys love Indian girls"; her seeming interest in meeting a man of color is qualified by her desire to meet a successful *celebrity* of color. When Mindy is invited to the VIP section of the New York Knicks, though, it is because the Knicks' white lawyer finds her attractive, turning her initial racial stereotyping on its head. Josh (Tommy Dewey), the lawyer, is nerdy and slightly awkward and represents reality intruding on the romcom fantasy Mindy creates in the episode, while also revealing that his attraction to Mindy is racially based. He asks her, "Are you the mistress of a black congressman?," claiming that it is a compliment, and although Mindy is initially taken aback, she eventually allows him to woo her.

The humor in this episode relies on Mindy's misconceptions about black men and South Asian women, yet having a white lawyer who likes Mindy's figure and dark skin as her love interest alludes to her racial identity without entangling it in a relationship with a man of color. In a sub-plot, Danny turns out to be an excellent hip-hop dancer; while whiteness is easily aligned with black music and style in this episode, Mindy is uneasily positioned as dark-*enough* for Josh but not too dark as to attract the attention of a black love interest. Blackness is circled around in another episode, "Mindy's Brother" (1.10), where we meet Mindy's younger brother Rishi (Utkarsh Ambudkar), who confesses to his sister that he wants to be a rap star rather than a doctor. The episode taps into a common second-generation South Asian experience, studied extensively by Maira, where East Coast Indian youth adopt and experiment with hip-hop music and style, but it also functions to associate Mindy with black identity at a safe distance via her brother, the only other man of color in the show. The show positions Kaling next to and against black identity, participating in, to modify Kamala Visweswaran's phrase, a millennial televisual "politics of alignment" that racializes her just enough—but not too much—for a primetime network sitcom (23).

Conclusion

As I write this essay, in the wake of the April 15, 2013, Boston Marathon bombings and subsequent fallout, the specter of 9/11 and racial profiling has turned into a more frightening reality. Both social media and "official" news outlets engaged in rampant speculation about the racial, ethnic and religious identities of the perpetrators; even after discovering that the Tzarnaev brothers are Chechen in origin, the public discourse struggles to reconcile their simultaneous Muslim and "Caucasian" identities, and a "brown scare" is in full effect in and around Boston.[6] Kaling, who is from Boston, has expressed support for her city via Twitter, but her tweets are distinctly a-political in relation to the calls for unity coming from South Asian and Arab American organizations such as South Asian Americans Leading Together (SAALT) and the National Network for Arab American Communities (NNAAC).

The lack of brown consciousness in Kaling's public persona and her work in light of the events in Boston points to the ways that American popular culture and politics in the millennium form tenuous and often tangential relationships, particularly in light of television's consumer-oriented postfeminist and multicultural ethos. Kaling began her television career on *The Office*, and her portrayal of the endearingly ignorant and narcissistic Kelly Kapoor fit into a new kind of millennial humor that was fast-paced, politically incorrect, and stylistically ground-breaking. The character of Mindy Lahiri builds on Kelly's quirky nature but is also granted depth, desire and privilege as the romantic lead of a single-camera situation comedy; while Lahiri does not acknowledge her heritage any more than Kapoor did, she adds a hint of color to the growing number of millennial comediennes bringing their writing and acting talents to the small screen. Kaling's creative control and influence on network television as a woman of color is ground-breaking and exciting, but I wonder when Mindy will date a man of color, have a co-worker or friend of color, or explore her identity beyond throwaway jokes or gags. As mentioned in the beginning of this essay, 9/11 has little to do directly with *TMP*, but as the definitive event of the millennium it continues to shape dominant perceptions of brown-skinned citizens, immigrants and members of the diaspora. Mindy Kaling's visibility as a South Asian writer, producer and actor on American television and *TMP*'s fragile relation to her ethnic identity raise questions about American multiculturalism and its visibility in popular culture. As Ramou Sarr says, "Women of color have been living under drought conditions when it comes to a woman who looks like us telling our own stories," and *TMP*, while a refreshing addition to the racially homogenous world of American television, presents a conflicted perspective on what those "stories" will look like.

Notes

1. See Brandon Maxwell.
2. In "*Revenge* as Postfeminist Dystopia," Anne Helen Petersen presents an excellent summation of postfeminism on TV and the ways that *Revenge* (ABC, 2011–present) highlights the movement's contradictions.
3. For a more detailed discussion on the subject, see Amanda M. Fairbanks, and John Halpin and Karl Agne.
4. See A. Vesey and K. Lambert for a look at the way contemporary female comediennes such as Tina Fey negotiate the boundaries of the single-camera situation comedy format.
5. See Michelle Flores' post about Mindy's problematic reaction to a female Arab patient in the pilot episode and the way it emphasizes racial privilege: "The framing of the Arab woman and Mindy's rhetoric construct a commodified vision of difference that casts the woman as worthless because of her inability to participate in capitalism and consumption."
6. For more, see Amanda Terkel.

The Big Bang Theory
Nerds and Kidults
JANICE SHAW

The Big Bang Theory (CBS, 2007–present) is a television series that exploits the current movement to adopt an adolescent lifestyle of its target audience of millennial adults in their twenties and thirties. This essay explores how the series engages with such a trend by depicting a group of friends who conform to the popularized concept of "kidults,"[1] or young adults who are still living like teenagers, and in the process promotes a reconsideration of the defining aspects of adulthood as they apply in a millennial context. The main characters of *The Big Bang Theory* are nerds, who are extensions of both the technological expertise and the consumerist lifestyle of Generation Y. The nerd is associated in popular culture with computer literacy, intelligence (especially in the areas of science and mathematics) and adherence to a sub-culture based on consumerism, as well as being resistant to routine employment, uncommitted in terms of relationships and lacking in responsibility.[2] These qualities are equally associated with the millennial young adults who form a large part of the viewing audience of the series. The popularity of this program with the 18 to 34 year old demographic[3] is indicative of the way it reflects the preoccupations of a generation characterized by a fascination with technological games and consumerism, a fascination that is also the basis of the popular conception of the nerd. *The Big Bang Theory* depicts nerds as the edge of a spectrum of behavior that is characteristic of millennials, and in doing so challenges previously held defining elements of adulthood.

In addition, *The Big Bang Theory* is an extension of earlier television programs such as *Sex and the City* (HBO, 1998–2006), *Friends* (NBC, 1994–2004), and *Charmed* (WB, 1998–2006) in presenting a lifestyle based on conspicuous consumerism and a prioritized allegiance to a peer group. But where these shows still present the markers of adulthood as desirable, so that the characters strive for stable relationships and use the peer group for comfort and security—often when such goals elude them—*The Big Bang Theory* infantilizes the main characters by having them live in a cohesive group structure where the peer social network is of more importance than those aspects which have previously defined adulthood in Western society: a spouse and children, stable employment, and independent living. The characters in *The Big Bang Theory* reject the stable elements that Western society has typically recognized as the markers of adulthood to the point that, according to Harry Blatterer, people in their twenties and thirties today are defined by "eschewed marriage and family formation, fragmented career trajectories, presentism" (787). Long-held concepts of what it means to be an adult are challenged in *The Big Bang Theory* by presenting the behavior of a marginalized group of nerds as the extension of a generation reassessing its priorities in reaction to a culture of consumerism and electronic recreation. This generation has grown up in a society that offers little financial or marital security, and instead prioritizes short-term goals and rewards.

The Big Bang Theory reflects a changing perception of appropriate lifestyles for young adults. It presents its four scientist main characters as having a network of allegiance not based on the traditional family or workplace structure, and entails an adherence to a largely consumer-based lifestyle. The series is a comedy based on the contrast between four Generation Y nerds who work in science departments at Caltech, a real-world university in California, and an attractive girl in her twenties who moves into an apartment across the hall from two of the characters. The two roommates, Leonard (Johnny Galecki) and Sheldon (Jim Parsons), are physicists who are cocooned in a world of science, computers and science fiction. Their friends, Raj (Kunal Nayyar) and Howard (Simon Helberg), are also scientists, Raj being an astro-physicist and Howard an engineer who designs equipment for NASA. Together, they are representative of a subculture of nerds who are isolated from the rest of the world by their intellect, but also by lifestyle choices. They inhabit a space dominated by electronic games, comic books, computers, science fiction collectibles and academic life. The girl-next-door, Penny (Kaley Cuoco), provides a contrast in both perspective and gender to the nerds, since she works in non-academic employment as a waitress, and functions within the series to represent a seemingly more conventional lifestyle. But even while a contrast is constructed in terms of the social exclusion of the nerds, both they and Penny still share lifestyle attributes associated with millennial adults.[4] All five of them are immersed in a consumer-based culture, own no large assets, are not in nine-to-five employment, and are reluctant to form long-term commitments.[5] In fact, they resist all the conventional *actions* associated with adulthood, according to sociologists such as Blatterer. He feels that the idea of being an adult is a socially embedded one, largely reliant upon certain practices accepted as defining it, and he takes the view that "adulthood holds a paradoxical position" because "it provides the unarticulated background [...] but it is largely defined by default as the taken-for-granted status of the social actor and the middle stage of life" (771). He defines this further since "[i]ts taken-for-granted status is evident in the representations and practices through which it is reproduced: working nine to five and beyond, dinner parties, jury duty and voting, marriages, mortgages and children, the family sedan, adultery and divorce, investment portfolios, life insurances, retirement plans, writing a will, and so forth" (Blatterer 773). A narrative analysis of *The Big Bang Theory* reveals a group of those in early adulthood who exhibit none of these attributes. The characters are in employment, but this is presented more like a school than a work environment, and it is so flexible in nature that there is never a presentation of it as a nine-to-five job. There is little sense of responsibility or accountability attached to the way their work as physicists is presented. Their recreations are what in a previous generation would have been associated with children, as they would have been termed "play."

The New Family

The Big Bang Theory actively promotes non-commitment except to the group. The main characters present a group of young adults living a communal way of life that constructs a group dynamic more like boarding-school friendships rather than an "adult" lifestyle of the traditional nuclear family. It is one of the situation comedies that John Hartley describes as "hybrids, joining family comportment (living together, couch-centric) and workplace (sexual exploration, flirt-centric)" (67) by uniting the typical aspects of the form: family and sexual exploration (Hartley 66). The adolescent lifestyle of the friends emphasizes the sexual exploration element of the program, in conjunction with examining a revised concept of the family for Generation Y. In effect, the group displaces and substitutes for an often dysfunctional family, in the same way that Rachel Hills claims that, for millennials, "forming kin-like relationships with your friends reinvents the family" (2). Certainly, in *The Big Bang Theory* the group provides the type of emotional, financial and cultural support normally associated with the family network. Even though this is, at times, as a result of their presentation as scientific geniuses, often it is as a result of a different lifestyle and perspective of their identity as Generation Yers.

The group functions as a pseudo-family, in contrast to the actual dysfunctional families of the characters. Each family reveals the limitations of its stereotype in a millennial society. For example, Sheldon's deeply religious mother (Laurie Metcalf) denies some of the scientific principles he holds most strongly. In "The Electric Can Opener Fluctuation," (Season 3, Episode 1), his mother challenges him about the validity of the theory of evolution, stating that it is "a matter of opinion" and that she prefers to believe in creationism and a literal interpretation of the Bible. When he replies that, "It's not opinion, it's fact," her response is, "And that's your opinion!" A further difference in perspective is revealed by Leonard's relationship with his mother (Christine Baranski) who, despite being a fellow scientist, maintains such coldness and clinical distance from him that Leonard relies on the group for emotional support. By contrast, Howard's mother is presented as needy, demanding and stultifying of his adult identity, so that he is the stereotype of the millennial still living at home in his late twenties. Just as Howard's mother is the stereotype of the Jewish mother, tellingly unseen onstage yet providing a ubiquitous absent presence, so Raj's parents are representative of the wealthy Indian family, anxious for ratification of success in capitalist terms; their main concern is Raj's low earning potential as a scientist.

The Big Bang Theory extends this presentation of the group as an isolated, cohesive entity by exploiting the stereotype of the nerd as a sub-culture within society. Simultaneously, it positions the characters as an extension of a mainstream trend within this age group. As Blatterer has explored, the notion of young adults refusing to "grow up" is of a global nature, shown by his documentation of Deirdre Van Dyk's 2005 findings of "the rise of 'adultescents' and 'kidults' in the U.S. and Australia; *Nesthocker* in Germany, KIPPERS (Kids In Parents' Pockets Eroding Retirement Savings) in the UK, *Mammone* in Italy and Boomerang Kids in Canada" (777).[6] The reasons for this phenomenon are debatable, and oscillate between the positive viewpoint of those such as Rebecca Huntley who view millennials as the "options generation" (7) and others like Lev Grossman, who describe eighteen to twenty-five or so years old as inhabiting "a strange, transitional never-never land between adolescence and adulthood in which people stall for a few extra years, putting off the iron cage of adult responsibility that constantly threatens to crash down on them" (n. pag.). This critical perspective, often presented in current media articles, is endorsed by research carried out by the British Economic and Social Research Council, which records that over sixty percent of this generation in America,

Australia and Britain has "failed" what they term the tests of adulthood, which are completing an education, becoming financially independent and moving out of the family home (Kate Crawford *Themes*).

This conclusion has prompted Crawford to challenge the validity of such a test, maintaining that these criteria no longer apply to a twenty-first century world. Crawford's view is that society needs to reconceptualize the terms by which it defines adulthood, so that it is "more interconnected, creative and collaborative than in the past" (Insecure Times 51). Rather than young adults today conforming to what may be an outmoded perception of an adult, Crawford's contention is that society should re-examine the terms of maturity in light of modern economic and environmental issues and the changes in relationships that may derive from these developments. Television fictional narratives such as *The Big Bang Theory* reflect this changing perception of appropriate lifestyles for adults. The series presents a network of allegiances not based on the traditional family or workplace structure, and it entails an adherence to a largely consumer-based lifestyle. But much of this consumerism is related to a millennial style of recreation and purchase, dependent on the electronic media so connected to both the nerd subculture and a generation allied to computer generated recreation.

The Kidult and Prolonged Adolescence

The emergence of such terms as "kidult," "rejuvenile" and "adultescent" indicates the ubiquitousness of the notion that millennials are suffering from an inability to move beyond the adolescent stage of life into adulthood. This has associations with the recent growth of adult fandoms based on Young Adult and tween texts and products like My Little Ponies, and such literature as the *Twilight* saga and *The Hunger Games*. The adult involvement in these children's areas has been so extensive that it has spawned terms like "Bronies" for adults, especially men, who love My Little Ponies,[7] and "Twi-Moms" for women interested in the *Twilight* saga.[8] Much of this adult interest has been attributed by scholars such as Crawford to the conflation of what were previously viewed as the different life stages of adolescence and adulthood. The appeal of products intended for a younger age group is indicative of a phenomenon also explored by Keith Hayward, who states that millennials are a generation for which "it is becoming ever-more difficult for young people to differentiate and dissociate themselves from the generation immediately ahead of them" (215).[9] Hayward attributes this to an increasingly consumerist society, in which "the century-old opposition between the adolescent/youth stage and adulthood is being challenged by a late-modern capitalist culture now functioning artificially to extend the former" (215).

The Big Bang Theory engages with a social phenomenon that Crawford suggests is emerging in people in their twenties and thirties: a type of Peter Pan syndrome characterized by difficulty with commitment, and a corresponding interest in the recreations and pursuits normally associated with childhood (Insecure Times 45). According to Crawford, young adults are "relating to career, relationships, property ownership and culture in problematic ways," so that they "consume forms of entertainment once reserved for children" (Insecure Times 45). The type of entertainment includes such areas as iPods, game consoles, animated films and adolescent fiction. This phenomenon problematizes the whole concept of what constitutes an adult, and much of *The Big Bang Theory* conflates the recreations associated with nerds, based on toy merchandising and computer games, with that associated with the millennial.

This changing nature of young adulthood being reflected in such series as *The Big Bang Theory* is, at least partly, the basis of their appeal with this demographic. Rebecca Feasey's examination of the popularity of such drama series as *Charmed* with a young adult audience suggests it is because "those themes, characters and intertextual reference points that appeal to the adolescent viewer also can be seen to speak to the twenty to thirty something generation who have turned their back on marriage, mortgages and secure employment in favor of a less rigid definition of adult maturity" (431). As *Charmed* depicts a group of three sisters who are witches, possessing supernatural abilities that they hide from the rest of the world, this plot taps into an adolescent longing for power and individuality while still being part of a fixed and elite peer group. This approach, which was intended for the teenage demographic, also appeals to an older age group of young adults. *The Big Bang Theory* similarly exploits a parallel situation where the "superpowers" of the group are that of the genius, equally establishing a sub-culture and constructing an elitist group that marginalizes its members. In both cases, the usual mundane concerns of adult life are subsumed by the imperatives of a comic book style double existence. Feasey reasons that this is precisely why *Charmed* appeals to a young adult audience, because areas which are of interest to a teen, that is "fantasy, generation, alienation and conformity" are similarly engaging for a "twenty to thirtysomething" (443) as a result of living a prolonged adolescence.

In agreeing with Valerie Walkerdine's argument about the appeal of teen dramas to adolescent girls, Feasey states that young adults empathize equally with these programs since "the fantastical presentation of difficult emotional issues and troubling circumstances encourages adolescents to identify with the heroine in the text without allowing them to dismiss these stories as being too close to their own lived reality" (437). The inclusion of the exaggerated lifestyle of the nerd in *The Big Bang Theory* functions in a similar way, so that its extrapolation of the millennial adult's concerns and preoccupations are presented in a non-threatening manner. The feelings of powerlessness, especially in areas involving physical strength, are symbolized in "The Justice League Recombination" (Season 4, Episode 11), where the friends dress up as the Justice League superheroes, and persuade Penny to adopt a Wonder Woman costume in order to win a competition at the comic book store. After winning the prize, they view a carjacking on the walk home. Fleetingly, they consider interfering in accord with their costumes, as they confuse reality with the fantasy of cosplay. Significantly, they realize that the identity they have adopted cannot be sustained in real life, and they run away, a direct reference to a life spent running away from bullies as a result of their marginalized position as nerds.

The series presents the friends as stultified in the emotional and social development of their teenage selves, still viewing the subculture of nerds like themselves as a haven from the ostracism and overt harassment of the wider school community. This relates, as well, to a conflicted and adolescent sense of gender identity, whereby, as Lori Kendall comments, while "nerds have an expected mastery of technology, which conveys masculinity," paradoxically, they have "low social skills and little or no sexual interaction, compromising their connection to hegemonic masculinity" (356). The friends often resort to utilizing these computer skills to construct a virtual presence that vicariously fulfills their adolescent desire to be physically more like a superhero role model; Howard's avatar, for instance, in "The Barbarian Sublimation" (Season 3, Episode 2) is a hypermasculinized version of himself.

Computers: Confusing Work and Play

Much of the humor and irony of the series is generated from the basic premise of the nerd subculture, that there is little distinction made between a real and a virtual existence, which is the result of so much of the millennials' life being associated with computers and electronic gaming. Both their work-life and recreation involves computers, to the point where Bogdan Costea, Norman Crump and John Holm claim that there is a confusion between work and play for this generation, because they rely on technology for both of these previously different aspects of life (149). A double irony is constructed here, because in the early episodes of *The Big Bang Theory* the social life of the friends existed mainly online, so that when in the "Pilot," Sheldon claims, "I have a very wide circle. I have 212 friends on MySpace," this leads to Leonard's retort that, "Yes, and you've never met one of them" (Season 1, Episode 1). This comment, intended to relate to the nerdiness of the character, has had its irony slowly eroded by current social trends that position such social networking as the norm rather than a marginalized approach. The extension of this Generation Y movement to online socializing is presented in "The Flaming Spittoon Acquisition," where Sheldon declares that he likes Facebook because he is "a fan of anything that tries to replace actual human contact" (Season 5, Episode 10). Even when Sheldon creates a "friendship algorithm" in the episode of the same name (Season 2, Episode 13), it is not for the purposes of socializing, but in order to exploit a friendship with fellow scientist, Barry Kripke (John Ross Bowie), to gain access to university equipment.

The irony of Sheldon's comment is all but lost in a context where millennials have "virtual" friends in conjunction with those viewed in the real world. These virtual friends are as much friends as those that the Generation Xs in *Sex and the City* or *Friends* saw daily in the coffee shop, the network of which form the focus of the programs. While *The Big Bang Theory* still depicts the physical presence of friends as important, of equal importance is the contact by iPhone, Twitter, Facebook and other electronic means. In addition, such contact has an immediacy that includes the absent friend as a real-time presence. For example, in "The Vacation Solution" (Season 5, Episode 16) Penny reminds Sheldon and Howard that the lives of the girlfriends in the nerd group intertwine, because "You know those girls text me every detail of their lives as it happens." The style of social and recreational contact has changed, not only for the nerds but for this generation. This is further shown since Sheldon's original contact with his girlfriend, Amy Farrah Fowler (Mayim Bialek), was through an online dating service, and much of their relationship is conducted at a distance through Skype and Facebook.

In addition, much of the irony of the dependence on a virtual world for a sense of "reality" by the four friends is generated by their online social engagements. The culmination comes in "The Boyfriend Complexity" (Season 4, Episode 9) where Penny's father visits and, under the impression that Penny and Leonard are dating, attempts to bond in the traditional male fashion with his prospective son-in-law. The subsequent scene shows them virtual fishing on a Wii Console in Leonard's living room. This displacement of what would formerly have been an adult real-world pursuit to a computerized adolescent substitute is further displayed in the episode "The Weekend Vortex" (Season 5, Episode 19), where the four males decide that they will have a gaming weekend of online play. When Sheldon's girlfriend, Amy, objects since he had promised to escort her to a family party, Howard encourages him to assert himself. His ironic advice encapsulates his position as both nerd and millennial, as he urges him to, "be a man. Tell her that you're going to have a sleepover and spend the weekend playing videogames with your friends."

The Big Bang Theory problematizes the concept of adulthood and how our society conceives of it by presenting characters who engage in pursuits and lifestyle choices that society has previously viewed as associated with adolescents. It challenges the current concept of adulthood by examining the practices that our society uses to define it. The characters' involvement with games relates to the way that "[i]n the 21st century [...] adults are encouraged to find and preserve the 'inner child,' to give up adult reserve and treat life as continuous play as the most important opportunity for free self-expression" (Costea et al. 148). A philosophy emerges that combines employment with games, especially when that work involves the very computers that form the basis of recreational pursuits for the millennial generation, so that, as Costea et al. explain, "playful work and playful leisure" blur the boundaries of each, creating a hybrid, more flexible concept of both (149).

Certainly, many of the episodes in *The Big Bang Theory* include the use of university facilities for games, such as the creation and fighting of the Mobile Omnidirectional Neutralization and Termination Eradicator (MONTE) robot that the friends challenge against a colleague's Kripke Killer robot in "The Killer Robot Instability" (Season 2, Episode 12). A more personal approach to robots and games is presented in "The Robotic Manipulation" (Season 4, Episode 1), when Howard has to be taken to the emergency room in the hospital as a result of the games he plays with the robotic arm he has constructed. Not only these comic aspects, but the mise-en-scène of the apartments and rooms, reveal that there is no clear distinction between work and the personal space of the characters, through the numerous whiteboards with formulae, models of DNA and computers in evidence. This is indicative, not only of the integration of science into all aspects of the lives of the characters, but also of the current shift from a "hard" to "soft" capitalist ideology in the workplace, so that "[i]n soft capitalist corporations, the employee ceases to observe a rigid distinction between work and leisure, but sees both as opportunities to express the self creatively" (Rachel Falconer 39).

The one character who is not able to integrate work and leisure, or see her employment in terms of gameplay, is Penny. But ironically, when she is feeling dissatisfied with the lack of progress of her career as an actress, even she turns to gameplay and finds fulfillment in the virtual world of *Age of Conan*, where she becomes immersed in the life of her avatar. In "The Barbarian Sublimation" (Season 3, Episode 2), Penny, previously aloof from the electronic games that Leonard, Sheldon and the others play constantly, becomes involved after continually being rejected for parts as an actress. Here, the lure of electronic games is linked to the millennial generation more generally, rather than specifically as a feature of being a nerd, through a reference to the escapism and vicarious satisfaction that games offer in a twenty-first century world where employment is uncertain.

Masters of Technology

The Big Bang Theory emphasizes the importance of the virtual world to the nerds, by relating it to their identity as scientists. However, the use of technology extends far beyond its scientific use to the common interaction in the millennials' social and cultural worlds. The computer skills that previously served to marginalize the nerd have now become a necessary and accepted aspect of Generation Y identity. The nerd stereotype, with its "expected mastery of technology" (Kendall 356), is inclusive of a now desirable but exploitable trait, so that in "The Vengeance Formulation" (Season 3, Episode 9) Leonard laments that the only time ex-girlfriends contact him is when their hard drive crashes.

Though seemingly desirable, this technological mastery is also associated with an inability to distinguish between the reality of the computer generated world and the outside world. In "The Zarnecki Incursion" (Season 4, Episode 19), for example, Sheldon contacts the police to report the theft of his virtual possessions in the online *World of Warcraft*, only to be astounded when they refuse to investigate the case of the stolen imaginary battle ostrich. To him, these possessions are as real as those he owns in the apartment. Throughout the seven seasons of the show, not only the interaction of the real and the virtual world is emphasized, but also the boundaries between the worlds are continually being transgressed, so that a virtual existence can seem to have more reality, and also be more satisfying, than a "real" life. Leonard, for example, points out the irony of the four friends adopting a heroic avatar and embarking on quests in their gaming existence, but refusing to act when a real quest is available to them, such as confronting Penny's ex-boyfriend to get her possessions back ("Pilot," Season 1, Episode 1) or the money he owes her ("The Financial Permeability," Season 2, Episode 14). This is also clearly shown by their collections of memorabilia, where they are attempting to bring the fictional world into their own.

The merging of the real and the virtual worlds also relates to the pervasive notion of the nerds as scientists engaged in a type of employment that is both unknowable and esoteric: so much so, that not only is it unproductive in the sense of a practical application, but other people have no access to it. On Leonard's date with Penny at the start of the series in "The Fuzzy Boots Corollary" (Season 1, Episode 3), she asks "So, what's new in the world of physics?" He replies, "Nothing... With the exception of String Theory not much has happened since the 1930s. You can't prove String Theory and at best you can say 'Hey look, my idea has an internal logical consistency,'" to which she reassures him in a way that shows no understanding, "Well, I'm sure things will pick up." This is reinforced later in Season 2, Episode 9, "The White Asparagus Triangulation," where another girlfriend, Stephanie (Sara Rue), asks Leonard what he did at work, and he replies, "I thought about stuff" and then belatedly adds, "I wrote some of it down."

But the episode where this is shown most clearly is in "The Pirate Solution," (Season 3, Episode 4) where Raj confesses that he had found that his project to predict the composition of trans–Neptunian objects was flawed months previously, and so for the past six months all he had been engaged in at the university was "checking his emails." As a result of his fear that he would lose his resident status and be deported back to India, he takes a job working for Sheldon. A montage of shots accompanied by the "Eye of the Tiger" theme from the film *Rocky* (1976) then reveal them pondering in various poses, reinforcing the abstract and abstruse nature of their endeavors and providing an ironic contrast to their mental rather than physical endeavors. Throughout the series, both the flexibility of the male protagonists' employment at the university and its unknowable nature subverts its legitimacy as work in the traditional sense.

Ironically, the strongest sense of responsibility to an employer or work colleague emerges in "The Benefactor Factor" (Season, 4 Episode 15), when Leonard "takes one for the team" by sleeping with a female patron in order to gain funding for new research equipment for the university. In addition, the few duties that the friends have imposed on them by Caltech are social; they are required by the Head of the Department, Dr. Gablehauser (Mark Harelik), to attend various fundraising cocktail parties and functions. This is an extension of the link between work and recreation for both nerds and millennials as a result of both being technologically based. In a Generation Y world, computers are used both for employment and recreation, creating a duality of function between what would previously have been viewed as quite separate areas of life.

The presentation of the main characters in *The Big Bang Theory* as scientists working at a university further displaces them from a conventional way of life, by reference to a popular perception of academics as impractical theorists who have never grown up and left school, in effect being perpetual school students. This is exemplified in "The Zarnecki Incursion" (Season 4, Episode 19), where, on their way from a fruitless quest to retrieve Sheldon's virtual gaming possessions from an internet thief, the car breaks down. In response to the question, "Who knows the theory of the internal combustion engine?" the scientists reply, "Of course." Then in reply to, "Who knows how to fix one?" there are negatives from them all. The culmination of the episode, where Penny not only rescues them from the stranded car, but leads the quest to retrieve the stolen goods, is indicative of their inability to perform in a practical or social situation that extends beyond theoretical knowledge. Even more, the adolescent nature of the four is intensified when, on the hunt to track down the goods, they discover that they are only able to contact the informant "after school hours."

Consumerism

The collectibles that are scattered around the apartments, workplaces at the university and even, in the case of Howard and Sheldon, as items they are wearing, function more than simply to provide an authentic mise-en scène in terms of the environment of the nerd or the millennial. They are also an attempt to bridge the gap between the virtual and the real world, as well as the fictional and the scientific. Their collections of *Star Trek* items, toys and collectibles function to bring the virtual world into reality, in conjunction with the cosplay they indulge in regularly.

Given the opportunity to adopt a costume, the male characters all choose The Flash, symbolizing their stultified adolescent longing to escape from situations in which they were bullied as a result of their identity as nerds. Often parodies within the series itself reinforce the extent of the immersion of the nerds in a fictional or online reality, such as where Sheldon is in a re-creation of a typical *Star Trek* setting in "The Transporter Malfunction" (Season 5, Episode 20). Similarly, in "The 21 Second Excitation" (Season 4, Episode 8) where the friends line up to watch the version of *Raiders of the Lost Ark* "with the extra 21 seconds," the end of the episode shows them re-creating a parodic sequence of the most famous scene of the original film, where Indiana Jones is fleeing from a rolling boulder. While they could order comics online, they refuse to do so, preferring to "find" the comic books themselves in a store so that the enjoyment of the book as physical artifact is preserved. This is in ironic contrast to their refusal to open their toys to play with them, because then its value as a collectible is lost.

A comparison with the consumerism in *Sex and the City* reveals the difference between the Generation Xers' conspicuous consumption and the consumerism of Generation Y. Where Carrie (Sarah Jessica Parker) spends enough on her Manolo Blahnik shoes to have paid a deposit on an apartment in Manhattan, as revealed in "Ring a Ding Ding" (Season 4, Episode 16), she does so as an engagement with the status of a named brand, and also, as it is shown in "A Woman's Right to Shoes" (Season 6, Episode 9), as a form of compensation for a "single woman's life." Carrie views the purchase of a status symbol and enjoyable item as solace for not being able to engage in the "adult" goal to which she aspires: a stable marital-style relationship with children. This is in contrast to the consumerism of *The Big Bang Theory*, which seems to have little to do with status as much as with indulging in an adolescent style of "play."

Where Carrie is initially amazed, and later remorseful, about the extent of her shoe-spending of over $40,000 that would have allowed her to buy her apartment when it went co-op without recourse to asking friends for a loan, there is little remorse about the money spent on collectibles in *The Big Bang Theory*. If any concern is expressed, it is in terms of being thought a "boy-man" by a woman, and that the model of the capital city of Krypton, Superman's home planet, "seems a lot cooler when a girl isn't looking at it" in "The Cooper-Hofstadter Polarization" (Season 1, Episode 9). The priorities are completely different and extend beyond just the nerds, as shown in "The Financial Permeability" (Season 2, Episode 14), where Penny is barely able to meet her rent, and so Leonard tries to help her to establish a budget to manage her finances. When he questions the need for her to spend money on cable, especially when her electricity is cut off for non-payment so that she cannot even use it, she is completely resistant to the notion of not engaging with what she considers to be one of the staples of life.

Similar comments that emphasize the allegiance to a consumerist ethic and its ties to an adolescent lifestyle are frequently presented in the series. "The Nerdvana Annihilation" (Season 1, Episode 14) details where the friends bid for and win a time machine online, only to find that when it arrives, it is full size and blocks the stairwell when Penny is on her way to work. In her anger, she accuses the men of acting like children in their attachment to science fiction and popular culture memorabilia, finally questioning, "You are grown men. How could you waste your lives with these stupid toys and costumes and comic books?" As a result, Leonard decides to sell all his collectibles, consisting mainly of *Star Trek* merchandise. The episode ends, though, with the endorsement of his lifestyle when Sheldon accuses Penny of hypocrisy, since she has an equally extensive collection of Care Bears, My Little Ponies and Hello Kitty clothing. The fascination with consumer products that was originally presented as related to the friends' identity as nerds is re-established as a product of a millennial culture, to which Penny is just as subject, despite being the symbol of normality in opposition to the nerd subculture of the scientist friends.

Conclusion

The Big Bang Theory exploits the popularized notion of the nerd as reliant upon a mastery of technology for a sense of identity and social contact, incapable of having a "real job" and unable to form a commitment apart from an association with fictional role models. This idea of the nerd forms the basis for the humor and much of the irony within the narrative, especially as it is dependent upon the typical device of situation comedy of introducing a disruption to the status quo. Within the series, this is achieved by the introduction of a "normal" perspective into that of the world of the geniuses through the character of Penny, who is intended to signify the mainstream perspective of the viewer. But this irony is continually being eroded by the tendency of the millennial viewers (who form much of its viewing audience), to themselves adopt a similar lifestyle to that of the characters in the show. Even though Penny is positioned as the symbol of real world normality, as demonstrated by her employment in a more conventional occupation as waitress and non-involvement in scientific areas, increasingly she reveals attributes popularly associated with the nerd, and the kidult viewer. These attributes challenge the previously accepted set of behaviors that defined adulthood: commitment, investment in large-scale assets rather than recreational items, and a secure and individual sense of identity. While *The Big Bang Theory* presents a discourse intended to depict a marginalized subculture, increasingly it appeals to and popularizes a trend within the mainstream of millennials, which is itself a reaction to an increasingly technological society with an uncertain economic context, and in the process exposes an alteration in the contemporary concept of adulthood and the practices that define it.

Notes

1. Rachel Falconer explores what she terms as "A cult of 'the inner child' or the 'kiddult'" as it was "permeating adult cultural life on many levels in the late 1990s" (32) in Britain, in *The Crossover Novel*. Here she cites the earliest use of the term "kidult" by Peter Martin in 1985 in a *New York Times* article, and explores other subsequent usage.

2. Lori Kendall refers to the "nerdity test" available online as indicative of the popular conception of the nerd:

> Although only one question on the nerdity test explicitly indicates gender, by and large, the test presents nerds as male. Nerds enjoy school and do well in it, especially math and science courses. The more types of computer experience, the higher the nerd score. Nerds have high IQs and possess large amounts of esoteric technical knowledge, but are socially inept. Nerds also collect objects connected with knowledge (atlases and maps; mathematical and scientific equipment such as telescopes and slide rules; etc.), and are avid science fiction fans. Section 10 of the text, concerning clothing and apparel, lays out several of the stock features of the nerd stereotype: uncoordinated clothing, pocket protectors, lack of personal hygiene, too-short pants ("high-water" pants or "floods"), and glasses, especially with ad hoc repairs (i.e., held together with tape or glue) [353].

3. After its second season, Edward Wyatt comments in an article in *The New York Times* that the show proved popular with the young adult demographic, in particular. At that time, he reported the series "has further expanded its audience, becoming the highest-rated live-action comedy among the sought-after young-adult demographic group" (n. pag.).

4. Lev Grossman presents a series of representative cases: "Michele, Ellen, Nathan, Corinne, Marcus and Jennie are friends. All of them live in Chicago. They go out three nights a week, sometimes more. Each of them has had several jobs since college; Ellen is on her 17th, counting internships, since 1996. They don't own homes. They change apartments frequently. None of them are married, none have children. All of them are from 24 to 28 years old." He goes on to contrast these case studies with previous generations, and points out that "Thirty years ago, people like Michele, Ellen, Nathan, Corinne, Marcus and Jennie didn't exist, statistically speaking" (n. pag.).

5. Harry Blatterer discusses such practices as previously being representative of adult life, and how these are being "eschewed" by millennials (773).

6. Deirdre Van Dyk's article lists the terms used for a similar phenomenon of delaying moving out of the family home, so indicating its global nature. While semantically the terms differ according to the national reason attributed to it, the trend is the same in each country listed: Canada has "boomerang kids" as a result of "a tight job market"; England has "KIPPERS" because of "rising costs"; France has "Tanguy Syndrome" in honor of a film based on a 28-year-old son who "refuses to move out"; Germany has "nesthockers" since the adult children "regard their parents as friends"; Italy has "mammonic" who "won't give up Mamma's cooking"; and Japan has the "freeter" who "job hops and lives at home."

7. According to "Bronies" on the internet site *Know Your Meme* a "'Brony' is an Internet slang term used to describe a teenage or adult male fan of the TV cartoon series *My Little Pony: Friendship Is Magic* (MLP:FiM). Though initially seen as a cult phenomenon outside of the show's traditional demographic of young girls, the Bronies have since grown into a

widely recognized fandom subculture and continued to retain their presence and influence on Internet culture and its hub sites" (n. pag.).

8. The article "'Twilight,' Take Me Away!" in *New York Magazine* concludes that "a large percentage of devoted fans of Meyer's four novels and two films [...] are smart, sophisticated, well-read mothers. Perhaps because the love story at the crux of the saga is unconventionally adolescent" (n. pag.).

9. Keith Hayward also makes the point that life stage dissolution is occurring for young adults in both preceding and succeeding generations, so that "the *bi-directional* processes of 'adultification' and 'infantilization'" are occurring simultaneously (215).

The Emotional Power of Technology, Community and Morality in *The Vampire Diaries*

MARGO COLLINS

In his latest book on vampires in film, Ken Gelder notes that "The encounter with a vampire is [...] an encounter with something old" (vii) and that this "affiliation of the old and the young" is generally a "catastrophic one that plays out with the vampire and its victim" (18). He writes that "The juxtaposition of old and new is, of course, central to vampire films broadly speaking, which so often gain their dramatic power through the narratives they build around an ageing or archaic vampire's experiences in the modern world" (24). While Gelder is certainly right—depictions of vampires do continue to center on the collision of young and old—those collisions have changed in recent years to accommodate the sensibilities of the millennials who now make up the primary audience of these depictions. In particular, the vampires themselves have become, if not actually millennials themselves, at least millennial-adjacent; if, as Nina Auerbach claims, each generation creates the vampire it needs, then the millennial generation's vampires reflect the values of Gen-Y, especially in their focus on individual moralism and emotions. The CW network's popular series *The Vampire Diaries* (2009–present) in particular illustrates the ways in which vampires become the millennials upon whom they feed.

Adapted for television from L. J. Smith's young adult book series published in the 1990s, *The Vampire Diaries* premiered on the CW network in 2009 to fan acclaim. Produced by Kevin Williamson (who also produced the highly popular WB's *Dawson's Creek*, 1998–2003), the show is clearly designed to appeal to the members of a young female audience who are already enthralled by the vampires of such stories as the *Twilight* novels and movies or HBO's *True Blood* series (2008–present) and aware of the conventions of teen melodramas such as the CW's *Gossip Girl* (2007- 2010) or *One Tree Hill* (2003–2012). Drawing on traditions of both teen drama and horror, the series begins as the story of Elena Gilbert (Nina Dobrev), a teenage orphan, who falls in love with Stefan Salvatore (Paul Wesley), a new classmate who, she soon discovers, is a vampire. The story quickly becomes more complicated, as many of her friends and family members either fall prey to or become supernatural beings themselves: cheerleader Caroline Forbes (Candice Accola) becomes a vampire, best friend Bonnie Bennett (Kat Graham) discovers she is a witch, football player Tyler Lockwood (Michael Trevino) triggers a curse and becomes first a werewolf and then a hybrid werewolf/vampire, and brother Jeremy (Steven R. McQueen) becomes a vampire hunter. Stefan's sometimes-evil brother Damon (Ian Somerhalder) becomes a second love-interest for Elena, and Elena herself turns out to be the descendant and doppelgänger of Stefan and Damon's first love, Katherine (also played by Nina Dobrev), who turned them both into vampires towards the end of the Civil War.

The series features a millennial cast, and as it progresses, the millennials and the monsters become more interpenetrating—the vampires take on more Gen-Y traits and virtually all of the teenage characters in the show take on supernatural traits; eventually, only high-school football star Matt Donovan (Zach Roerig) is left among the millennials to nominally represent humanity. However, despite the characters' shift into the monstrous, the series implies that these monsters are representative of millennials in general. Asa Simon Mittman writes that

> Monsters do a great deal of cultural work, but they do not do it nicely. They not only challenge and question; they trouble, they worry, they haunt. They break and tear and rend cultures, all the while constructing them and propping them up. They swallow up our cultural mores and expectations, and then, becoming what they eat, they reflect back to us our own faces, made disgusting or, perhaps, revealed to have always been so [...] all "monsters" are our constructions [...] through the processes by which we construct or reconstruct them, we categorize, name, and define them, and thereby grant them anthropocentric meaning that makes them "ours" [1].

In the case of *The Vampire Diaries*, the monsters are indeed our own. In particular, they are our own millennials made monstrous—but in doing so, the series underscores the values of the millennial generation. In particular, *The Vampire Diaries* posits a particularly millennial concern with the value of emotions, especially as shown through the characters' actions and interactions with technology, community, and morality.

Some of the series' depictions of millennials are drawn from popular conceptions of the "Y-Generation" and its values; portrayals that claim that millennials "are prolific communicators" (Richard Sweeney) who "have a reputation for being attention sponges" (Jeanne C. Meister and Karie Willyerd), and who "are lazy, lack emotional intelligence, and don't take criticism well" but "can be easily won over by the latest gadget" (Jonathan Becher). However, *The Vampire Diaries* pulls away from these easy criticisms of the generation it represents, ultimately delineating a generation whose members "display little appetite for claims of moral superiority" ("Millennials: Confident. Connected. Open to Change," 7) and who prefer instead to place value on "strong team instincts and tight peer bonds" (Neil Howe and Reena Nadler 18). Ultimately, the series suggests, these tight peer bonds should be predicated on emotional ties rather than any more traditional moral stances[1]; indeed, most decisions in the series are depicted as being based on emotional alignment to such a degree that this emotionalism becomes associated with the millennials who rely upon it in their decision-making.[2]

Technology

Nina Auerbach writes that in general, "vampirism springs not only from paranoia, xenophobia, or immortal longings, but from generosity and shared enthusiasm" (vii). For the millennial generation, these enthusiasms tend toward the technological. This is certainly true in *The Vampire Diaries*, which initially sets up a divide between the young, technologically savvy humans and the older, less technologically capable vampires. However, this distinction quickly blurs, highlighting the ways in which the series casts all of its primary, adolescent characters—both human and monsters—as inherently millennial, no matter how long they have been alive.

The title of the series focuses on communication and self-discovery; however, the show's emphasis on diaries fades quickly. This is perhaps unsurprising, as current millennials (unlike the books' original audience in the 1990s) are almost certainly more likely to post a blog than they are to write in a diary, particularly a hand-written diary like the one Elena carries with her to the cemetery in order to sit by her parents' grave and record her thoughts. Elena is set up early in the series as a reader, when she says that she wants to read *Wuthering Heights* again—this time in a first edition Stefan lends her ("The Night of the Comet," 1.2). Later, she says she wanted to be a writer but that she can't see herself pursuing that goal after the death of her mother ("The

Turning Point," 1.10). This writerly characterization isn't developed in the series; Elena's claim that her dream of becoming a writer died with her parents seems particularly designed to eliminate any need to continue the diary theme (despite the series title). Indeed, by the second season, the diaries have been all but eliminated, leaving only the title-sequence voice-overs as remnants of the diary-writers season one included. By the third and fourth seasons, the title sequence includes voice-overs from several characters, making this a series about the entire cast rather than simply Elena and Stefan. In this, the series itself becomes a sort of video "diary" recording the lives of the characters—a move that is more than a little reminiscent of the increasingly popular (and public) YouTube videos that often function as a form of diary for the millennial generation. Thus the title serves both as a reminder of the inherently self-revelatory nature of the series' characters and as a link between the old (vampires and diaries) and new (millennials and videos).

Examples of millennial comfort with technology abound in the series. In Caroline's car, a Ford Fiesta, Elena attempts to change the subject during an uncomfortable discussion by suddenly announcing "I love this song." Caroline asks aloud "What's playing?" and the car replies, 'Playing: 'We Radiate,' by Goldfrapp" ("Memory Lane," 2.4). In addition to being an obvious example of product placement, this moment also highlights the ease with which the millennial characters use technology. The series attempts to set up a distinction between the millennial, human characters and the older vampires early in the series. In the second episode, "The Night of the Comet," Elena and her best friend Bonnie discuss the fact that Elena and her potential love-interest Stefan have not communicated except in person. For the viewer, who already knows that Stefan is a vampire, his failure to offer Elena the information she would need to contact him by texting is a reminder of his status as an outsider, a non-millennial pretending to be a teenager. Later, Bonnie attempts to give Stefan the information that he lacked by offering him Elena's cell-phone number on a slip of paper. She says "I'm gonna give you Elena's cell number and her email. She is big on texting, and you can tell her I said so." As she reaches out to give the paper to Stefan, her hand brushes his and she is overcome by a psychic vision, one that she later calls "a really bad feeling" ("Friday Night Bites," 1.3). As Elena begins to suspect that Stefan is not what he claims to be, his lack of technological connection serves as one more piece of evidence for her to ponder.

Once Elena discovers Stefan's secret identity, however, that distinction disappears. All of the vampires throughout the show are shown as becoming remarkably adept at using cell phones and computers—even those who have lain dormant for many years and are, presumably, unused to these innovations.

Despite one scene in which the vampire Anna works to explain television remotes to a group of newly revived vampires ("There Goes the Neighborhood," 1.16), the implication seems to be that those vampires who are connected to the millennial humans in the series both learn the new technology quickly and become as dependent upon it as the millennials themselves, though the series often downplays that dependence in favor of physical, personal communication. In part, of course, this issue is due to the nature of television—the series needs action, and constant communication through electronic means does not make for good TV. But the plot itself is often predicated on technology and its ability to apparently erase distance. At the end of the third season, Elena, concerned that both Stefan and Damon will die, must decide which brother to join. She has a long telephone conversation with Damon, but the implication is that the phone and its electronic communication does not suffice, does not take the place of joining Damon physically, a clear plot device that highlights the show's inconsistencies in its attitude toward technological communication when a scene can be played for emotional impact.

Nonetheless, instant communication and its possibilities do play a part in the series. In season two, for example, Elena's friends develop a plan to eliminate Elena's ancestor-turned-vampire Katherine—a plan that is dependent upon the use of cell phones and particularly texting. Each character completes his or her portion of the plan and sends a text to alert the others. As they are creating their attack plan, Bonnie enters the room and says "I got Stefan's message." Thus, even the creation of the plan begins with the use of technology; Bonnie and Stefan did not speak directly. Indeed, it's unclear whether they are discussing a voicemail or a text, and the lack of distinction highlights how little the characters differentiate between the two forms of communication. Similarly, Elena realizes that something is awry when no one communicates with her. She says "I haven't heard from anyone all day. It's like everyone's been avoiding me." A lack of communication for a single day is enough to cause Elena concern, indicative of her position as a millennial. As Alice Marwick and Danah Boyd note,

> Far from being a source of isolation, the teen's phone is a tether to loved ones; it is a personal object, a crucial connection. A study by the International Center for Media and the Public Agenda asked one thousand students in ten countries to engage in a 24-hour media fast. The students had no problem giving up TV, newspapers, or magazines. But cutting them off from the Internet made them feel alone and isolated.

Thus, Elena's concern is valid; if a millennial desires constant (and instant) connection, then the sudden disappearance of that contact is cause for worry.

Elena's fears are validated when Alaric Salzman (Matthew Davis), Elena's history teacher (and a vampire hunter), keeps her from answering his ringing cell phone—his unwillingness to share communication indicates his desire to keep information from Elena.

Moreover, this episode sets up Stefan and Damon as more like their millennial friends than other vampires, in this case Katherine. The plan to capture Katherine is intricate: Damon texts Bonnie and Jeremy; Jeremy delivers a verbal message from Stefan to Katherine ("He and Damon want you to meet them at the edge of the lake by the woods. They brought the moonstone."); Jeremy texts Caroline; Caroline allows herself to be captured by Katherine and tricks Katherine into a room designed to keep her magically contained; Damon and Stefan are waiting in hiding to stake Katherine.

It's significant here that Katherine is depicted as being utterly dependent upon verbal communication—unlike the others, she is not part of the community of cell-phone users texting to one another. Indeed, this plan would not have been possible were it not for the characters' ability to communicate instantly via text—this way they cannot be overheard and their plan cannot be disrupted. Stefan and Damon, despite being over 140 years old, are adept in their use of technology. Katherine, at least in this episode, is not.

However, this episode also suggests that it is possible to rely too much on technology, as Katherine is able to prevail through the very reliance upon physicality that the other characters used to trap her by arranging for a magical connection to Elena. Elena feels every blow that Katherine takes, and when the vampire brothers attempt to stake her, they almost kill Elena. Although Bonnie is eventually able to break the magic connection, the episode suggests that it is perhaps unwise to rely solely upon technology to the exclusion of other means of communication, and that the physical is at least as important as the technological. This emphasis on the physical is highlighted at the end of the episode by the fact that Elena is kidnapped immediately after talking to her brother on her cell. She tells Jeremy, "Tell Bonnie that whatever she did, I'm starting to feel better. Yeah, you can drive her home. I'm just gonna go straight to bed." But of course that's not what happens at all, underscoring the fact that technology is no more reliable than any other form of communication and that trusting implicitly in anything communicated via that technology is at best naïve and at worst dangerous. Indeed, it is not until Jeremy speaks to Stefan in person at school the next day that anyone realizes Elena is missing—Jeremy assumed that she was with Stefan; Stefan assumed she was at home.

Similarly, Bonnie decides she can trust Lucy, the witch working with

Katherine, when they touch hands and arms—because they are both witches and are blood-related, Bonnie is able to tell that Lucy is on her side. Once again, then, this episode seems to privilege the physical over the technological. But when Lucy meets with Katherine, she uses her new knowledge to disable her, tricking Katherine into verbally discharging the debt Lucy owed her. As soon as she is free to do so, Lucy uses her magic to render Katherine unconscious. Katherine's reliance upon verbal communication unmediated by technology leaves her vulnerable, whereas the millennials and their allies prevail, in part because they were able to communicate with one another through technological means. The series suggests that the most effective communication is that which comes from personal connection supplemented by technology, a fact that highlights the overarching emotionalism of the series; indeed, in *The Vampire Diaries*, everything is better when it is connected to emotion and personal communication.

Community

Sarah Rees Brennan notes that in *The Vampire Diaries*, Elena has had a strong support system from the beginning, unlike heroines in other recent vampire tales such as Stephenie Meyer's *Twilight* books (2005, 2006, 2007, 2008) or the *Twilight* saga films (2008, 2009, 2010, 2011, 2012) or even *Buffy the Vampire Slayer* (The WB, 1997–2003); Bella and Buffy, the heroines of those works, begin their respective series alone in a new school setting, without a support system in place. Elena, on the other hand, has a fairly wide-ranging group of friends. This support is in itself particularly millennial; a 2011 Pew study found that "someone who uses Facebook several times per day averages 9 percent more close core ties in their overall social network compared with other internet users" ("Technology and Social Networks")—echoing the idea that "virtually connected Millennials have more close friends (yes, 'real-life' friends!) than any other generation. And they're more likely to maintain these connections longer" ("5 Millennial Truths"). For Elena, this support system grows to include more and more millennials (and monsters-made-millennial), even as she loses the more traditional connections to authority figures. As first her parents, then her aunt Jenna (Sara Canning), and finally her guardian Alaric all die, she develops stronger connections to those around her who are (or, in the case of the vampires, who appear to be) her own age.

In addition, the paratextual elements of the series, when read in conjunction with the plot itself, reveal the series' link between emotional connection and community—again, an especially millennial trait. In particular, the voice-over elements of various episodes illustrate the development of a community drawn together by both proximity and emotional connection. In season one, the series opens with Stefan saying "For over a century I have lived in secret; hiding in the shadows, alone in the world. Until now. I am a vampire. This is my story... I shouldn't have come home. I know the risk. But I had no choice. I have to know her." The images are all of Stefan—staring into the sunrise, jumping off a roof and landing smoothly. As he announces, this is initially his story. By season four, on the other hand, the episodes open with a montage of characters and the voice-over is performed by virtually the entire cast:

> STEFAN: Mystic Falls. I was born here. This is my home.
> DAMON: And mine.
> ELENA: And mine.
> STEFAN: For centuries, supernatural creatures have lived among us.
> CAROLINE: There are vampires, werewolves, doppelgängers –
> BONNIE: Witches.
> KLAUS: And even hybrids.
> BONNIE: There are those who protect them –
> JEREMY: And those who want them dead.
> ELENA: There are friends –
> STEFAN: Our enemies –
> ELENA: The ones we love –
> MATT: And the ones we've lost.
> ELENA: And then there's me. I'm human. At least I was.

In each episode of season four that uses this opening, the lines change after Klaus (Joseph Morgan) says "hybrids." In the third episode, Jeremy says "Our town has always been different. But now there are strange things happening that no one can explain," and Elena says, "And there's a new hunter in town who wants people like me dead" ("The Rager," 4.3). Gérard Genette argues that "the text rarely appears in its naked state, without the reinforcement and accompaniment of a certain number of productions" (261). He defines paratext as every instance of text that stands next to the "proper" text,

> like an author's name, a title, a preface, illustrations. One does not always know if one should consider that they belong to the text or not, but in any case they surround it and prolong it, precisely in order present it, in the usual sense of this verb, but also in its strongest meaning: to make it present, to assure its presence in the world, its "reception" and its consumption [261].

In the case of *The Vampire Diaries*' fourth season, the paratextual voice-over introductions orient the audience not only to the plot elements, but to the desired emotional response. In particular, on the one hand, these voice-over openings function as paratext, taking the place of the "previously on" segments that many shows use, as the lines are interspersed with scenes from previous episodes. On the other hand, though, this new title sequence highlights the communal nature of the series and its focus on relationships and connections, as villains become friends and friends become family. For example, the second episode changes Elena's final line and gives it to Stefan: "And then there's Elena. She's one of us, a vampire, and I'll do anything to help her survive" ("Memorial," 4.2). His use of "one of us" connects Elena to the vampires, but it is echoed in later voice-overs, as well. In episode four's introduction, Klaus says "Now there's a hunter in town, determined to kill us all, and only I know his secret" ("The Five," 4.4) and in episode five, Stefan says "The hunter holds the key; he'll stop at nothing to kill us all" ("The Killer," 4.5). In each of these cases, the use of "us" ties all of the characters together, particularly because it echoes the fact that the characters band together first to overcome the hunter and then in a search for the cure to vampirism. The individuals within the group have different reasons for wanting the cure, as the voiceover for "After School Special," episode 10, notes:

> ELENA: My name is Elena Gilbert and I'm a vampire, but there are complications. But there's hope now [the cure].
> STEFAN: Everyone wants it for a different reason.
> TYLER: For revenge.
> REBEKAH: To be human and in love.
> DAMON: For the truth.
> ELENA: And some will stop at nothing to get it.

Nonetheless, the characters are united in their desire to find that cure. When the sheriff Liz Forbes notes in her eulogy for Tyler Lockwood's mother that "Carol Lockwood always said that togetherness in times of tragedy leads to healing, that one community is stronger than a thousand of its members" ("After School Special," 4.10), she could very well have been talking about the community of supernaturals in Mystic Falls.

This form of community identification is also especially millennial and, like the other millennial aspects of the series, is based upon emotional connection. Thus, the story arc tracing out the group's search for a cure spends quite a bit of time on the emotional state of the characters, as noted in the introductory voice-overs. The most important element here is how Elena feels. As Stefan says, "Since she's turned, everything about her is different" ("We'll Always Have Bourbon Street," 4.8)—and that difference is almost entirely emotional. Elena's change into a vampire is more an emotional change than a physical one; she is, as she notes, no longer the Elena of seasons one through three: "Things changed the minute that I went off that bridge [and became a vampire]. Even if I could be human again, I wouldn't be the person that I was. So it's about time that I accept the person that I am now and figure out a way to start living the rest of my life" ("Down the Rabbit Hole," 4.14). The focus on emotions is underscored by the fact that the communal voice-overs end after the episode in which Elena disconnects herself from her feelings in order to avoid dealing with the pain caused by her brother Jeremy's death. The paratextual opening of episode 4.16 reverts to "previously on The Vampire Diaries"—at this point, Elena has turned off her emotions, and despite the fact that the other characters are still working together to find the cure and save Elena, her lack of emotion eliminates the community bond that has held the group together up until this point. In fact, season four suggests it is better to have an excess of emotion than a lack. Thus, the series wavers between depicting extreme individualism in millennials and strong bonds among peers, reflecting the apparent disparity in millennial identity as both deeply connected and potentially isolated by the very technology that so often virtually connects them.

Morality

Perhaps one of the clearest distinctions between millennials and those who came before them is a difference in the ways in which morality is perceived and enacted. It is, of course, not unusual for a culture's elders to bemoan the unruly ways of their successors, and that's certainly been true of many of those observing Gen-Y. In a September 2011 *New York Times* editorial, David Brooks claims of the millennials that "It's not so much that these young Americans are living lives of sin and debauchery, at least no more than you'd expect from 18- to 23-year-olds. What's disheartening is how bad they are at thinking and talking about moral issues." He cites a study that had polled millennials and found what Brooks calls "an atmosphere of extreme moral individualism—of relativism and nonjudgmentalism" that doesn't necessarily lead to immoral behavior, but that Brooks nonetheless characterizes as problematic. What Brooks and other critics like him fail to acknowledge as they decry the possibility that we are "raising a generation of deluded narcissists" (Keith Ablow) is that the very connectedness that defines the millennial generation implies that the members of that generation are not functioning without any moral consensus—rather, the consensus among millennials is that morality is subjective and often a matter of individual determination. Carson Lane points out that the millennial generation "has had access to the Internet and a diverse range of viewpoints and topics during their most inquisitive years. Its members therefore have more flexibility to choose the standards they agree with." Valarie Kaur suggests that "It's not that we [millennials] don't have a shared vocabulary to address moral issues—we just don't have theirs [older generations']" (qtd. in Lane). Similarly, Tom Krattenmaker notes that, "It's not that there's a shortage of morality among the so-called Millennial generation, which reached adulthood post–2000. It's just that they have different morals, and different ways of articulating them." These differences loom large in *The Vampire Diaries* and, rather than separating the vampires and the teenagers, serve to unite them. These vampires are the essential moral relativists, functioning almost entirely on emotion. Indeed, when Stefan trains the newly turned vampire Caroline to function on animal blood rather than human blood, he tells her that this is the natural state of the vampire. Thus, these vampires, all turned when they are adolescents, become the epitome of overly emotional adolescence. As Vera Nazarian writes,

> The vampire archetype is the immortal young sociopathic wild thing inside all of us—selfish and focused entirely inward, frequently making choices regardless of the effect of its actions on others; focused on regaining its bearings after a confusing transformation and understanding (and learning to meet) unfamiliar new needs. The vampire stands in for our very own hormone-powered predator-self, dangerous and untamed and filled with the raw life-force that drives us onward [99–100].

While this is certainly true of many vampires, the vampires of Mystic Falls are only considered moral when that "raw life-force" is directed by appropriate emotion. Brooks writes that

> [i]n most times and in most places, the group was seen to be the essential moral unit. A shared religion defined rules and practices. Cultures structured people's imaginations and imposed moral disciplines. But now more people are led to assume that the free-floating individual is the essential moral unit. Morality was once revealed, inherited and shared, but now it's thought of as something that emerges in the privacy of your own heart.

What Brooks misses here, though, is the idea that morality based on individual feeling can itself gain communal approbation. In *The Vampire Diaries*, this dependence upon a sort of "emotional morality" emerges as the primary marker of character. That is, characters are judged not on what they do, but on how they feel. In part, this is an outgrowth of the sentimentality typical of dramas pitched toward adolescents—but more than that, it's a clear sign that millennial morality, situational and subjective morality, rules in the world of Mystic Falls. Krattenmaker writes

If you're around Millennials much, you know they tend to voice their morality with more humility, even hesitation, than the old guard. That's partly because they are legitimately suspicious of easy answers to complex questions, and their moral compasses tell them that condemning others is rarely the right way to treat people.

In this series, the "complex questions" include, for example, what the consequence of murder should be—and the answer seems to be a typically millennial "it depends." Most of the characters commit murder at some point—though the term "murder" is rarely used, perhaps because condemning others for killing might not be "the right way to treat people."

The first major character to kill with impunity is Damon, initially presented as the "bad" brother who returns to Mystic Falls to torment his brother and mock what he calls Stefan's "sulking and Elena longing and forehead brooding" ("History Repeating," 1.9). In Damon's first on-screen appearance, he kills a couple on their way home from a concert ("Pilot," 1.1). As a new vampire, Caroline feeds on and drains a carnival worker. The original hero, Stefan, is something of a blood addict, a former "ripper" who not only fed on and killed humans, but tore his victims apart in a way that was exceedingly vicious, even among vampires. And when Elena herself is turned into a vampire, she kills the vampire hunter Connor Jordan (Todd Williams). And that list doesn't even cover the number of non-humans the characters kill: Damon rips out the heart of werewolf Mason Lockwood (Taylor Kinney) and dumps his body; Stefan stakes the vampire Vicki Donovan (Kayla Ewell) when she threatens Elena and Jeremy; Tyler Lockwood accidentally kills his classmate Sarah (Maiara Walsh); Elena kills Jolene (Samantha Kacho), a waitress who knows Katherine. Brennan claims that the series "refuses to flinch from how dangerous vampires can be, and thus how much danger a human mixed up with them might find herself in. Vampires are shown as having an approach to things that truly is inhuman—even the good vampires" (9). But more than an inhuman approach, the series takes a millennial approach. That's not to suggest that millennials would necessarily condone murder, but they are perhaps more likely to be drawn to a series that highlights moral relativism like *The Vampire Diaries* does. The distinction in this series between murder and acceptable killing is apparently the feeling that accompanies it. When Caroline kills the carnival worker, Bonnie reacts with revulsion. Stefan takes Caroline to a bathroom and begins to wipe the blood from her mouth. Caroline, shaken, begins by saying "She hates me. Bonnie hates me." Their conversation highlights the relativistic nature of killing. Although Caroline's reaction is to label herself a murderer, Stefan works to naturalize her actions—she is not a murderer, he implies, but merely acting according to her nature. And if that is true, then killing someone is not immoral, but merely innate. Equally significant is the fact that Caroline is initially more concerned about her relationship with her friends than she is with the man she killed. And although Elena asks what happens to the body of the man Caroline killed, she accepts Stefan's evasive reply that "It's been taken care of." Indeed, she seems much more concerned with her own issues.

The phrase "It is what it is" permeates *The Vampire Diaries*. Things are what they are, and examining them too closely is a bad idea. The characters feel what they feel and act on those feelings, rarely delving explicitly into the morality of those actions. As Mary Borsellino notes, "the battle of good versus evil is, at best, a secondary consideration for all the sides of the fight in *The Vampire Diaries*; personal alliances and enemies are of far greater importance" (137).

The entire fourth season is predicated on the idea that vampires are highly emotional and that those emotions are the bedrock of morality, good or bad. Elena, turned into a vampire at the end of season three, spends virtually all of the fourth season dealing with her vampiric emotions, first by fighting against them and then by cutting them off entirely. In the season premier, she begins laughing uncontrollably at her use of the cliché "cross that bridge when we come to it," and Stefan says "You're laughing. I'm pretty sure you don't actually think that's funny... Your emotions are a bit heightened today. A lot heightened" ("Growing Pains," 4.1). These heightened emotions continue to underscore the season's plot. Damon and Stefan disagree about Elena's ability to transition smoothly into a vampire, and that disagreement is based on their assessments of Elena's emotional ability to deal with feeding from humans. Elena's emotional state as a vampire is more than a barometer of her concern for others, however; it is the essence of her morality, as it is for all of the other characters. This emotional morality overrides all other considerations; it is not a character's actions that determine his or her moral state, but the feelings that motivated those actions. In *The Vampire Diaries*, good intentions pave not the road to hell, but the road to redemption—a fact that clarifies some of the more chaotic and potentially confusing plot points of the series. The season four finale in particular illustrates the redemption to be found in correct feeling, particularly in the characters of Rebekah (Claire Holt), Klaus, and Damon.

The episode "Graduation Day" is the culmination of the events of not only season four, but the series to date. As the episode opens, the witch Bonnie has opened "the veil to the other side," where supernaturals with unfinished business go after death. Mystic Falls is flooded with old friends, allies, and enemies, all intent upon dealing with those they left behind when they died. The

Original vampire Rebekah and the human Matt are caught by a group of formerly dead vampire hunters, including Rebekah's former lover Alexander (Paul Telfer). Alexander places Matt on a pressure-sensitive plate connected to explosives, and it is only through Rebekah's ability to correctly align her emotions that he is saved. When she turns up at Matt's door later, he agrees to spend the summer traveling with her.

The fact that Rebekah "almost killed" Matt—and did, in fact, kill Elena, prompting her switch into a vampire—is no longer significant once she feels right. She loves Matt, so all is forgiven. Similarly, the original vampire Klaus is exonerated of his misdeeds when he shows up just in time to save Damon from death by werewolf venom. Despite his continual threats and attempts to kill other characters, his love for Caroline ameliorates those actions. When he tells Caroline that his gift to her is to allow the return of Tyler, banished from Mystic Falls by Klaus's threat to hunt him down, the audience is meant to see the shift in his emotional state. Klaus's former actions matter less than his current feelings, illustrating a distinctly millennial morality.

Jessica Hatch claims that the reason Stefan loves Elena is "not that she's smart or she's funny," but that "her only value lies in how she reacts to his actions." More than that, though, it's the emotional register of those reactions that matters. Elena's continual need to choose between the Salvatore brothers also illustrates this tendency to focus on emotions rather than actions. In the final season, Damon and Stefan both discuss the need to allow Elena the opportunity to revert to humanity by taking the single dose of a cure for vampirism. The need for action falls to the wayside, though, when emotions come into play.

For Stefan, Elena's ability to correctly define her emotions takes precedence over "how to protect the world." Moreover, any actions are predicated on those feelings—Elena's emotions determine how he will act. Stefan might say to Damon "You reap what you sow, buddy," but he's not entirely right—on *The Vampire Diaries*, characters reap what their *emotions* sow. They gain only when their emotions are correctly aligned. Elena says to Alaric and Jeremy "I did some pretty terrible things," but because she feels strongly, she does not suffer any consequences; emotional morality, that millennial touchstone, functions to ameliorate actions.

Conclusion

Unlike, for example, the *Twilight* movies, *The Vampire Diaries* does not shy away from fairly graphic depictions of blood and gore. In "The Birthday"

(3.1), Damon and Alaric track Stefan, who has temporarily succumbed to his blood-lust. In a farmhouse in Tennessee, they find the pale bodies of two women, sitting straight up on a sofa, blood coating their blouses. Damon declares that they are clearly Stefan's victims, because Stefan is a "ripper" who "feeds so hard he rips them apart, then feels remorse, so he puts the bodies back together. It's the damndest thing." He nudges one of the bodies with his foot and her head rolls off her neck and onto the floor. Yet, neither Stefan's murderous actions nor Damon's callous response seem to call for any horrified reaction from the audience. In addition to potentially illustrating a millennial audience's habituation to screen violence, the scene illustrates the series' demand on its viewers to regard feeling over action. It is Stefan's remorse that the series underscores, even as it gives the sort of visual cue that in slasher films of earlier generations, for example, would have been designed to produce revulsion and dismay.[3] *The Vampire Diaries* expects its audience to be more invested in Damon's desire to save his brother and in Stefan's salvation than in the carnage that transpires because of Stefan's lapse into active, violent vampirism.

Ultimately, even at its bloodiest, *The Vampire Diaries* is a show about emotions, despite its depictions of vampires, werewolves, and other monsters. The characters' emotions influence everything from their use of technology, to the value they place upon community, to the very morality they embrace and espouse. In the series' focus on emotional alignment, *The Vampire Diaries* illustrates its clear ties to a millennial value system for all of the characters, whether they were born millennials or became millennials through contact. In this series, an encounter with a vampire is not, as Gelder claims, an encounter with something old that in some way changes the modern world; instead, it is the millennial characters who change what they touch, including vampirism itself.

Notes

1. To some degree, this focus on emotions can be ascribed to *The Vampire Diaries*' presumed audience of young women; television series geared toward women often concentrate on emotion over action. However, the idea that these emotions should be the basis of morality seems to be a millennial-generation addition to supernatural teen dramas. For example, in *Buffy the Vampire Slayer*, emotions were important in characters' decision-making, but the series presumed an understanding of moral and ethical imperatives; the need to save the world always outweighed any personal emotional entanglements. On the other hand, MTV's *Teen Wolf* (2011–present), a supernatural teen drama that the head of MTV programming David Janollari calls "a terrific foray into the scripted world for the millennial MTV audience" ("MTV Howls"), does not necessarily have the same obviously gendered appeal to women as does *The Vampire Diaries*, yet similarly ties morality to emotions.

2. It's important to note that although the series appears to target young women as its ideal audience, the depictions within the show make no distinctions in terms of millennial emotionalism—that is, both female and male characters in the series make decisions based on emotion rather than logic or any moral underpinnings.

3. See, for instance, *Halloween* (1978), *Friday the 13th* (1980), *A Nightmare on Elm Street* (1984) or *I Know What You Did Last Summer* (1997).

Generational Conflict, Twenty-First-Century Horror Films and *The Cabin in the Woods*

KAREN J. RENNER

An examination of millennials in popular culture would hardly be complete without consideration of the genre perhaps most deliberately designed for their viewing pleasure: horror. In addition to being the largest consumers of horror—and, indeed, likely because of this fact—they dominate the genre's cast of characters as well.[1] And yet, horror is not a genre made by millennials so much as a genre *about* them, for they have little to do with its production: even the youngest directors today still tend to be Gen Xers.[2] The representations of millennials in the horror film therefore are not self-portraits but rather constructions created by an older generation.

As a result, the depictions of youth in the horror film are deeply rooted in the varied biases and motives of their makers. Producers of horror films might pander to their largest demographic in hopes of currying favor (and generating revenue). Filmmakers could also base characters upon the most negative stereotypes of millennials and then employ the conventions of the genre to destroy these delinquents, thereby giving what they perceive as a condemnable generation its just desserts. Most frequently, however, horror films incorporate both attitudes, reserving grotesque deaths for those who display negative traits while allowing only the most meritorious to make it out alive. As a result, many contemporary horror films function as ideological vehicles, spelling out the most praiseworthy traits and deplorable flaws of their millennial characters, as horror movies and the gothic texts that are their forebears have long been wont to do.[3]

It is worthwhile to briefly mention another complexity posed by the horror film's popularity: there is no way to really know *why* millennial audiences are attracted to the horror genre or to specific movies within it. Certainly, horror has long appealed to young viewers, and many critics have made guesses about why that might be.[4] However, the reasons why a particular film attracts a large audience may have little to do with its ideologies or "message." Ticket sales are not always accurate indications of a film's appeal, nor can we assume that rave reviews reflect millennial assessments: after all, the most influential film critics still derive from older generations. Since millennials are more likely to communicate over the internet, online ratings may be more reflective of their opinions, yet it is impossible to know the ages of the oft anonymous authors of these reviews. To complicate matters further, some scholars, like Neal Gabler, have argued that millennials feel the need to be familiar with current releases, good or bad, since so many of their conversations revolve around popular culture; their penchant for movie-going might therefore be the result of their seeing pop culture literacy as a sort of social responsibility—as other people view an awareness of current events—that allows them to actively contribute to ongoing discussions, many of which revolve around entertainment.[5] In short, the popularity of a horror film tells us little about its primary consumers—the millennials.

I bring this up because there is a tendency to assume that the popularity of a horror film implies its viewers' silent approval of the ideologies and values it conveys. Consider, for example, Roger Ebert's review of the 2003 remake of *The Texas Chainsaw Massacre*, in which he claims that the film "confirmed [his] suspicion that the movie was made by and for those with no attention span" or his comment, regarding the 2007 remake of the 1997 Austrian film *Funny Games*, that "if you liked those pictures from Abu Ghraib, you'll *love* 'Funny Games.'" Both comments suggest that one would not see these films or enjoy them unless one were either undiscriminating, sadistic, or both.

In this essay, I argue that disputes over the merits and demerits of horror films duplicate debates over the relative "goodness" or "badness" of the millennial generation that abound within the media. While every generation has, in their youth, been viewed with skepticism or even contempt to some extent, the millennials seem to be a special source of concern and disdain. Dan Black, for example, claims that the millennials are "one of the most maligned generations ever to enter the workforce," and certainly Hara Estroff Marano's 2008 *A Nation of Wimps: The High Cost of Invasive Parenting*, Mark Bauerlein's 2009 *The Dumbest Generation: How the Digital Age Stupefies Young Americans and Jeopardizes Our Future (Or, Don't Trust Anyone Under 30)*, Jean M.

Twenge and W. Keith Campbell's 2010 *The Narcissism Epidemic: Living in the Age of Entitlement*, and the cover story of a May 2013 issue of *Time* "The Me Me Me Generation," together suggest little hope for the millennials. For these writers, millennials are entitled, narcissistic, focused on money and fame, and socially minded only insofar as it will help their own success: volunteerism may have increased, Twenge points out, but only because it dresses up resumés.

However, the millennials are not without their champions, as is evident in such texts as 2000's *Millennials Rising: The Next Great Generation* by Neil Howe and William Strauss, 2008's *Generation We: How Millennial Youth Are Taking Over America and Changing Our World Forever* by Eric Greenberg and Karl Webber, and 2011's *Millennial Momentum: How a New Generation Is Remaking America* by Morley Winograd and Michael D. Hais. These writers interpret the millennials' supposed sense of entitlement and narcissism as confidence, see millennial focus on extrinsic things as only one goal among many (and a rather natural ambition at that), and also view millennial volunteerism as a marker of their optimism in their ability to realize social change.

To demonstrate how these contrasting views of millennials are reflected within horror film criticism, I will first give a brief survey of twenty-first-century horror films, demonstrating how alarms about the state of the genre resemble key concerns about the millennial generation. From there, I move into an examination of *The Cabin in the Woods* (2012), dubbed "this generation's *Scream*" by dreadcentral.com. *Cabin* has earned this moniker by the particularly relevant meta-discourse it offers that presents horror films as a collaborative effort between filmmakers, studios, and their fans. More importantly, however, *The Cabin in the Woods* suggests that the demonization of the young, as we see currently occurring with the millennials, is an unavoidable and perhaps even necessary social cycle.

Foreign and Domestic Remakes, Torture Porn and Found Footage

In the introduction to his 2010 edited collection *American Horror Film: The Genre at the Turn of the Millennium*, "They Don't Make 'Em Like They Used To: On the Rhetoric of Crisis and the Current State of American Horror Cinema," Steffen Hantke notes that twenty-first-century horror is widely considered to be in a period of dramatic decline. This perception, Hantke argues, seems largely related to the genre's current reliance on several key formulas: he mentions in particular contemporary foreign remakes and remakes of classic

1970s and 1980s movies and gestures toward the "cycle of torture porn films" (xii) initiated by Eli Roth's *Hostel* (2005). Had Hantke written his introduction a year or two later, he would undoubtedly have added found footage films to the list of current horror subgenres that many feel are being recycled to the point of ridiculousness and which are thus degrading the genre as a whole.[6]

Hantke, however, is skeptical about the reasons given for the deficiencies of the contemporary horror film. He claims that much of the disdain for current horror production is the result of a romanticization of "1970s neo-horror" (xviii), necessitated by the need for "real" horror fans to distinguish themselves from Johnny-come-latelys who have embraced the genre only in response to its recent mainstreaming. Hantke also notes that there is considerable irony in the fact that contemporary horror films are dismissed in favor of their 1970s predecessors since critics are, in essence, "validat[ing] a period in the horror genre for the same qualities that incurred its condemnation in its own time" (xviii). Ultimately, Hantke concludes

> Once we see all of these complaints—about sequels, remakes, and foreign imports—in the larger historical context, what begins to emerge is one possible, albeit broad, response to the complaint that American horror film is in a crisis, which goes like this: things have always been this way. What appears as a sorry state of creative attenuation is, in fact, nothing more than a local manifestation of industrial practices that are a tried-and-true element of Hollywood filmmaking [xvi].

Hantke's claim that the horror film may always be perceived from the present as in crisis, while retrospectively as a meaningful cultural product, applies to discussions of youth as well. The young, it seems, are always misguided, always lacking, always on the brink of collapse—until, of course, they get a little older and start having children of their own about whom they can complain. Joel Stein, author of *Time*'s recent "The Me Me Me Generation" cover story, even acknowledges this trend, stating, "I am about to do what old people have done throughout history: call those younger than me lazy, entitled, selfish, and shallow." Elspeth Reeve takes Stein's claim one step further, literally demonstrating through an array of magazine articles dating back to 1907 that most young generations have been viewed with skepticism and dismay. As Black points out, "it wasn't too long ago when Gen Xers were 'slackers' and Boomers were 'hippies.'" Just as current horror films never seem able to rival the classics of the past, especially for viewers who find their old favorites forgotten, the youngest generation never seems to quite measure up to the generations of the past.

Many of the more specific complaints about the subgenres that have dominated millennial era horror—foreign and domestic remakes, so-called torture porn, and found footage—bear an uncanny resemblance to those made about the millennials themselves. Beginning with the 2002 film *The Ring*, a remake of the Japanese film *Ringu* (1998), remakes of contemporary foreign films have been a Hollywood horror staple.[7] The response to individual foreign remakes varies, but when criticized as a genre, it is, as Christina Klein points out, either because they "homogenize[e] the distinctive creative visions" of the source material or because they are proof of an underlying racism in Hollywood that demands that foreign faces be replaced "with white ones" (5).

Not surprisingly, the millennials have also been criticized for an equivalent penchant for cultural homogeneity. In 1991, William Strauss and Neil Howe predicted that the millennial generation "will be more clean-cut and homogenous than any seen since that of the circa–1930 G.I.s" (419), and their prediction seems prescient of what other contemporary scholars have to say. "Individuation is not a key phrase for [the millennials]," writes Myna German. "[T]hey would like nothing better than to wear uniforms to school, be like everyone else, have the same i-pod as their friends, and watch the same shows." Even though they are often noted to be the most ethnically diverse generation yet, critics of the generation feel that they have become white-washed into conformity nevertheless.

Around the same time that foreign remakes became popular, filmmakers also began remaking well-known horror films from the 1970 and 1980s. One reason for this cross-national and domestic creative plunder seems to be that the slasher film, long a domestic staple, lost its oomph after one last hoorah in the late 1990s that included the first *Scream* cycle (1996, 1997, 2000), *I Know What You Did Last Summer* and its sequel (1997, 1998), and *Urban Legend* (1998). In addition to looking abroad for new horror formulas, filmmakers attempted to bank on the draw of familiar titles. Although not the first of its kind, the 2003 remake of *The Texas Chainsaw Massacre* catalyzed the trend. Though the extensive list of remakes made since encompasses all manner of horror movies, the slasher film remains the most popular choice.[8] Slasher remakes stray in varying degrees and ways from their original storylines, some changes necessitated by new technological devices (such as cell phones) that render some plot devices anachronistic; other revisions involve an obvious attempt to appeal to the increased number of female horror movie fans.[9] Evaluations of these domestic remakes often divide over issues of ingenuity and respect for the original. If a remake is embraced (and this is rarely the case), it is because it is viewed as engaging with the original in meaningful and respectful ways; if rejected, it is often because the remake has dumbed-down a masterful, multi-layered original or perhaps bears little in common with the original beyond its title.

The millennials' relationship with the past and the older generation has been probed along similar lines as these American horror remakes. Although identified as embracing a "retro" style, more so than many other generations, millennials are also criticized for being all style and no substance. Gabler, for example, notes their tendency to dismiss cultural heritage by neglecting to watch classic films. Likewise, in a *New York Times* article entitled "Generation Sell," William Deresiewicz attacks millennials for adopting the costumes of an older generation but none of its politics: "unlike those previous youth cultures, the hipster ethos contains no element of rebellion, rejection or dissent." "Today's ideal social form," Deresiewicz continues, "is not the commune or the movement or even the individual creator ...; it's the small business.... Call it Generation Sell." Like the ineffective remake of the American horror film, the millennials adopt the past for its symbolic capital, as a fashion statement rather than a show of political solidarity.

The debate over millennial engagement with the past is also evident in discussions of their relationships with their elders. While advocates claim that millennials have a deep and intense investment in and admiration for family and therefore for the older generations, others, such as Ron Alsop, argue that the millennials' supposed sensed of entitlement, the result of having been treated as the "trophy generation," has given them a healthy disregard for their higher-ups: millennials, according to Alsop, "tend to be highly opinionated, and fearlessly challenge recruiters and bosses. Status and hierarchy don't impress them much.... They want to be treated like colleagues not subordinates" (28–29).[10] Like the horror movie remake, the millennials have a contested connection to the past and its people.

Another general trend in the domestic horror remake is an increased emphasis on graphic violence. This characteristic is likely influenced by the concomitant popularity of torture porn, a term coined by David Edelstein in a review inspired by his viewing of *Hostel*.[11] The ethics of torture porn has been hotly debated. Critics like Edelstein, Reynold Humphries, and Christopher Kelly tend to consider torture porn as a morally inquisitive genre rather than an amoral morass.[12] Furthermore, as Blair Davis and Kial Natale demonstrate in their quantitative analysis of horror films from 1998 to 2007, displays of gore have actually been decreasing since 2004 and even before then seem to have negatively affected box office sales. In other words, the fact that torture porn films have been made for and viewed by millennials does not necessarily mean that millennials themselves covet these films.[13] Others, however, see the supposed rise of torture porn as a direct result of the millennial generation's general lack of empathy.[14] Either way, the ethics of torture porn is linked to perceptions regarding millennials' treatment of others: those who see torture porn as more than just splatter often view the films and their audiences as willing to engage the disconcerting and disturbing prevalence of violence in our world; those who dismiss torture porn feel it could only find a foothold amongst the sadistic and indifferent.

In recent years, the argument has become mostly moot, for blood-and-gore lust has apparently dwindled, with torture porn being for the most part replaced by films favoring the supernatural and, in particular, the found footage approach. Although *The Blair Witch Project* announced the potential popularity and profitability of the genre in 1999, found footage did not come to prominence until almost a decade later, with the release of *Paranormal Activity* in 2007.[15] While some have received positive reviews, the genre as a whole seems to prompt more thumbs down than up, especially lately. Critics have claimed that since the found footage film requires little technical knowhow, financial backing, or celebrity figures—indeed, those ingredients could very well diminish the sort of gritty verisimilitude the genre tries to generate—everyone can try their hand at it (and do), with most attempts failing cinematically and narratively.[16]

Not surprisingly, the millennials are directly related to the found footage genre, with their penchant for and proficiency with the new forms of media and technology that have arisen in recent years. Millennials, also known as the Facebook and YouTube Generation, have been both commended and criticized for their adeptness with various technologies and networking media. At best, they are praised for their know-how; at worst, they are defamed as a generation interested only in becoming rich and famous but without putting a lot of work into it.[17]

In short, then, discussions of contemporary horror revolve around many of the debated shortcomings and strengths of the millennial generation. What is striking is that the preferences of young horror film viewers are presumed to be already established rather than constantly evolving in response to the movies produced. This is a standard approach to youth as well: they are already defined, born with a particular set of traits and solidly set on a certain course through life. Little attention is given to the idea that the discourse about a generation might actually shape its perception of itself as well as its subsequent behavior. *The Cabin in the Woods* directly engages the ways in which the young are negatively constructed to suit the needs of the older generation and suggests that their awareness of this unfavorable discourse makes them all the more likely to reject their assigned roles as the scapegoats—and sacrificial lambs—of societal failure.

The Cabin in the Woods: Critiquing Horror, Exposing Generational Conflict

Held up for three years due to MGM's financial troubles, *The Cabin in the Woods* was finally released by Lionsgate on April 13, 2012. It has since achieved high critical acclaim, as its 92 percent rating on rottentomatoes.com and 72 percent score on metacritic.com indicates. In many ways, the delay aided its appeal, since it allowed one of its stars, Chris Hemsworth, to gain notoriety and also because, as a result of the lag, it appeared just a few months before co-creator Joss Whedon's long-anticipated *Avengers* (2012). At the same time, however, the film's intentional critique—Whedon referred to it as a "loving hate-letter" to the horror film industry for its depictions of "kids acting like idiots, the devolution of the horror movie into torture porn and into a long series of sadistic comeuppances"—came a bit late; as one reviewer puts it, "So-called 'torture porn' has been supplanted at the box office by the shaky-cam creep-verité of the *Paranormal Activity* series [...] *Cabin* does a superb job of hanging torture porn from its own meat hooks, but you can't kill what's already dead."[18]

However, *The Cabin in the Woods* remains an elegant exposé of both the horror film industry as well as the treatment of youth by older generations and, indeed, implies that the two may in fact be linked. On the surface, the film looks like the most conventional horror plot ever: five young adults head to a cabin in the woods to party and are soon beset by beasties—in this case, The Buckners, a "zombie redneck torture family," according to a description given later in the film—that are intent on butchering them one-by-one. But rather than simply employing these conventions, *Cabin* offers a meta-critique of them. What we discover along the way is that the five characters are part of an elaborate ritualized sacrifice. In the *Cabin*-verse, the world is at the mercy of the "Ancient Ones," evil gods who will destroy all of humankind unless they are routinely appeased with a satisfying offering of blood. Every time the Ancient Ones threaten to rise, countries across the globe, in a concerted effort, each offer up their culturally specific versions of horror in hopes that one will succeed in temporarily staving off the threat.

The film switches back and forth between the young adults selected to be sacrificed and those orchestrating and ensuring their demise, mostly two men named Sitterson (Richard Jenkins) and Hadley (Bradley Whitford), who work for the American "company." This corporation includes many employees and divisions, including chemistry, zoology, demolition, accounting, and even "wranglers." As *Cabin* begins, Sitterson and Hadley are informed that Japan and America are the last hopes for success, all other nations having failed to bring their sacrifices to fruition. However, the two men hardly seem worried since Hadley says, "It's going to be a long weekend if everyone's that puckered up," and then invites Sitterson over for drinks the coming Monday. People concerned about the impending end of the world would hardly engage in such banter.

The American version of the sacrifice involves the five young protagonists of the film, who roughly correspond to various archetypes common to American horror: the whore, the jock, the scholar, the fool, and the virgin. In Japan's version, however, victims are far less distinctive than the monster, which is what is commonly known as a "dead wet girl," a sopping young female, dressed in white, with dark hair hanging in her face, a figure popularized by *Ringu* and its American adaptation *The Ring*, but who appears in countless other Asian horror films as well. Ultimately, Japan's dead wet girl fails to achieve a single fatality amongst the class of little Japanese schoolgirls she attacks, who join hands, sing, and transform the spirit into a "happy frog," and the Americans are left on their own.

Cabin provides a hearty meal for "true" horror fans. Not only can they recognize references to key films in the genre, but the movie also alludes to the conventions of not only American horror in general but also international variants.[19] In that regard, *Cabin* is hardly original: after all, a large reason for the popularity of *Scream* was its metatextual referencing of the "rules" of the slasher film while simultaneously employing and breaking these rules within its own narrative. *Cabin* has a more complicated agenda than cleverness, however. On one level, the film examines the complex relationship between the creators of horror films, the studios that purchase, produce, and distribute them, and their consumers. However, on a deeper level—and one more relevant to this article—*Cabin* comments on generational conflict, suggesting that the scapegoating of the young for problems caused by older generations is a standard, cyclical part of history.

Cabin's critique of the horror genre is relatively straightforward. Sitterson and Hadley roughly correspond to creators of horror films, such as Whedon and Goddard, who co-wrote the film.[20] They are responsible for ensuring that the story unfolds correctly, with the virgin dying last—or emerging as the sole survivor only after a great deal of suffering.[21] At the same time, Sitterson and

Hadley are required to not simply tell this story but to tell it well. For example, by controlling temperature, pheromone mists, and strategically creating a shaft of romantic moonlight, the two ensure a sex scene immediately before the first killing, complete with full-frontal nudity. When a newbie asks why the baring of breasts is necessary, Hadley states, "We're not the only ones watching, kid," and Sitterson quickly echoes his sentiment by saying they've "[g]otta keep the customer satisfied."

But perhaps the most obvious evidence that marks Sitterson and Hadley as symbolizing the creators of horror occurs during a celebration that takes place when the workers believe that they have accomplished their mission. Two young employees praise Hadley for the dramatic unfolding of events. The male exclaims, "Classic dénouement. When the van hit the lake—." He is promptly interrupted by the woman, who declares, "I screamed." Obviously, the men are considered the authors of the narrative.

If Hadley and Sitterson represent the creators of horror, they answer to higher authorities who mediate between them and the Ancient Ones. These upper-management figures may signify the studios and other executives who often exert creative control over the films. The Ancient Ones then represent the horror fans who ultimately have the final say over a film's success or failure. To an extent, it would seem that the film excuses creators and instead blames more powerful forces—fans and the production companies ever seeking to satisfy them—for the violent content of their creations.

However, Sitterson and Hadley, though comic and likeable characters, are hardly innocent. In fact, the film several times makes a point of showcasing the coldness that they—and all their minions—exhibit toward their victims. Although trapped in a binding agreement they didn't negotiate with forces far more powerful than they are, what makes the employees distasteful—Sitterson and Hadley among them—is the aloofness with which they perform their tasks. Almost all members of the company, for example, participate in a betting pool in which they bid on which creature will be chosen to kill the selected victims. At another point, Hadley—believing that they have succeeded in their sacrifice—expresses sympathy for the virgin, Dana (Kristen Connolly), who appears to be the last one standing: "I'm actually rooting for this girl. She's got so much heart. And you think of all the pain and the –" However, he quickly becomes distracted by people entering the room bearing celebratory cocktails and blurts out, "Tequila is my lady!" immediately forgetting about Dana who is still being tormented. During the party that ensues, Dana is shown being brutally attacked by one of the Buckners on screens all over the room; none of the employees take any notice but instead drink and mingle, behaving like stereotypical attendees of an office party. The film thus launches a multi-layered critique, indicting creators, corporations, and consumers for the sadistic and exploitative aspects of the horror film.

The movie thus offers a somewhat contradictory view of millennials. As the primary consumers of the horror film, they are partly responsible, for the treatment of horror characters as occasions for gruesome deaths. However, they also constitute the bulk of the victims within horror films and in that capacity, refuse to participate in this sort of objectification of each other. Early on in the film, as the group of young adults settles into their respective rooms in the cabin, Holden (the scholar, played by Jesse Williams) discovers a one-way mirror through which he can see Dana begin to undress. Rather than enjoy this "free show," Holden knocks on the wall, reveals the mirror, and offers to switch rooms. Dana is then placed in the same predicament, for Holden then begins to take off his clothes, and Dana is given the opportunity to secretly watch. However, though Holden's physique is tantalizing, she refuses to take advantage of his trust and covers the mirror. The scene then becomes an image on one of the many screens that Hadley and Sitterson are monitoring in preparation for the sacrifice. The millennial protagonists are thus revealed to treat each other far more humanely and respectfully than the older generation does. In short, in *Cabin* we again see the conflicted view of millennials present in other critiques of the horror genre: as the consumers of horror symbolized by the Ancient Ones, they demand violent deaths, but as characters they refuse to engage in sadistic objectification. They are both empathetic and cruel, conscientious and self-serving.

While the commentary on the horror film that *Cabin* puts forth is certainly astute, more incisive is its claim that generational conflict is an inevitable and even necessary aspect of cultural change. This is most apparent in the film's revelation that the young adult victims of horror films so frequently fit negative stereotypes because the older generation *needs* them to. Jules (Anna Hutchison), the whore, for example, is in actuality a pre-med student and loyal friend to Dana who is involved in a sexual but monogamous and loving relationship with the jock, Curt (Hemsworth). However, the company manages to transform her into a "whore" by infusing her blond hair dye with chemicals that slow down her cognition and increase her libido. Once transformed into the whore, she makes out with a stuffed wolf's head on a dare and dances sexily for the entire group. Curt whoops encouragingly during Jules's performance, but we discover that he, too, is hardly himself. Curt is a football player, but he is also established as an intellectual and a genuinely nice and funny guy in his first scene. However, whatever chemicals the company feeds him change him into a stereotypical jock who bullies the other men and makes fun of his smart teammate. His change in character is so dramatic that it prompts Marty (the fool, played by Fran Kranz) to figure out that something strange is going on: "[S]ince when does Curt pull this alpha-male bullshit? I mean, he's a sociology major. He's on full academic scholarship, and now he's calling his friend an egghead?" Each of the characters are compelled to conform with expected stereotypes.

The ritual also demands that the victims choose their fates of their own free-will. First, they must decide to ignore warnings dispensed by a "harbinger," a character common to horror films who tries to dissuade the characters from going wherever they are headed but who is routinely ignored. In *Cabin*, this figure is a cantankerous, creepy old man at a gas station who gives thinly veiled warnings about the dangers that face them at their get-away destination. Second, they must also choose which monster will dispatch them. This choice occurs in the basement, which is filled with objects typical of horror films that, when meddled with, often initiate the horror plot proper. It is because Dana reads Latin phrases in a diary that the Buckners—the family of "zombified, pain-worshipping backwoods idiots," as both Sitterson and Hadley call them—are resurrected. The element of choice, Sitterson and Hadley explain, is essential to the sacrifice. When newbie Truman (Brian White) asks how it is fair to wager when they "control the outcome," the following exchange occurs:

> HADLEY: We just get them in the cellar. They take it from there.
> SITTERSON: No, they have to make the choice of their own free will. Otherwise, the system doesn't work. It's like the harbinger. Some creepy old fuck, practically wears a sign, "You will die." Why do we put him there? The system. They have to choose to ignore him, and they have to choose what happens in the cellar.... [I]n the end, they don't transgress—
> HADLEY:—they can't be punished.

But while the creators claim to allow the victims to choose their fates, this is obviously not the case. Their decisions and personalities are constantly influenced by the chemicals to which they are exposed, and they are prevented from escaping their fates by manufactured cave-ins and invisible, electrified fences. The appearance of choice is just a façade.

Ironically, however, the film's millennials do ultimately get to make a choice: after breaking into the company's facility and destroying it by freeing all the monsters in its "stable," Dana and Marty decide to honor each other's lives and, in doing so, make a choice to let the world end. As Marty tells the "Director," a sort of CEO for the company played by Sigourney Weaver, the ultimate Final Girl of sci-fi horror, "If you've got to kill all my friends to survive, maybe it's time for a change." Whedon describes this decision in the commentary track of the DVD as choosing "people over humanity." Ultimately the choice is—as seems to be the case with so many behaviors of the millennials—a conflicted one, incredibly generous while also exceptionally selfish, meaning, as it does, the end of existence for everyone who isn't a "friend" as well. Aware of their betrayal by their elders, they see little reason to serve as either scapegoat or sacrifice.

Conclusion

Joel Stein's May 20, 2013, cover story of *Time* magazine, "The Me Me Me Generation," has, as I finish this essay (on May 15 no less), already incited many angry responses. One I find particularly compelling is an article on www.policymic.com by Zainab Akande that has collected parodies of the cover. The original *Time* cover featured the image of a young woman lying on her stomach taking a picture of herself with her cell phone. Above her are the words: "The Me Me Me Generation. Millennials are lazy, entitled narcissists who still live with their parents. Why they'll save us all." In most of the parodies, the image of the young woman remains while the text has been changed. One reads: "The Unemployed Generation. Millennials are Narcissists because we fucked their entire generation over and they don't have anything better to do than jerk off and look at Tumblr. Why they'll starve to death." Another: "The Doomed Generation. We pissed their future away on endless war, golden parachutes for bankers, and handjobs for stockbrokers. Why? Fuck 'em, that's why." The last image, however, has swapped out the reclining young woman photographing herself for a motherly looking figure laughing. The caption: "The Indentured Generation. We trampled their rights, tanked the economy, and trashed the planet for our benefit—but expect them to foot the bill. Why we call *them* narcissists."

All of these examples snidely and obliquely gesture toward the same argument made in *The Cabin in the Woods* and to the same lack of self-awareness displayed in many of the critiques of the millennials—whether direct ones or those filtered through discussions of secondary matter, such as the contemporary horror film. Regardless of whether the accusations made against the millennials are accurate, it is apparent that the older generation often needs to shape the young into scapegoats to dodge their own complicity. And it is equally apparent that the millennials are plenty aware of what's going on. Who's to say, then, that the supposed deficits in their behavior are not responses to what's being said about them?

Notes

1. Viewers inhabiting the six-year time span between 18–24 constitute 22.4 percent of the audience of horror films, according to audiencetargeting.com, while visibilitypr.com suggests that horror is even more popular with an even younger demographic: according to an October 2011 report, "high-schoolers (32 percent) are more than twice as likely as collegians (15 percent) to say horror movies are among their favorites."
2. 1967 was the average year of birth of the 44 directors of the top ten grossing films during the five most recent years (2008–2012) for whom biographical information was available. The youngest directors of this group are Henry Joost and Ariel Schulman, co-directors of *Paranormal Activity 3* and *4*, both of whom were born in 1981, which makes them older millennials.
3. In a review of *The Biology of Horror: Gothic Literature and Film*, Carol Joan (Kay) Picart refers to "the well known thesis that horror/the Gothic, despite their indulgence in shattering taboos, are ultimately conservative in their thrusts; these genres eventually punish transgressions, thus enabling the return to 'normalcy'" (36).
4. I find particularly compelling Bryan Alexander's claim that horror films, like Gothic texts, "repeatedly threaten their younger, post-adolescent characters with a mixture of unwanted marriage, disinheritance, rape, and the death of parents" (146). Alexander notes that horror films replicate this plot: "Casualties are characters who fail to become adult, while protagonists grow through defeating these fears, organizing themselves, and mastering situations to cross the liminal spaces of the later teen years into normal adulthood" (148).
5. According to the "Theatrical Market Statistics" for 2012, available at www.mpaa.org, age groups from 12 to 24 constituted 36 percent of frequent moviegoers (moviegoers who go to the cinema once a month or more). The 12 to 24 age group also made up 24 percent of those who attended at least one film in 2012 and 31 percent of the total tickets sold, even though they comprised only 18 percent of the total population. These figures do not even take into consideration the number of millennials who, either legally or illegally, view films streaming online, download them, or rent them shortly after their release.
6. In the strictest sense of the term, a found footage film is a movie that purports to be composed entirely or primarily of footage shot by its characters, who have since died or gone missing. I am using the term more broadly to refer to these types of films as well as those supposedly pieced together from footage from surveillance cameras and other types of recording devices that have no human operator and mockumentaries focused on horror subject matter. For an extended discussion of the found footage genre, see Kristin Thompson and David Bordwell's "Observations on Film Art: Return to Paranormalcy."
7. Although the Asian market has been the primary supplier, Scandinavian and Spanish-speaking countries have also gained attention. Well-known horror remakes include the following (with the year of American release as well as information about the original film's title, if different, year of release, and country of origin in parentheses): *The Grudge* (2004; *Ju-On*,2002, Japan), *Dark Water* (2005; *Honogurai mizu no soko kara*, 2002, Japan), *Pulse* (2006; *Kairo*, Japan, 2001), *Quarantine* (2008; *[Rec]*, 2007, Spanish), *Shutter* (2008; Thailand, 2004), *The Uninvited* (2009; *A Tale of Two Sisters*, South Korea, 2003), *Let Me In* (2010; *Let the Right One In*, Sweden, 2008), *Silent House* (2011; Uruguay, 2010), and *Come Out and Play* (2012; Spain, 1976). Two more significant foreign horror films are rumored to be in production: *The Orphanage* (Spain, 2007) and *Troll Hunter* (Norway, 2010).
8. Prominent examples since *Texas Chainsaw* include (by year of remake) *Dawn of the Dead* (1978, 2004), *The Amityville Horror* (1979, 2005), *The Fog* (1980, 2005), *Black Christmas* (1974, 2006), *When a Stranger Calls* (1979, 2006), *The Omen* (1976, 2006), *Halloween* (1978, 2007), *April Fool's Day* (1986, 2008), *The Hitcher* (1986, 2008), *Prom Night* (1980, 2008), *Children of the Corn* (1984, 2009), *Friday the 13th* (1980, 2009), *My Bloody Valentine*

(1981, 2009), *Nightmare on Elm Street* (1984, 2010), *Evil Dead* (1981, 2013), and *Carrie* (1976, 2002, 2013). Many more are rumored to be in the works.

9. See Joshua Alston and Lorenza Munoz for further discussion on the increasing popularity of horror films amongst young women. Pamela Craig and Martin Fradley claims that the genre does tend to "foreground ... troubled (and frequently female) teen protagonists" (87). Visibilitypr.com claims that the genre is even more popular amongst females than males, stating that "24 percent of girls vs. 17 percent of boys say horror films are among their three favorite movie genres."

10. For discussions of millennials' respect for older generations, see Thom S. Rainer and Jess W. Rainer, especially pp. 54–60. Emily Matchar acknowledges millennial lack of deference for superiors in the workplace but concludes that the changes that may result might ultimately prove positive.

11. Significant contributions to this subgenre came in several franchises, including *Final Destination* (2000, 2003, 2006, 2009, 2011), *Wrong Turn* (2003, 2007, 2009, 2011, 2012), *Saw* (2004, 2005, 2006, 2007, 2008, 2009, 2010), and *Hostel* (2005, 2007, 2011), as well as in single films, such as *The Devil's Rejects* (2005), *Wolf Creek* (2005), *Vacancy* (2007), and *The Strangers* (2008). The decisions to remake *The Hills Have Eyes* (1977, 2006), *The Last House on the Left* (1972, 2009), *I Spit on Your Grave* (1978, 2010), and the Austrian film *Funny Games* (1997, 2007) were likely influenced by the popularity of this subgenre.

12. Edelstein, for example, considers the genre part of a larger debate about the morality of torture ongoing since 9/11, and Ashley M. Donnelly sees the idolization of the dispensers of torture (such as Dexter from the show that bears his name) as part of a larger need to distinguish righteous from unrighteous violence in the wake of war. Kelly believes torture porn is "a modern strain of horror that takes us straight back to the politically conscious, deeply despairing 70s classics" like the original *Texas Chainsaw Massacre*.

13. Davis and Natale also importantly distinguish between active gore "caused by violent acts as they are happening" and passive gore "caused by violence that has already occurred" (41) and note that the cinematic "uses" of gore have changed as well. They also point out that Mel Gibson's 2004 *The Passion of the Christ* easily outdoes any of the horror films they studied in terms of the number of screen minutes devoted to displays of gore, leading them to argue that "when used to inspire fear or disgust in a horror film images of gore often inspire different reactions than when equivalently gory images are used for alternative purposes in different genres" (50–51). In other words, evaluations of the ethics of "gore" are largely linked to perceptions of its viewers and creators.

14. One particularly virulent attack came from an Amazon review of Rebecca Huntley's *The World According to Y: Inside the New Adult Generation* by "Utah Jack Squint," who referred to the millennials as "the lappers-up of bloody delicacies proffered by the latest cinematic torture-porn... Abu Ghraib or Grindhouse—it's all the same to them, just as long as the current geopolitical situation doesn't prevent them from plunging headlong into the economy to snatch up dollars." See Ray B. Williams's "Is the 'Me Generation' Less Empathetic?" for a discussion of both sides of the issue.

15. Since then, three sequels have been made (2010, 2011, 2012) and a fifth film is slated for release in 2014; the film has also prompted more than a few hopeful imitators. Other well known found footage films include *REC* (2007) and its American remake *Quarantine* (2008), *Cloverfield* (2008), *The Last Exorcism* (2010), *Grave Encounters* (2011), *Apollo 18* (2011), *The Devil Inside* (2012), and *Chronicle* (2012).

16. Director Andrew Weiner discusses many of the perceived shortcomings of found footage films in a blog entry he wrote for the *Huffington Post*. Among the several reasons that he points to as to why this type of film is "frequently dismissed by critics," Weiner cites the perception "that any guy with a video camera can make one."

17. See, for example, Stein, Christine Rosen, and Twenge.

18. See "Joss Whedon Talks Cabin in the Woods" and Alex Pappademas.

19. Most prominent are the references to *Evil Dead*, which include the cabin in the woods itself, which contains a basement filled with objects that each summon a different creature (much like the Necronomicon), and even the inclusion of an "angry molesting tree" within the company's monster menagerie; the film also nods at *Hellraiser* and *The Strangers*. In addition, *Cabin* obviously gestures toward more general trends in the horror film genre, such as the recent reliance on Japanese horror and its conventions.

20. According to the "Trivia" section of the entry for *The Cabin in the Woods* on imdb.com, in *The Cabin in the Woods: The Official Visual Companion*, Whedon directly states that Sitterson and Hadley represent him and Goddard.

21. In this regard, *Cabin* is quite obviously referring to Carol Clover's concept of the Final Girl. See Chapter 1 of Clover's *Men, Women, and Chainsaws: Gender in the Modern Horror Film*.

The Scream of a Generation

"Generation Me" in Scream 4

SOTIRIS PETRIDIS

Introduction

This essay will examine the representation of the millennial generation in the postmodern slasher *Scream 4* (2011).[1] I argue that the film's young characters typify the so-called group of "Generation Me" with their characteristic emphasis on the self. The essay will also discuss the traits this group of people carries, and their impact on the slasher subgenre. Slasher films constitute a fruitful site for the examination of Generation Y, as the subgenre is usually addressed to a young demographic.

The main feature of the slasher subgenre is that evil is embodied in human nature. Most of the time, the "monster" is a male serial killer, hunting potential victims who are usually teenagers. Women constitute the majority of the victims and they face a more brutal death than the male characters. In the end, a girl, usually a virgin, survives, confronts and defeats the serial killer. Darryl Jones has summed up the basic narrative structure of the slasher as follows:

> A past misdeed creates a psychopathic killer. In the present, on a specific date, the killer returns to the site of the misdeed. He stalks and kills with a knife (or some kind of blade) a group of teenagers of both sexes. One girl survives to thwart the killer, at least temporarily [114].

Young people are featured in these films because the filmmakers are trying to target teen audiences (Vera Dika 87). Other characteristics of the slasher films include the punishment of the sexual act, having relatively few adult characters and the point-of-view (POV) shots of the serial killer. An example of this POV shot, which is today considered a classic example of this technique, is the opening sequence of *Halloween* (1978); the audience sees the whole action through the eyes of little Michael Myers (Will Sandin), who will grow up to become the killer of the franchise. The sequence is also a great example of the punishment of the sexual act. Moments before the murder of Michael's sister by Michael himself, she was having sex with her boyfriend. The convention of being punished for having sexual desires is considered a very common trope and narrative motif of slasher films and, as Carol J. Clover says, "sexual transgressors of both sexes are scheduled for early destruction" (33).

Another characteristic of the slasher is the many sequels and spin-offs that are created after the mainly commercial success of the original film.[2] It is precisely due to the standardization and repetition of the same formula, however, that the subgenre started to decline in the early 1990s and as a consequence, most of the new and original slasher films were unable to find national distribution (Adam Rockoff 177).

Nevertheless, the slasher renaissance arrived quite soon, in 1996 with the first film of the *Scream* franchise, which questioned the previous narrative norms and initiated a new, postmodern era for the subgenre. Of course, before 1996 there were some other movies with postmodern elements, like *New Nightmare* (1994), but *Scream* is considered to be the starting point of the postmodern slasher period because the whole film is imbued with those ideas and techniques (Andrew Syder 78–79).

Postmodernism, as both a critical theory as well as an aesthetic attitude that arose in the historical period of late capitalism, assisted in the creation of this new group of horror films. This is not something peculiar because postmodern theory and horror films share some common values. As Syder points out, "both postmodern theory and the horror genre are fundamentally concerned with parallel questions about how we perceive and make sense of the world around us, and as such both offer comparable models for ordering the knowledge we possess about the external world" (79). Isabel Pinedo goes a step further and describes the postmodern world of the horror films as "an unstable one in which traditional categories break down, boundaries blur, institutions fall into question, enlightenment narratives collapse, the inevitability of progress crumbles, and the master status of the universal subject deteriorates" (86).

Slasher films are one of the most popular expressions of postmodern horror. The first *Scream* came out in a period when the Gen Xers were still teenagers and it was a film about them and for them. We could also argue that *Scream* was a film "made" by this generation because the screenwriter, Kevin Williamson, is a member of Generation X. So, Gen Xers were responsible for the postmodern turn of the subgenre. In order to better understand the dual influence of postmodern slasher films and Gen Xers on the conventions of the subgenre, we have to look at some of the characteristics of this generation.

The term "Generation X" was introduced by Douglas Coupland in 1991 to describe the generation after the Baby-Boom of 1946 to 1964. People who were born after 1965 belonged to a new generation. This group, termed Generation X, constituted an enigma to their political and culturally rebellious parents (Kendall R. Phillips, 172). The characteristics of Gen Xers were mainly their cynicism, their antipathy towards the baby boom generation and their belief that nothing is sacred and no one can be trusted (Phillips, 172).

I would argue that the above traits, combined with postmodern narrative elements, helped to define the tone and storylines of the *Scream* franchise. In the original film, whose main characters are primarily Gen Xers, we watch how Sidney (Neve Campbell) tries to escape from a murderer, whose identity remains secret until the end. The victims, the female protagonist and the killer, belong to Generation X and this affects the whole film; due to the cynical perspective of the characters, *Scream*'s point of view embodies parody and sometimes this changes the essence of the norms. The characters are hyperconscious about the structure of the narrative and they try to alter the conventions by making fun of the subgenre's formula. A characteristic example is at the end of the film when Randy (Jamie Kennedy) asks Sidney to be careful because usually the killers of slasher films come back to life for a last scare; Sidney immediately shoots the killer in the head, responding: "not in my movie." Thus, Sidney breaks a well-known slasher convention while she accepts the fact that she is in a movie.

Sidney, the girl who survives at the end, constitutes a good example of the postmodern turn of the subgenre. According to Clover, the Final Girl[3] is the only character to be developed in any psychological detail and the viewers understand that hers is the main story line, from the attention paid to her onscreen (44). Sidney is smart, intelligent and does not have sexual desires, something that stands in contrast to the behavior of the other female teenage characters of the movie. Although Sidney is the girl who survives at the end, she does not possess all the characteristics of Clover's Final Girl theory. Sidney is popular, bright and has a boyfriend, as opposed to the virginal and lonely stereotype of the Final Girl. Even though *Scream* follows and at the same time plays with and/or subverts the conventions of the subgenre, it breaks one basic rule of the classic slasher films; punishment of sexual desire. In the *Scream* franchise, the murders have nothing to do with sexual activity and the characters are mocking this convention by referencing previous slasher films.[4]

Three sequels followed the first *Scream*; *Scream 2* (1997), *Scream 3* (2000) and *Scream 4* (2011). The first two were released only a few years after the first film while the last one came out fifteen years later. All the movies enjoyed financial success, with *Scream 4* grossing the least of the films' franchise.⁵ *Scream 2* and *Scream 3* obey the conventions initially set out by the original. The viewers follow the same basic characters from adolescence to the first stages of adulthood. Even the new characters and the potential victims are approximately the same age as the characters from the first movie. In fact, the characters in the first three movies of the *Scream* franchise are all primarily Gen Xers.

Fifteen years later, when *Scream 4* was filmed, the teenage target group, to which the majority of slasher films are addressed, was no longer part of Generation X. In 2011, a new generation was going through puberty with different characteristics, likes and dislikes, and therefore, other issues had to come to the cinematic fore. The basic three characters, Sidney, Gale (Courteney Cox) and Dewey (David Arquette), remain the same but the murder plot and the killer are about new, younger characters with entirely different behaviors compared to the other three *Scream* films.

This generation has a lot of names, such as Generation Y, Yers, Millennials, the Internet Generation, or the Net Generation (Mici L. Halse and Brenda J. Mallinson 59). For the purposes of clarity, this essay will use only the terms millennial generation or millennials to avoid confusion.

Scream 4: The Millennials and the Generation Me Approach

The millennials are the people who were born, roughly, from 1982 to 1999 (Jean Twenge "The Greatest Generation"). As Ed Grabianowski points out, "there doesn't seem to be a defining cultural characteristic that binds them together, however. With the possible exception of 9/11, no unifying, singular, generation-defining world event took place for them" (1). Nevertheless, despite the absence of a single, connecting occurrence, millennials do present some common traits.

First, they are characterized as demanding. Charles Woodruffe claims that this stereotype is about exigent young people who are difficult to recruit but easy to lose, and he refers to them as Generation Whine, an alternative epithet which comes from a derivation of the term Generation Y (31). Woodruffe's list of millennial traits includes high ambition, inability to take criticism and self-confidence of possessing the capacity for achievement (32).

There are two major theories around the millennial generation personality; the "Generation We" and the "Generation Me" view. The Generation

We theory posits that millennials are more community oriented, caring, activist, civically involved, and interested in environmental causes than previous generations (Twenge, W. Keith Campbell, and Elise C. Freeman, 1046). At the other end, there is the Generation Me view which postulates that millennials care more about themselves than anything else. In her book *Generation Me*, Twenge presents data showing generational increases in self-esteem, high expectations, assertiveness, self-importance and narcissism.

This view is also supported by an article by Twenge, Campbell and Freeman, which examines the generational changes in community feeling. The article summarizes the results of three studies on three different generations (Baby Boomers, Gen Xers and Millennials). The first study is about generational differences in terms of life goals; the second one examines generational changes in terms of their concern for others and the third one examines trends in civic orientation and social capital. The results of those studies primarily support the "Generation Me" view because there are findings of an increase in individualistic traits and a decline in civic engagement (Twenge, Campbell and Freeman, 1058). These contrasting perspectives on the millennials raise the question of which set of character traits the millennials in *Scream 4* exhibit.

As was already noted, *Scream 4* focuses on millennial characters and is also addressed to them but it is not made by this generation like the original *Scream* was made by Generation X. The story takes place in the same fictional town of the first film, Woodsboro, California. Now, Sidney is the author of a book about her experience with the murders and Woodsboro is the last stop in her book tour. There, she reconnects with Sheriff Dewey and Gale, who are now married, as well as with her teenage cousin Jill (Emma Roberts) and her Aunt Kate (Mary McDonnell). Unfortunately, the Ghostface[6] is back and the whole town of Woodsboro is in danger once again. Most of the victims are friends of Jill's, which means they are in their late teens. In the end, it is revealed that Jill herself is behind the killings and that she did it all for the sake of fame. Jill is assisted by a "secondary" killer, Charlie (Rory Culkin), who ends up dead in her hands.

Scream 4 belongs to a franchise initially created for Generation X. Nevertheless, since the fourth installment was released fifteen years after the first film, it had to "fill the gap" between the two generations that constitute its main target audience. *Scream 4* opts, therefore, to represent both generations and is also addressed to both. Millennials, on the one hand, could not have remembered the impact of the first *Scream* because they were very young. Gen Xers, on the other hand, had grown up and their tastes and interests had changed over the years. Commenting on the issue, Wes Craven, director of all of the *Scream* movies, explains: "You're addressing a generation of young fans, but also the generation that has gone with you for three, as well as a decade worth of other films. You have to be as good, or better, than all these films" (in Portman, "Debate over *Scream 4*"). Craven also adds that "We had to do something distinctive and unique to its time, not just do a repeat of something we've done before with *Scream*... Keeping that freshness called for a lot of work. I think what we have is original and wonderful" (in Johnson, "Craven Promises New Twist").

Before we go any further, a plot comparison between the first and the fourth films is in order; if the ending of *Scream 4* is not taken into account, there is a significant number of similarities between the two films. Their plot description could be summed up as follows: "a girl lives in Woodsboro; her mother dies; she has a boyfriend; Ghostface comes and hunts her and kills all of her friends." The main difference in the fourth film is that, apart from this storyline, the storyline from the previous films is also followed. In other words, the "remake storyline" is about the millennial characters of the film and the "old storyline" is about the Gen Xers. The old storyline concerns the lives and actions of the characters of the first three filmic texts (Sidney, Sheriff Dewey and Gale). The new narrative elements are connected with the millennials of the film and their structure is reminiscent of the first *Scream* movie; thus, the new elements of Jill's life and friends constitute the remake of the original storyline. *Scream 4* even mocks the fact that it looks like a remake of the first *Scream*. For example, when Sidney goes to the school's Cinema Club, Robbie (Erik Knudsen) and Charlie tell her that they believe the killer acts according to the conventions of a remake horror film. There is a similar reference at the end of the film, when Sidney kills Jill and tells her, "you forgot the first rule of remakes; don't fuck with the original."

In addition, there are even scenes that are created in order to look like parts of the first *Scream*. One of them is when Jill's boyfriend, Trevor (Nico Tortorella), comes into her room from the window so he can talk to her, the same way Sidney's boyfriend, Billy (Skeet Ulrich), did in the first *Scream*. The similarity does not go unnoticed, even in the fictional world, since when Sidney sees Trevor she "self-referentially" tells Jill, "you remind me of me." The characters from the first and fourth film of the franchise become more and more linked and are represented as two different versions of the same person.

Another example of the remake structure of *Scream 4* is the ending. Jill and Charlie, her accomplice, kill all of their friends but they want to accuse Jill's boyfriend of the crimes. So, they capture and kill him and then try to alter the evidence of the last crime scene in order to make it seem as if Trevor was the killer. In other words, the real killers want to recreate the ending of the first *Scream*, so that the boyfriend is revealed to be the killer and Jill the final survivor, like Sidney.

The first *Scream* is considered innovative because it dared to defy some of the conventions of the subgenre. A characteristic example is the now classic first sequence in which Drew Barrymore is murdered. A Hollywood star actress, who would be the Final Girl in a traditional slasher film, is being slashed in its first minutes. What *Scream 4* introduces is another way to toy with the conventions of the remakes of the first slashers, as in fact the majority of the millennial slasher films are remakes of older films, such as *Halloween* (2007), *Friday the 13th* (2009) and *A Nightmare on Elm Street* (2010). The structure of *Scream 4* resembles a remake of the first *Scream*, but at the same time it is also a sequel of the same film. *Scream 4* essentially parodies the new subgenre trends, one of those being the remakes of classic slashers. Parody, or according to Fredric Jameson pastiche, has a vital role in postmodernism. "Pastiche is, like parody, the imitation of a peculiar or unique, idiosyncratic style [...] the imitation of dead styles, speech through all the masks and voices stored up in the imaginary museum of a now global culture" (Jameson, 16–17). An example of parody in *Scream 4* is the scene where the killer talks to the phone with Kirby (Hayden Panettiere) and Charlie is tied in a chair outside the house. The killer asks questions in order to give Kirby a chance to save Charlie and the last question is about the remakes of horror. Kirby's answer includes a lot of film titles, something that mocks the trend of the remakes. Apart from this, the scene also parodies the opening sequence of the first *Scream,* because the set and the action are almost identical.

The main characters of *Scream 4* are separated into two broad categories, the Gen Xers and the millennials. The basic Gen Xer characters, Sidney, Gale and Dewey, come from the previous films, and all the millennials are new characters in the franchise. Due to the 15-year span between *Scream* and *Scream 4*, a lot of things are different in the story structure. The most important is that technology has become an integral part of everyone's lives. Millennials were born during a period in which social networks and the internet as a whole have increased people's interest in their public image. Facebook and Twitter accounts, blogs and chat rooms are part of the everyday life of almost every millennial. They care more about how they are viewed than how they really are. Craven observes: "The growth of social networking, smartphones, video cameras and recorders has a tremendous presence in every nook and cranny of our life, and we're very much in that world. I can't imagine doing a film set in today's world without those things being important to plot and character" (Johnson, "Craven Promises New Twist").

In the first *Scream*, it was rare for a teenager to have a cell phone. Billy was even accused of being the killer because he was near the attack against Sidney and had a cell phone on him. On the other hand, in *Scream 4* every teenager owns and is seen using a smartphone onscreen. A characteristic example of this is the scene where a whole classroom of millennials learns about the first murders. While the teacher is speaking, all the students' smartphones begin to ring and the tragic news is spread in no time. This kind of instantaneous communication of events in almost real time represents the everyday life of this generation. Every aspect of their lives is dependent on technological gadgets that deliver information at warp speed.

Another feature that the new technology brought is that it has allowed millennials to engage in multitasking, or doing several things at the same time. Halse and Mallinson point out that millennials "expect learning to be more exciting and engaging than their predecessors, are accustomed to changing their focus frequently from one thing to another and back (multitasking)" (59). Of course, multitasking is highly influenced by the internet. Nowadays, one can have as many internet tabs open as he/she pleases, go from one tab to another in no time and take in a lot of information at once. *Scream 4* incorporates this trait into the narrative.

The opening sequence is indicative; three very similar scenes succeed one another, each with two female characters and at least one killer. The first is a scene from *Stab 6*, which is watched by the girls in scene two. Scene two is a scene from *Stab 7*, which is watched by the girls in the third scene who are the first "real" characters from *Scream 4*. The *Stab* movies are part of a fictional film franchise within the *Scream* franchise and they are supposed to adapt the events from the first *Scream*. The first ten minutes of the film are based on the combination of pastiche with multitasking. In the first part of the sequence we have a lot of references to the relationship between millennials and technology. Facebook, texting, smartphones and an internet stalker are parts of the narrative of *Stab 6*. The second part of the opening sequence, *Stab 7*, is a comment on the postmodern elements of slasher films. Two Hollywood stars, Anna Paquin and Kristen Bell, make cameo appearances as the stars of the scene, reminding the "older" and/or knowledgeable viewers of the Barrymore sequence of the original *Scream*.[7] There is also a dialogue between them, with Paquin arguing that postmodern horror films are "the death of horror" and Bell disagreeing. This dialogue is even more interesting if we take into account that is a part of the opening sequence of a postmodern horror film. Finally, the last part of the sequence represents "real life" in Woodsboro. The opening sequence of *Scream 4* has all the characteristics essential to the whole narrative: postmodern elements, the rise of technology and the millennials, all of which are framed within a multitasking montage.

Even some of the killings are based on the multitasking trait. Olivia's (Marielle Jaffe) murder is one example. Olivia is Jill's friend and lives next to her. Jill is in her room with her friend, Kirby, watching a movie. Olivia is seen returning home while talking on the phone with the two girls. The killer calls and threatens Jill and Kirby but there is a misunderstanding about his/her whereabouts. At the end, the viewers and the two female characters see the killer murdering Olivia in her room. In this case, the narrative not only incorporates multitasking, but also includes live streaming. With the evolution of technology, millennials can interact with others through voice or even image. So this murder is represented as a sort of bizarre video chat which allows the caller to witness the murder almost live.

Another example of these multitasking/live streaming murders is when Ghostface tries to kill Gale during the *Stab* Marathon.[8] Gale goes where the "Stabathon" takes place to secretly install some cameras in an effort to find the killer, only to stumble upon another hidden camera. At the same time, Dewey arrives outside the area where the Stabathon takes place and looks at Gale's laptop in her car. Dewey watches the killer approach Gale on the screen while her attempted murder is captured by the killer's camera. So, the audience has the capacity to view the murders through many perspectives by virtue of three different camera angles and shots; two fictional cameras (the killer's and Gale's) and also the camera recording the film itself.

The representation of the millennial generation as a whole reflects the Generation Me view. Every millennial in *Scream 4* cares only about his/her needs while no character and/or scene suggests the possibility of a complement by the Generation We theory. The main representative of the millennials is Jill, and as the film progresses, the viewers are led to believe she is going to be the Final Girl, although it turns out that she is in fact the killer. This twist breaks the conventions of the subgenre, because the Final Girl and the killer have always been two characters and their final duel a staple of the subgenre. *Scream 4* decides to merge the two in a single character, thus annulling a basic convention. Clover claims that by confronting the killer, the Final Girl enters the adult world and "is what the killer once was; he is what she could become should she fail in her battle for sexual selfhood" (50). According to Clover's theory, the Final Girl and the killer share common elements as the first one is the evolution of the other. In other words, these two characters can be interpreted as two sides of the same coin. *Scream 4* breaks an obvious convention by substituting it instead with a more extreme, though less obvious convention.

Jill is the embodiment of the Generation Me theory. Grabianowski asserts that the main traits associated with this theory are the millennials' intense belief in themselves, their feeling of entitlement regarding wealth and fame and their reluctance to take on hard work (2). Jill will do anything to succeed. She becomes the murderer, because she is driven to do so by an entirely selfish motive. Among the victims are her friends and her mother whom she sacrifices for her own success. Jill's representation as part of the Generation Me view is obviously a negative one. The main representative of the millennials in this film is portrayed as willing to kill almost every one of her closest friends in order to achieve immediate success and fame. In the scene where the viewers and Sidney finally learn about her real actions, Jill tells Sidney: "My friends? What world are you living in? I don't need any friends! I need fans! Don't you get it? You had your fifteen minutes, now I want mine!"

Jill's obsession with fame is also in accordance with the consolidation of celebrity culture that took place in the 1990s and 2000s as a result of the technological revolution. Today, anyone can be famous with the help of social networking. YouTube, Facebook and Twitter are some of the examples that can help any act done by an individual, however trivial and insignificant, go viral and be seen and/or commented upon by millions around the world in a matter of a few minutes. *Scream 4* comments on this reality when Jill says: "we all live in public now; we are all on the Internet. How do you think people become famous anymore? You don't have to achieve anything." It can be argued that the millennials are, in a way, obsessed with "showing" and/or exhibiting a significant part of their lives. They upload every minute and aspect of their everyday life, with the explicit desire to create an impression of perfection to others. This is why in *Scream 4* the murders are filmed. As Gale points out when she discovers the murderer's cameras: "this time, he is making the movie." Another line that refers to the fact that the murders are filmed comes from Jill when she tells Sidney: "with you, the world just heard about what happened but with us they're gonna see it... it's not like anyone reads anymore." In other words, the millennial generation believes that the fifteen minutes of fame can best be achieved through images (whether still or moving) on the internet. By the end of the film, Jill gets her fifteen minutes of fame as the reporters outside the hospital describe her actions, comparing her to "an American hero right out of the movies," as they are not aware of Jill's true nature and actions. The sequence ends with a close-up of Jill's dead face, which can be regarded as an ironic comment on how media represent true events.

Jill may be an extreme example of this tendency of obsession with fame; she is after all the "monster" of a slasher film that has to obey certain conventions, but there are also other millennial characters in the film that support similar views. There is Charlie, who helps Jill with her plan until she kills him as well and Robbie, who has a mini camera "installed" on his head and broadcasts all his life live on the internet.

Juxtaposing Jill with the first *Scream*'s Sidney, it could be argued that the former is the latter's alter ego, a millennial version of her. Both the young Sidney and Jill are in high school, with a lot of friends and a bad-boy boyfriend. Their difference lies in their narrative function, with Sidney meant to be the Final Girl and Jill the killer. In addition, Sidney does not want all that publicity and tries to have a private life. Jill, on the other hand, aims for exactly this kind of publicity and even sacrifices human lives to achieve it. As she says: "sick is the new sane." Sidney and Jill's antithetical perspectives can be summed up with the phrase Sidney tells Jill, when the latter asks her how she is handling all this publicity: "I try not to think about me. I have people I care about. I focus on them." This is the complete opposite of what Jill said about not needing any friends and only having fans.

Millennials are represented negatively in *Scream 4*, exhibiting the worst traits of the Generation Me view, while Gen Xers, by contrast, are portrayed as selfless and community-oriented. Sidney, Gale and Dewey try to solve the murders by risking their lives while the millennial characters seem indifferent, at best, as to whether the perpetrator will be arrested or not. An example of their insensitivity is that, despite the recent murders, Stabathon still takes place due to a kind of lack of respect for the value of human life and indifference to suffering and tragedy. As Dewey says in the film, "one generation's tragedy is the next one's joke." Taking into account the positive representation of Gen Xers in the narrative, it is no wonder that the Final Girl is not a millennial, but a member of the Generation X.

As I have argued, in almost the entire film, the audience believes that Jill is going to be the Final Girl. At the same time, there is Sidney, a character who has been a Final Girl for the last three movies. Sidney is represented as an adult Final Girl or, in other words, as a Final Woman, more active and fearless than ever before. This is one of the first times that we see a Final Girl become a Final Woman through the filmic texts of a franchise. Another example is Laurie (Jamie Lee Curtis) who decides to confront the killer, Michael Myers (Chris Durand) in *Halloween H20: 20 Years Later* (1998) despite having the opportunity to run away. Four years later though Michael kills Laurie in *Halloween: Resurrection* (2002), punishing her for her fearless actions.[9] Sidney is also one of the first Final Women in slasher films who does not run away to survive, as most Final Girls would do. Instead, she actively hunts down the killer and risks her life in her effort to save the others. When Olivia is killed, Sidney is in the house across the street and sees the murder from the window. Other Final Girls would have screamed and tried to call the police, yet Sidney runs to the other house, finds the killer and fights.

Usually, the single constant element in all slasher film franchises is the killer. Victims and Final Girls may come and go but the only character who manages to survive in more than one film is the murderer. Not so in the *Scream* franchise; the female protagonist is the constant element and we follow her from adolescence to adult life; from Final Girl to Final Woman. A very characteristic scene which encompasses the traits of the Final Woman is the one in the hospital where Sidney and Jill fight. Jill tries to kill Sidney but Sidney inevitably survives, in the same way as the "monsters" of other slasher films do. In the end, Sidney kills Jill and completes her task as Final Woman.[10] So, Sidney takes over and she is the final survivor, along with the other two Gen Xers, Gale and Dewey. At the same time, all the millennial characters and even Jill herself, end up dead.[11]

Scream 4 can be viewed as a struggle between two generations.[12] The adult community of the town and the figures of authority belong to Generation X. These characters try to solve the murders and their actions aim at the greater good. On the contrary, the young community belongs to the millennial generation. Their representation is mostly negative and makes the majority of these characters look bad. Thus, the Gen Xers prevail in this peculiar generational conflict.

Conclusion

Slasher films are a very important part of modern pop culture and *Scream* constitutes one of the most well-known franchises of the subgenre's history. The majority of the representations involve teenagers and youth, who also constitute the target group of the films. The four *Scream* films were instrumental in ushering in the creation of new norms and innovative perspectives in slasher films. The representations of the first three movies are about Generation X. The first film was created especially for the teenage Gen Xers of the mid 1990s. *Scream 4* was released fifteen years later when the teenage audience was inevitably different. The millennial generation was experiencing puberty and *Scream 4* was addressed to a new generation. *Scream 4* becomes, therefore, a fictional site of struggle between those two generations.

The millennials' portrayal is heartless and harsh. These characters seem to not care about anyone except for themselves. They place their selfish needs first, and they are not concerned about what the others want. Even the killings are justified through the millennial fascination with instant fame and popularity. On the other hand, Gen Xers are portrayed as the complete opposite and care about the greater good, a trait that further accentuates the negative side of the millennial characters. There is a clear-cut opposition between the "good" adult Gen Xers and the "villainous" millennials who only care about their public image.

Scream 4 represents the new generation through the eyes of the older ones (mainly the filmmaking team) and assumes a rather critical and condemning outlook. The film does not fill the gap between the two generations and instead creates a sense of conflict between Gen Xers and millennials. Millennials end up murdered and the Final Girl of the *Scream* franchise is once again a Gen Xer. The narrative of the filmic text has picked a side in this generational struggle and it ultimately comes as no surprise why it favors Generation X.

Notes

1. Horror films are one of the most popular Hollywood genres and constitute an integral part of pop culture. Horror made its appearance almost at the same time cinema was born and a lot of subgenres were created since then, such as demonic films, vampire films and splatter films. One of the most well-known and important subgenres of horror is the slasher film; filmic texts about the story of a psychokiller who slashes to death mostly female victims until he is subdued or killed, usually by the one girl who has survived (Clover, 21). *Halloween* (1978) is considered to be the starting point of the subgenre although two other movies which came out four years before 1978, *Black Christmas* (1974) and *The Texas Chainsaw Massacre* (1974) are said to have influenced slasher film. However, *Halloween* is considered to mark the formal beginning of slasher films, for it combines all the characteristics of the subgenre. Since then, a lot of slasher films came out using different conventions and cinematic techniques, depending on the socioeconomic conditions of the period in which the movie was produced.

2. The *Halloween* franchise consists of eight original films and two remakes, *A Nightmare on Elm Street* has eight original films and one remake and *Friday the 13th* has eleven original films and one remake. An example of a spin-off is the film *Freddy vs. Jason* (2003) in which the two well-known killers from *A Nightmare on Elm Street* and *Friday the 13th* meet.

3. Clover says about the survivor, or in her words the Final Girl, that she "is presented from the outset as the main character [...] she is not sexually active" and "she is also watchful to the point of paranoia. [...] Above all she is intelligent and resourceful in a pinch" (39). Clover continues to analyze the characteristics of the gender of the Final Girl and says that the gender is compromised by her masculine interests, her sexual reluctance and her "active investigating gaze" which is normally reserved for males (48).

4. In the first film of the franchise, Randy talks about the conventions and rules that you have to follow in order to survive in a slasher film, such as abstinence and no consumption of alcohol.

5. *Scream 4* opened at No. 2 at the box office with $19.3 million (Associated Press, "Moviegoers"). According to data from the website Box Office Mojo, the original *Scream* grossed $173 million worldwide, followed by $172 million for *Scream 2*, $161 million for *Scream 3* and $97 million for *Scream 4*.

6. Ghostface is the killer of the *Scream* franchise. The name originates from the famous mask which looks like a ghost. Even though Ghostface is the killer in the entire franchise, the person who wears the mask is different in every filmic text.

7. Anna Paquin is one of the leading characters of *True Blood* (HBO 2008–present), a mystery horror TV show, and Kristen Bell is known for her role in *Veronica Mars* (UPN, CW 2004–2007), a mystery TV show. It can therefore be argued that the selection of those two Hollywood stars was not random.

8. *Stab* Marathon, or Stabathon, is an annual movie marathon in which all the *Stab* films are screened.

9. Slasher films are often accused of gender bias. Laurie's murder in *Halloween: Resurrection* is a proof of how patriarchy can sometimes pretend to provide women with power only to take it violently back. It would be interesting to examine feminism's course and general conditions during the first *Halloween* in 1978 and Laurie's victory and the 2002 movie which claimed her life but this goes beyond the scope of this essay.

10. This scene is also interesting if we analyze it through a lens of gender representation. We have four women who are affecting the progress of the narrative and one unconscious male policeman.

11. It should be added that the screenwriter, Kevin Williamson, who is also the writer of the scripts of *Scream* and *Scream 2*, and the writer of the characters in *Scream 3*, was born in 1965. So, the script of *Scream 4* is written by a Gen Xer.

12. The struggle between the young generation and the older community is a very common trope in slasher films. The big difference between older slasher films, like *Scream*, and *Scream 4* is that in the latter the Gen Xers are not teenagers anymore and they have take the place of the old community.

"Comedy Natives"

Generations, Humor and the Question of Why Smart + Funny Is the New Rock and Roll

MARGARET TALLY

Introduction: Mapping Humor on to the Millennials

In a recent online post in Ypulse, an online magazine about the millennial generation, the observation was made that a majority of TV comedies about millennials is being created by or marketed to millennial women specifically. For example, *2 Broke Girls* (CBS, 2011–present) is produced by Whitney Cummings, who also created and starred in *Whitney* on NBC (2011–2013), as well as her own talk show on the entertainment channel *E!* Similarly, Zooey Deschanel has created, developed and stars in several millennial comedies, including *New Girl* (Fox, 2011–present). Mindy Kaling, who is between a Gen X (those who were born after the baby boomers, from the early sixties to the mid-seventies), and a millennial, that is, those who have been born between 1980 and 2000), has also created and stars in *The Mindy Project* (Fox, 2012–present). Finally, Lena Dunham wrote, directed and stars in her culturally cutting-edge HBO television series titled *Girls* (HBO, 2012–present) and recently signed a multi-million dollar contract for a book which is billed as a millennial memoir. Taken together, these young women were described in the online post as having created their own "media empires."

While the term "media empire" may be overstating the case, these young women are nevertheless impressive for their ability to leverage their comical talents in several different realms, including writing, producing, directing and oftentimes starring in their own programs and films. And though there are certainly male comics, such as Jonah Hill and Aziz Ansari, who, as millennials, have also found success, their roots are more often than not in stand-up comedy or ensemble acting, while the millennial female comics draw on earlier role models in Hollywood, including Amy Poehler, Kristen Wiig and Tina Fey, as inspirations for creating media "empires," to showcase their talent.

In some ways, this rise of millennial women turning to comedy as a vehicle for creative expression is by no means a new phenomenon. Since Mae West first offered her famous one-liner about guns in pockets, for example, to Lucille Ball and her stint in a chocolate factory, women have been actively creating humor in popular culture since the beginning of the medium of film and television itself. However, during a time in Hollywood where women have continued to struggle for recognition and airspace, the rise of female humorists in our recent historical period is a welcome new development. This period, roughly between the 1990s and 2000s, has also coincided with the "third wave" of feminism and these millennial women have reached maturity during a time when women's rights have been taken for granted, hence the ubiquitous phrase of this generation, "I'm not a feminist but..." For this group of women, humor has been used as a way to voice their political views, which is arguably different from the more radical and angry associations with second wave feminism. For example, Tracy Clark-Flory, in a 2012 article entitled, "Mockery: Women's New Weapon," has explored the ways in which women are using strategies, such as proposed sex strikes or restricting access to Viagra, to fight against attacks on their reproductive rights.

In addition, this may be the first generation to actively learn about political events of the day through a comedy show, *The Daily Show with Jon Stewart* (Comedy Central, 1996–present), which offers a biting satire and is geared towards the desirable 18- to 34-year-old demographic. The election of Barack Obama was won in no small part due to the enthusiasm of the millennial men and women, and comedians like Jon Stewart as well as Stephen Colbert of *The Colbert Report* (Comedy Central, 2005–present) were influential spokespersons for rallying young people to get out the vote for Obama in both elections, even as they also criticized some of his shortcomings, particularly during the second campaign (Alexander Heffner).

The Daily Show with John Stewart and *The Colbert Report* are both on Comedy Central, which is part of MTV Networks, which in turn is part of the mega media giant corporation, Viacom. Comedy Central has been pitching their shows towards millennials, based on research which indicates that millennials believe humor is a central feature of their lives. The channel also commissioned research about how millennials view humor (Chanon Cook).

Writing about their findings, Tanya Giles, the executive vice president for research at MTV Networks, Comedy Central's parent company, noted "Comedy is so central to who they are, the way they connect with other people, the way they get ahead in the world. One big takeaway is that unlike previous generations, humor, and not music, is their No. 1 form of self-expression" (qtd. in Bill Carter).

While some critics, including Carter, have commented on the self-serving attitude of such a study, there are some insights that can be garnered from this research (Carter). For example, the research found that comedy is very important to this group of millennials, not simply as a means of self-definition, but also as a way to reach out to others quickly, via technology and their use of social media, such as YouTube, tweets and texts. Comedy Central also found that their audience is primarily male (65 percent), and, despite losing market shares to other social media, younger males are their primary viewers (Cook).

This essay will critically interrogate the claim that millennials are indeed "comedy natives," by exploring some recent examples of humor that have been generated by and/or marketed to, this demographic group. For the contemporary reading of millennials in the larger culture is that they are somehow uniformly different from earlier generations, precisely because they define themselves as both humorous as well as being most comfortable with a comedic take on the world. As part of this investigation, I will also see whether and how gender becomes one of the key differences in terms of both the millennials' sense of humor, that is, what they find funny, as well as the potential for this age group to help re-define a prevailing stereotype of women as somehow not being funny.

In fact, one of the central reasons for undertaking the study conducted by Comedy Central was to learn how to recapture the coveted young male millennial market, and young women were only a secondary consideration. The channel needed to create a "new business model" based on their findings about the millennials, and one of the strategies they employed was to create shows like the scripted *Workaholics* (Comedy Central, 2011–present), which stars young male millennials, as well as *Tosh-O* (Comedy Central, 2009- present), which offers satirical commentaries on real videos. Together, these two shows would be the "new face" of Comedy Central.

While the findings above are driven by a tighter focus on young male millennials, there are, nevertheless, some implications that can be drawn from the Comedy Central study regarding millennial women and comedy as well. These include the notion that millennials view almost any subject as being potentially funny; that absurdist humor is more congenial to their world outlook than irony and that they like their comedy to come at a fast pace (Cook). Part of the reason why speed is important is that millennials have the opportunity now to turn to multiple platforms and screens to watch comedies, which requires television programs to be as current as possible to attract their viewers.

New Generation or Endless Recycling: Constructing the Millennial?

These findings about specific millennial behaviors and preferences tap into larger debates about whether it makes sense to even speak of distinct generational characteristics, or whether this is itself a kind of facile shorthand for market researchers to try to pitch certain ideas to their clients? While there may be no clear answer to this question, one indication of the *constructed nature* of defining millennials are the contrasting interpretations of millennials as either the "Generation Me," or the "Generation We" (Joanna Chau). For every negative trait that is cited in research on this generation, a corresponding positive trait is also provided.

To refer to one example, Thomas Pardee gives the same trait both positive and negative spins. Pardee's article cites a 2010 Pew Research study, which found that 37 percent of 18- to 29-year-olds don't have jobs. As a result, millennials are considered to be more frugal than past generations, with the notable exception of Depression-era individuals. The Severe Recession, which commenced in 2007, has shaped their life choices, including delaying marriage and home buying, fueling the inclination to live at home after college for longer periods than the Gen Xers and Baby Boomers. Since they never left home, some argue they developed closer and, therefore, better relationships with their parents, who made them the center of the household (Tom Rainer). At the same time, this view of millennials as remaining at home after college is alternatively referred to as "failing to launch," and "delaying adulthood" or, more simply, living off their parents and not taking responsibility for their own lives.

Whether millennials are viewed in positive or negative terms, there are some general attitudes of both male and female individuals that have been garnered in such large research studies as the Pew Research Study. In this large-scale survey, millennials stated that they are both trying to make ends meet and stay afloat economically. At the same time, they are optimistic about their futures (Pardee). Likewise, because they never had to reject anything, as the

Baby Boomers did during the culturally turbulent period of the 1960s, they are arguably more open to the idea that they can be successful by building on what already exists. Technology, finally, is also seen both positively and negatively as a feature of millennials' lives. As the 2010 Pew Research study also found, millennials identify themselves as the *networked generation*, and technology plays a key part in helping them to solve problems, communicate with others and entertain themselves. At the same time, since some respondents indicate they devote 15 hours per day on average to technology use, legitimate questions might be raised as to the impact of this usage on other aspects of millennials' lives.

For media marketers, constructing some idea of what millennials like and don't like allows for a shorthand way of helping clients to pitch their products. This is never more apparent than in *Advertising Age*'s marketing "tips" or strategies they advise their clients to use to market to millennials, which includes advice such as "be clever," "be transparent," "don't "technologize" everything, and finally, "give them a reason to talk about you" (Pardee). Humor is viewed as a key marketing technique to engage and create loyal millennial customers, who they believe it necessary to obtain allegiances from earlier in their lives so that they will remain as faithful customers in the future as well.

In terms of a provisional summary, then, we can say that millennials may indeed constitute an age cohort that demonstrates some similar characteristics as a result of real social and economic changes in their lives and the resulting pressures that the age group of 18- to 32-year-olds are facing, including the Severe Recession, unemployment and underemployment. Concurrently, however, the specific claim that millennials are somehow a radically different generation than the one before it is not by any means irrefutable.

For example, even if one could identify a specific age cohort with certain attitudes and behaviors, this is different from a generational construct, because it is entirely conceivable that individuals from other generations may also possess some of these attitudes and behaviors. Suppose, in addition, it is possible to identify certain characteristics of this cohort, or a subset, such as those who are now living at home more, delaying marriage and parenthood, taking longer to find or build a career, and living with the help of parents, this does not define the entire age cohort of 18- to 32-year-olds. A sizable minority of this age group may hold opposite views and make considerably different lifestyle choices.

What we may be able to say, given the limited nature of speaking of a particular generation with a defined set of values, is that there are currently many young people in this cohort, as well as older individuals who are trying to attract this age group and who are mining the material conditions of this group and using it to explore the social and inner lives of people in this extended adolescence. This includes young women such as Dunham, as well as several of the comic artists already mentioned. What has happened in terms of the media system, including, for example, advertisers, television channels, and filmmakers, is that in the competitive pressures to court this demographic, they have not only embraced shows that represent it, but have elaborated a heterogeneous set of discourses that seek to map the trends and tastes of this group.

Interestingly, this kind of cultural forum that media can serve as a way to talk about millennials, has offered up *humor* itself as a way to distinguish this age cohort from others who have come before it. Media scholars such as Gaye Tuchman and Todd Gitlin have relied on the concept of "framing" to explain the role that media discourses can play in mapping meaning onto experiences and, in particular, media frames as a way of organizing social reality. The mixed discourses now arising around the generational construct of "millennials"—by media marketers, media critics, as well as television series and films representing this age cohort—has coalesced, to some degree, around the idea that they have a specific sense of humor or comedic sensibility which distinguishes them from other generations. By focusing on a single issue as it cuts across these discourses—the attempt to specify the role that humor plays in the lives of millennials—the media have created a particular frame or mapping onto of a generational trend of this group. Moving forward in our own analysis, we can say that this kind of framing of the millennials as "comedy natives" is a central work of the media system, one that mirrors sociological efforts to understand the social and economic changes that young people are now negotiating.

How, then, are the representations of the millennials as having their own sense of humor being framed in contemporary media? What are the qualities they are attributing to millennials as specific to their comedic sensibility? Take a show like *The Office* (US Version), that only recently ended (2013) after a lengthy run which began in 2005. The show was one of the first of its kind to use the idea of a reality TV show for a fictional comedy. The premise was that there were interviewers shooting a documentary about the offices of Dunder-Mifflin, a paper supply company, and each of the fictional characters, including Michael, the boss, played by Steve Carrell, were interviewed in between the story-line scenes. Other shows were soon to adopt this mode; *30 Rock* (NBC, 2006–2013), *Parks and Recreation* (NBC, 2009–2013) and *Portlandia* (Independent Film Channel, 2011–present), among others, followed in this path of subverting conventional situation comedies with both faux-vérité and absurdist elements. These shows found that the demographic most interested in them was in the 18–34 year old range (Grant).

With the popularity of unconventional comedies like *The Office* appealing to this younger demographic, the description of millennials as seeking absurdist humor becomes one of their defining features. Elizabeth Charlotte Grant, for example, outlined some of these "laugh values," as she calls them, which millennials believe in, including authenticity: "Our generation of 20- and 30-somethings is no longer interested in Disney's happy-go-lucky characters. We need the truth of a Wes Anderson film in a 30-minute TV bite, and we find it in these dark comedies" (Grant). To be authentic in this time period, however, requires a kind of hipster absurdist outlook, as a way to define themselves in opposition to earlier groups who were either earnest, or silly, or ironic.

A second "laugh value" that millennials hold is that humor does not need to have a "larger agenda," but rather allows the viewer to just inhabit the absurdist world of the characters. Linked to this idea is the way in which millennials find humor in taking things to an absurdist conclusion, even if it is skewed towards something disturbing. Speculating on why a focus on the absurdity of life is appealing to millennials, Grant offers:

> Viewers under 35, in particular, have been touched by the absurdity of life-we have vivid memories of 9/11, not to mention the high rate of people under 35 who have therapists to deal with their own personal tragedies. Life can feel chaotic and nonsensical. To be able to laugh, then, in the face of life's absurdities relieves us and gives us hope for the future.

Vulgarity: The New Normal?

Another area where millennials are described as differing from other generations is that vulgarity is the new normal. While vulgar humor has existed for as long as comedy has, what is different in this historical juncture is the extent to which this kind of humor, created and disseminated through social media, has spread into the larger culture. In addition, whereas in earlier times comic magazines for young people, such as *Madman,* may have gently poked fun at certain cultural events, recent periodicals, like the satirical magazine *The Onion,* highlights the specific turn towards vulgarity that has arisen in trying to market material to the age cohort of 18- to 32-year-old males.

The Onion, for example, was recently accused of becoming more vulgar and brutal in its tone, with coarse humor that is meant to shock and entertain its target audience of 18- to 34-year-old, tech-savvy males. In an increasingly saturated market for comedy, with different platforms for drawing viewers to multiple sites for comedy, *The Onion* has responded by pushing the limits of its oftentimes self-mocking humor. In a recent 2013 piece, for example, it offered the following supposed viewer response to the story about three women who were kidnapped in Ohio, entitled "Men are the Best":

> And, look, we're not saying men don't have their flaws. Oh, sure, once in a while they'll get you pregnant and then lock you in a darkened room for 10 or so years while they viciously beat you until you lose the baby and almost die, but hey, we all have our own little quirks, right? [qtd. in Daniel D'Addario].

Other examples of the use of raunchy and vulgar humor directed toward a millennial audience can be seen in several other recent television shows, including *Workaholics* and *It's Always Sunny in Philadelphia* (FX, 2005–present). In these shows, both of which are about twenty-something slackers, conversations about erections, semen, booze, bathroom humor and drugs form the bulk of the dialogue. The episodes invariably include absurd situations, and the three characters in *Workaholics* are shown amiably and essentially not working in their job as telemarketers. In fact, the lack of ambition for more challenging work is implicitly linked to the notion that jobs for millennials are supposedly few and far between in a bad economy. Here, however, this "slacker" attitude is played for laughs, and much of the humor revolves around the ways in which the three friends contrive situations to maximize their opportunities to avoid work; hence the humorous play of the title of the series, *Workaholics*.

While it could be said, then, that market competition is driving the push towards increasing vulgarity to reach the 18- to 34-year old millennials on television, we may ask, whether this also is true for other media, including films? Examining recent comedies geared toward millennials, box office receipts do suggest that there is a shift towards films that are R-rated and far more graphic than earlier comedies, and this marketing shift has been very successful for the film companies. *Hollywood Reporter* reported that these R-rated comedies passed the $1 billion mark in the summer of 2011 alone (cited in Lindsey Kirchoff).

Defining Male versus Female Millennial Humor: "We Saw Your Boobs!"

In exploring these marketing constructions of vulgar and absurdist humor as a way to create and map onto millennials a particular sense of humor, it may be helpful to further explore whether this kind of humor is fundamentally different for millennial women than men? Further, if there are differences, why would creating "gendered" forms of comedy for millennial men versus women be beneficial from both an audience as well as marketing standpoint? This brings us back not only to the opening of this essay, and the question of why young women are leading the pack in creating media empires based on comedy, but also gets to the question of what kinds of humor are being created for millennial men as opposed to women?

One recent event that highlights this question was the 2013 Academy Awards or Oscars, hosted by the creator of *Family Guy* (Fox, 1999–present), Seth MacFarlane. During the show, MacFarlane did a song and dance number, "We Saw Your Boobs," in which he orchestrated a musical gag that included mentioning several famous actresses whose "boobs" were shown on screen in various films. He also included jokes about women's weight and domestic violence (Andrew O'Hehir). Whether MacFarlane was successful in his attempts at mocking the Hollywood Establishment's requirement that actresses take their shirts off in major films as a way to gain the status of being "serious" actresses may depend on who was watching the skit, that is, the subjects of the humor as well as the objects.

In this case, many have argued that MacFarlane, as a younger male, was chosen as the host precisely because he would bring in the younger, male demographic viewing audience who would gladly respond to this kind of humor (O'Hehir). In fact, the producers of the Oscars, Craig Zadan and Neil Meron, who chose MacFarlane, stated just this intent: "We looked at ratings and said, 'Men are not watching, and young men are not watching, and why does that have to be?'" (qtd. in Bryn Elise Sandberg). Zadan and Meron's choice did pay off in the end, in spite of or perhaps because of, the controversies surrounding their choice of MacFarlane. Millennial viewers between the ages of 18 and 34 increased in viewership from the previous Oscars, growing over 20 percent compared to the year before.

In this sense, there is still a considerable bias in favor of believing that raunchy humor is more "male," than female, and that young men should be the coveted group for whom humorous television programs and movies are created. So, one way we can answer this question of whether there are different forms of humor pitched to millennial men versus women is to say that, for the most part, young males have been the sought after group by marketers. Accordingly, it can't be determined whether this is because they are different in their comedic tastes from women, or whether they are simply the group whom marketers have been pursuing.

In either case, that is why it is all the more surprising that comedies for millennial women are beginning to be created and green-lighted in the entertainment industry, both in film as well as television. One example, in addition to the television shows created by Kaling, Deschanel and others, includes the recent film *Bridesmaids* (2011) which was written by and starred Kristen Wiig, a Gen X woman and cast member of *Saturday Night Live* (NBC, 1975–present). This film, which is considered a raunchy female counterpart to *The Hangover* (2009) and the string of Judd Apatow comedies that star mostly men, includes a cast of funny women who are portrayed in humorous situations that include a lot of scatological humor. The film earned more than $280 million worldwide, and the audience was one-third male (Rebecca Traister).

Interestingly enough, in terms of the media surrounding *Bridesmaids*, which included an online campaign by a female producer to encourage women to see the film on its opening weekend, was the sense that supporting the film would be an important way to send a message to Hollywood that they should make more films directed to women. Universal Pictures, which produced *Bridesmaids*, was initially uncertain about the film's box office prospects, despite the fact that it received positive film reviews, and achieved a 91 percent "fresh" rating on Rotten Tomatoes. The film, which is "about a group of comical women who are helping their friend prepare for her wedding," did eventually appeal to a primarily female audience. In fact, the audience was 67 percent female. Because it was an R-rated female-oriented comedy, however, of which there are few at the box office, it was initially felt that it would not generate strong ticket sales and would likely gross approximately $15 million in its first weekend. The film was made together with Universal Pictures and Relativity Media for $32.5 million, which is relatively modest by Hollywood standards, and ultimately attracted a sizable opening weekend audience that produced box office receipts of over $24.4 million (Amy Kaufman).

Mike Haverty, writing in 2011 about whether the film was marketed toward younger women or not, makes the point that it subverts itself just as it appears that it is going to offer a conventional view of the sexes. For example, when Annie (Kristen Wiig), the main character, starts to date a nice cop, it looks like he will allow her to hold his gun. Yet, instead the camera shows her holding a speed detector, which inverts the image of a macho police officer "packing" a pistol, to the goofy image of Annie holding a speed detector and aiming it at cars passing by. In another scene, when it appears as if the director is going to replicate a scene from *The Hangover* by having the main characters go on a drunken bender to Las Vegas and wreak havoc there, the characters instead end up being escorted off the plane because Annie incited a commotion by being drunk and disorderly after taking pills and drinking to quell her fear of flying.

More generally, *Bridesmaids* offers a comedic sensibility that both embraces and moves beyond stereotypical female humor, portraying women as competitive, obsessed with weddings, while at the same time revealing how painful it is when friends find that they are being replaced. The one character in the film who moves beyond the stereotypes is played by Melissa McCarthy. She is more masculine in her behavior compared to the other women; she is comfortably overweight and doesn't complain about her sex life or her husband. She takes "ownership" of her sexuality by repeatedly flirting with a man who turns out to be a federal agent on the plane, and she is the only consistently happy character in the film.

As Haverty noted, the character of Megan, whose weight is used as a comedic note throughout the film, is in many ways the most interesting character in the film, as she offers both a bizarre counterpoint to all the conventional females and yet is the happiest of them all. Far from simply being a joke because of her weight, she instead offers a vision of being both "out there," and yet far happier than the other women who are more conventional. Reflecting on the ways in which *Bridesmaids* must navigate its own sense of humor within a male-dominated comedy landscape, Haverty concludes that:

> *Bridesmaids*, like any film marginalized by focusing on anyone but white straight males, defines itself in relation to what the dominate culture finds comfortable. As a comedy, it achieves its goal beautifully through parody, using a language recognizable in popular movies to show how it sets itself apart. The parodic separations from masculine comedy in *Bridesmaids* show why the gender-defined genres must be different. To simply recreate a masculine movie as a "chick flick" discredits any positive influence of the female voice. By dissecting differences, it frames women's issues in something easily digestible to the average comedy fan, regardless of gender.

Though *Bridesmaids* moves beyond a simple re-appropriation of male humor, some of the humor is directed specifically towards males, in particular the "bridal-shop barf-fest" (Dana Stevens) as a way to draw in male viewers. Although some of the raunchy humor was directed toward men, the larger point is that the film itself offers both women and men a way to appreciate women in comedic situations, as it highlights the many funny women who audiences would love to see.

Changing Scripts for Millennial Women: Reinventing Rom Coms?

In considering why a film like *Bridesmaids* is appealing to millennial women, another factor comes into play, and that has to do with the fact that it is unlike more conventional chick flicks or romantic comedies, which are light-hearted comedies with romantic plotlines. Some writers lament the decline in quality of romantic comedies over the past three decades. In 2013, Reuben Fisher-Baum, of the female online magazine *Jezebel,* did an infographic that charted the decline in ticket sales of romantic comedies over the past thirty years. As he was able to illustrate by statistics from Box Office Mojo, the romantic comedy genre, typically thought to be the most popular comedy film genre for women, has plummeted, even as there have been a large number of releases of these films. Though these films have not done well at the box office, other genres of films, such as male-oriented Superhero movies, continue to rise. Similarly, Meredith Lepore, writing for *The Jane Dough,* notes that from 2004 to 2006, while more rom coms were released than at any point before in films, the total receipts fell by 40 percent. Lepore continues by observing that the way that women are portrayed is not realistic to audiences, and their romantic woes appear contrived, at best. As she notes:

> The women are always earth-shatteringly beautiful and yet we are supposed to believe they are single because they are clumsy, and everyone always plays a friggin' magazine editor[....] As Mindy Kaling wrote in her book, *Is Everyone Hanging Out Without Me?*, "I simply regard romantic comedies as a subgenre of sci-fi in which the world created therein has different rules than my regular human world. Then I just lap it up."

Other film critics, like Tracy Moore, believe that rom coms are almost passé, because couples no longer face the same sort of social taboos on the path to true love. Whether it is parents, or some social barrier and especially pre-marital sex, the usual issues that the lovers had to overcome are no longer as relevant. In other words, if millennials can now routinely engage in "hookups" without being in a relationship or marriage first, then one of the prevailing plot bases for rom coms no longer make sense.

Addressing this new social milieu, Alyssa Rosenberg believes that the turn inward for rom com characters could be one way for the genre to respond to millennials' changed landscape of love and relationships: "If romantic comedies have gotten harder to do well, maybe it's actually not because so many barriers to finding love have fallen, but rather because modern love's gotten more difficult, and more difficult to capture" (Rosenberg).

So, how does a film like *Bridesmaids* specifically offer millennial women a way to turn inward, to fix "herself," rather than fix something external to her? Moore writes about some of the strategies that films like *Bridesmaids* offer younger women that speak more relevantly to their experiences in this era. One is to portray the female protagonist as "love-resistant," in other words, to not totally abandon their careers whether they were going well or not, when the man comes along. In these films, the man is held somewhat at bay while the woman tries to "work out her own shit" (Moore).

Another strategy is to move away from the man-child male lead and the overly serious and boring female character who tries to get the male to grow up. *Knocked Up* (2007) was a classic of this genre. For millennials, however, there are several situations in which the male millennial is more "together" than the female, and this kind of role reversal moves away from the stereotype of the woman always having to somehow "fix" or "tame" the man. Part of this idea of gender-bending, which is very comfortable for millennials—since they were raised to see men as needing to be as responsible around the house—could also be shown by having the male character as more sensitive than the traditional male rom com character. Moore concludes by advising that we explore how sex itself, once taboo in rom coms, could instead be depicted as easy to initiate for millennials, but "problematic" to keep. In other words, while sex is not something that seems to be an insurmountable burden to attain, there are all kinds of ways where it doesn't meet one's expectations and where the casual nature of it is precisely what makes it such an unsatisfying thing, whether or not the woman wants a relationship attached to it.

Part of this dilemma is that young women may be friends with a man or "friends with benefits," but this can lead to multiple complications when either one or both get a significant other. All of these situations, which, arguably, are dilemmas that millennials confront and which didn't arise in earlier generations, could be comic fodder, and the more successful comedies for young women employ these dilemmas as their starting points.

Younger Women, "Shit Girls Say"

The discussion of the popular reception of *Bridesmaids* by millennial women raises the question more broadly of whether millennials have a different sense of humor from other generations and, second, whether millennial women have a different comic sensibility than millennial men. To some extent, there is some validity to the idea that there is a more coarse and vulgar sense of what's funny and what's acceptable to be part of the mainstream culture. This vulgarity is driven, at least in part, by the sense in Hollywood and by advertisers that the best way to appeal to the coveted 18- to 34-year-old audience is to feed them a steady diet of films like *The Hangover* comedies (2009, 2011, 2013). These films, directed towards young men, have led to an understanding in the larger culture that the younger generation has both a cruder and more absurdist sense of what's funny than earlier generations. The fact that *The Hangover Part III* (2013) did poorly at the box office may portend the fading popularity of this genre, or it could simply mean the franchise had exhausted itself. Still, it may be instructive to think about whether it is signaling some movement away from this type of humor.

In terms of whether this kind of humor similarly appeals to millennial women, less is known, but the newer spate of comedies in both film and television directed towards younger women indicate that Hollywood believes that what is appealing to young men might also be similarly appealing to younger women. Interestingly, female audiences in general have had a hard time getting recognition as consumers until recently, and Hollywood has been notorious for not creating vehicles that are directed toward female audiences. That is why there has been, for quite some time, so much interest in and pressure to perform coming from women directors and stars, as a way to prove Hollywood executives wrong. Unfortunately, as of this writing in 2013, it is still an uphill battle to have women, whether younger or older, represented with any parity in terms of participating in Hollywood's creative output (Melissa Silverstein).

While the statistics on female comedy writers in the industry remain dismal, the popularity of TV shows such as *The Mindy Project* do offer some hope. In addition, new female millennials continue to emerge on the horizon, promising additional opportunities to see how these young women will take on the established turf of male comics.

One recent example of this strategy to cross over into male turf is the new Comedy Central show which stars Amy Schumer and called, *Inside Amy Schumer* (2013). This comedy show is an attempt to, in a sense, outdo younger men with raunchy humor, offering what one critic described as a "female-centric take on bro-comedy, dedicated to exploring the ways girls can be crazy" (Willa Paskin). Another example is Rebel Wilson, who is also in *Bridesmaids*, playing the British roommate of Annie. Wilson, a twenty-something Australian female comic, recently won the "Best Musical Moment" award for her role as Fat Amy in the movie *Pitch Perfect* (2012). In addition, she was the first female host since 2007 for the MTV Movie Awards, and has also now starred in several movies and currently has a television show being built around her.

These current examples suggest that millennial women's humor has a place in the cultural line-up, even though the overall state of women in Hollywood remains limited. Some young women have been able to get through that glass ceiling by offering up humor that is both self-referential and which acknowledges their own foibles while at the same time offering a sense of being "in" on the joke.

For this Facebook generation, who are exposed at virtually all times in their waking life and creating their own real-time reality shows about their lives, the ability to poke fun at themselves, while being in on the joke, can be a wonderful way to triumph over any potentially embarrassing situation. At the very least, the young women in this generation may ultimately be in a better position than young men, if they can truly not only be in on the jokes, but actively making them, thereby having the last laugh.

The Romantico-Sexual Narrative and Intertextuality in *Friends with Benefits* and *No Strings Attached*

Betty Kaklamanidou

Introduction

This essay will study a new cycle in the romantic comedy genre that emerged in the 2000s and addresses sex and love in the context of millennial hookups, that is, casual sexual encounters that do not necessarily lead to serious commitment. I will be examining the narrative consequences of the representation of sexual encounters in a genre that usually promotes committed relationships and I will also be assessing how these cinematic stories become mythic texts that can inform and educate us through explicit and/or implicit intertextual commentary.

One would expect that since the Hollywood industry is notorious for its obsession with youth not only in terms of the age of its films' heroes and heroines but also the age of its target audience, fictional millennial characters would certainly abound in the romantic comedy genre. However, as I was going through the corpus of around 200 mainstream Hollywood romantic comedies released between 2000 and 2010,[1] I was surprised to discover that only rarely did these comic love stories feature millennials—that is, primarily protagonists in their twenties; the top-twenty of the most commercially successful rom coms featured heroes and heroines in their thirties (*Hitch*, 2005, *The Break-Up*, 2006, *The Ugly Truth*, 2009), their forties (*What Women Want*, 2000, *My Big Fat Greek Wedding*, 2002, *The Proposal*, 2009, *Knight and Day*, 2010, *The Proposal*, 2009), and even in their fifties and sixties (*Something's Gotta*

Give, 2003, *It's Complicated*, 2010). Only *Knocked-Up* (2007), starring Katherine Heigl and Seth Rogen, managed to represent the millennial generation—even if both protagonists were in their late twenties in both the fictional world and real life—and address cinematically some of their peers' generational dilemmas and anxieties.[2]

The second decade of the millennium did not seem to change this trend with the exception of 2011, when *No Strings Attached* and *Friends with Benefits* made their way into theatres worldwide only seven months apart; released in January and July of the same year respectively. These two films not only star millennial characters, and/or focus on millennial angst, but were preceded and/or accompanied by titles such as *Forgetting Sarah Marshall* (2008), *Zack and Miri Make a Porno* (2008), *Love and Other Drugs* (2010), *Hall Pass* (2011), *Bridesmaids* (2011), and *What's Your Number?* (2011). Taken together, these films established a new tendency; that of the raunchy romantic comedy. *Friends with Benefits* and *No Strings Attached*, in particular, place sex in the middle of the narrative in a genre that, despite celebrating romantic relationships, omits the representation of on-screen carnal relations, only hinting at them in the same way ancient Greek tragedies never represented murders or vile acts on the stage. Although sex was present in the past romantic comedies of the 1970s, Tamar Jeffers-MacDonald observes how a number of contemporary romantic comedies—which she names neo-traditional—"greatly de-emphasize[s] sexuality," which "provides a real problem," since many films "have to work hard to find ways to explain why sex is not happening for [their] main couple" (97).

Another characteristic of the two films is their intertextuality, that is, their continuous reference to popular culture film and television artifacts which, according to Jeffers-McDonald, were also present in the 1970s rom coms (67–68).[3] However, the intertextual references that appear in *Friends with Benefits* and *No Strings Attached* are somewhat different from a repetition of a classical film line—as in *What's Up Doc?* (1972)—or the heroine's obsession with a specific romantic drama—as in *Sleepless in Seattle* (1993).

The tendency for intertextuality, which is obvious in *Friends with Benefits* and subtler in *No Strings Attached*, cannot be exhausted as "ironic, detached self-awareness," a postmodern playful game for both characters and viewers, although this function is accomplished as well; I would argue that the films' intertextual moments are part of a collective memory system of popular characters and texts which, despite their relative young age, have become modern-day myths in the definition of Roland Barthes, who defined myth as "a system of communication" (202); a narrative which is repeated continuously until it is no longer of use for the society that created it. That is, providing that whatever issue, problem, conflict it "magically" deciphered has found its solution in real life. Thus, it can be argued that romantic comedies are still in existence because men and women are still struggling to find and maintain a committed and loving romantic-sexual relationship with the "one."

Hookups and the Romantico-Sexual Narrative

Just as the introduction of sex in the romantic comedies of the 1960s and 1970s (*The Graduate*, 1968, *The Goodbye Girl*, 1977, *10*, 1979, *Annie Hall*, 1979, among others) is linked to "the final abandonment of the Production Code and its replacement by a ratings system" (Jeffers-McDonald 61) and the general societal acceptance of freer sexual mores, the "raunchiness" of *Friends with Benefits* and *No Strings Attached* can be attributed to the characteristics of the generation that is represented.

One of the main traits of the millennial generation, aside from financial and job insecurity, technological dependence, political and ecological conscience, outlined in the Introduction to this volume, is that when it comes to matters of the heart, twenty-something men and women tend to favor hookups—that is casual sex encounters which are not expected to lead to anything more permanent—instead of a series of dates that can lead to a committed relationship. Numerous internet and print articles have been discussing this new phenomenon in an attempt to discern the consequences of this change in the North-American sexual landscape of young millennials, focusing mainly on college students where the practice is thought to prevail. Hookup is defined as a sexual interaction "between partners who are not dating or in a romantic relationship and do not expect commitment" (Robyn L. Fielder, M.S. Kate B. Carey, and Michael P. Carey, 1).

Consequently, hookups can have different meanings to different people and do not necessarily need to be equated with vaginal penetration, although most "practitioners" find that intercourse and hookup are synonymous concepts. Most journalists, such as Debby Herbenic, Katie J.M. Baker and Hanna Rosin, argue that this new phase in the romantico-sexual relationships represents another empowering tool for young women who can now experiment with different suitors without having to commit to a long-term relationship early on and/or carrying the stigma of promiscuity—at least less often than in the past. Kathleen A. Bogle (2008: 2) claims that the two main reasons for this new path that romantic/erotic relationships have taken in the new millennium is the postponement of marriage later in life and the fact that most "emerging adults" "are spending the early years of their adult life on college campuses" (2). Boggle rightly notes that even though most "hookup" studies and/or articles started to appear from 2000 onwards, the practice of just "hooking up" have been in existence since the 1980s. It should be noted, however, that although Boggle refers to the consolidation of this liberal sexual practice in the 1980s, the "hookup" is actually a product of the 1960s, and more specifically a direct result of the introduction of contraceptives, as most literature on the subject exhibits (see, for instance, Susan Thistle, and Thomas Borstelmann).

Bogle adds that sexual behavior is also socially dictated and uses Gagnon and Simon's "sexual scripts" theory to underline how men and women "internalize" those scripts "in order to interact with the opposite sex" (8). I would propose that it is not just the script—that is a series of lines of dialogue—but the whole narrative of sexual behavior for young adults that has incurred a significant restructuring in the 2000s. This "re-write" has witnessed various alterations in the way two individuals flirt, decide to have sexual relations, form a more committed relationship or resolve to also add casual sexual encounters, AKA "booty calls," or hookups to their sum of sexual and romantic life experience. Similarly, film narratives had to accommodate this new trend in the genre of the romantic comedy, the *par excellence* cinematic site of examination of romantico-sexual mores. The use of the two adjectives, sexual and romantic, will be used to describe what has been summarily called just "romantic" life in the romantic comedy bibliography, as I believe that the use of just one epithet—especially in the filmic texts of this essay—does not do justice to the carnal part of the relationship, which offers not only enjoyment but is a significant factor in the narrative plot and the fictional relationship as well. Therefore, I will be introducing the compound adjective "romantico-sexual" to designate those narratives and experiences that combine emotional as well as sexual expressions.

The 2000s operated as the moment that witnessed the coming-of-age of the millennials and the simultaneous consolidation and acceptance of the hookup. It is, therefore, easily explicable why millennial men and women showed more interest in hookups than traditional dates; they simply followed the prevailing narrative. Just like children today who cannot use an older phone dial set as they have never seen it, several young men and especially young women grew up feeling they could express their sexual desires without having to commit necessarily to a single person. How do *Friends with Benefits* and *No Strings Attached* represent their millennial characters and their romantico-sexual entanglements? Do they teach us anything new about how these twenty-something individuals view sex, relationships and marriage or do they simply "update" the genre's formula with younger protagonists, only superficially and frivolously addressing one of life's and art's, for that matter, greatest subject, love?

The Films

Both films share a similar plot which would put them in the same genre cycle; that is, a number of genre films that share many characteristics, usually released during the same time, with each one building on the commercial and/or artistic success of the other (Rick Altman). In *Friends with Benefits*, Los Angeles–based Dylan (Justin Timberlake), a twenty-something IT entrepreneur, accepts a lucrative job offer as the art director of *GQ* magazine in New York via head hunter Jamie (Mila Kunis) and moves to the Big Apple. As both protagonists are single, and Dylan is quite lonely in his new surroundings, they start to spend time together. While they face problems in the romantico-sexual department—Dylan does not express his emotions and Jamie is "emotionally damaged," according to an ex-boyfriend—they decide to add sex to their friendship on the condition that they do not become a couple. In *No Strings Attached*, intern doctor Emma (Natalie Portman) "reunites" with Adam (Ashton Kutcher), whom she met and became friends with as a teenager at a summer camp. The two also decide to begin having sex with "no strings attached," provided they do not fall in love with each other.

Both films' premise is important not only because it addresses the millennial generation's romantico-sexual dilemmas but also because it changes the genre's syntax; the infamous boy meets girl—boy loses girl—boy gets girl in the end is transformed into boy meets girl—boy and girl become sex buddies—boy and girl form a relationship. It is true that on a macro-narrative level, the change may be insignificant, as the object of love / romantic union is finally attained by the protagonistic couple, but the journey of the two individuals is transformed because of their initial decision to just maintain a casual, sexual relationship. Thus, the plot does not include awkward first dates (*Hitch*, 2005, *Going the Distance*, 2010), initial antipathy (*New in Town*, 2009, *Leap Year*, 2010), and/or any kind of masquerading (*How to Lose a Guy in 10 Days*, 2003, *Failure to Launch*, 2006).

A true and meaningful romantico-sexual relationship that can lead to marriage and a utopian "and-they-lived-happily-forever-after-the-credits," is not the object of the protagonists' narrative arcs. *Friends with Benefits* begins with Dylan and Jamie breaking up with their respective better-halves in a quite funny parallel montage sequence. During their break-ups, we learn that Dylan is a workaholic and Jamie is "emotionally damaged." Once their exes leave, Jamie decides "to stop buying into the Hollywood cliché of true love" and then she shouts at a poster of the Katherine Heigl rom com *The Ugly Truth*, accusing the actress of being a liar. At the same time Dylan decides to "just work and fuck. Like George Clooney," while a cut to Jamie shows her saying that she will "shut down emotionally. Like George Clooney." Both individuals' use of the name of George Clooney is a comic moment that leads to laughter, but is also indicative of how differently a popular icon can be perceived by different people.

No Strings Attached opts to "reunite" cool and "not affectionate" Emma with Adam, after showing them in two scenes, one at a camp 15 years ago and another five years ago. In the former, teenage Emma is trying to console Adam about his parents' imminent divorce. While Adam is crying, Emma hesitantly tries to pat him in the back and tells him: "Look, I'm not really an affectionate person. People are not meant to be together forever." In the second scene, Emma and Adam meet by accident at a fraternity party. Emma invites him to attend a "stupid thing" with her the next day, which turns out to be her father's funeral. Despite this surprising "date," Adam seems interested in seeing Emma again, to which she calmly retorts: "Adam you're wonderful. If you're lucky you'll never see me again." This brief à la *When Harry Met Sally...* montage, notwithstanding, Emma and Adam's "relationship" results, in their third encounter in the present time, in a mutual decision to "use each other for sex at all hours of the day," as Emma puts it, "until one of [them] starts feeling something."

Both couples seem to embrace "hookup culture," that is, a relatively new romantico-sexual practice. Hanna Rosin examines studies of this phenomenon conducted in the 2000s and shows that despite those mainly conservative voices that oppose this sexual practice—such as William J. Bennett's 2012 CNN article entitled "Hookup Culture Debases Women"—hookups represent part of the sexual practices of the majority of millennial collegians, but are not responsible for the disappearance of intimacy. In fact, according to Fielder, Carey, and Carey's study, "sex in the context of a relationship was more common than sex through hookups with a casual partner." Adam Hoffman further notes that "Fielder's findings are consistent with *The Herald* poll conducted in 2011, which found that 73.9 percent of students had 0 or 1 sexual partners that semester. A poll conducted last month found that 73.3 percent of students were currently involved in an exclusive relationship with one other person or no sexual relationship at all, with 56 percent seeking an exclusive relationship."

Despite all the data that focuses on the numbers of sexual encounters and/or sexual partners, hookup culture is changing how individuals relate to each other in a "romantic" context, challenging the traditional gender balance, empowering female and male sexual expression and can lead to a new level of honesty between individuals which could in turn foster a heightened level of intimacy. For instance, when Jamie and Dylan start to undress before having sex for the first time in *Friends with Benefits*, they unashamedly share their sexual likes and dislikes, something they would probably not do if intercourse were to take place in the context of a series of dates. Jamie reveals that her nipples are sensitive, she doesn't like dirty talk and she would have shaved her legs that morning had she known she was going to have sex. Dylan confesses he is a little ticklish, he sometimes sneezes after ejaculation and he keeps his socks on because of intimacy issues. Once they finish undressing—Jamie is wearing only a pair of panties while Adam gets completely undressed, although the viewer never sees any part of Jamie's breasts or the protagonist's genitalia—the sex scene ensues.

What is interesting in this scene is that both protagonists show that they are comfortable with their bodies and the concept of sex. They know what they like and how they like it and they are not embarrassed to even tell the other person what they are doing wrong. When oral sex is performed, Jamie advises Dylan on how he could help her climax and Dylan follows suit without feeling awkward. Although both protagonists feel a little uneasy the following day, they can't help but end up in bed again while a "sex" montage shows them enjoying each other's bodies in different sexual positions. Interestingly, the sequence includes the same kind of honest discussion between the two lovers, which is a rarity in the romantic comedy universe, as well as in most cinematic love stories—whether they are dramatic or comic—and I might add even in real life.[4] As health educator and author of books on sex and relationships Dr. Emily Nagoski argues, sex is not the easiest discussion topic "even for couples who plan to share everything with each other" (Ian Kerner). Dr. Nagoski rightly observes that while the majority of people "have had some sex education somewhere in the past," "nobody ever taught us how to have a constructive conversation with a partner about the sex we're having" (Kerner).

No Strings Attached is as frank as *Friends with Benefits* in the representation of the sexual chemistry and encounters of Adam and Emma. Although Adam is obviously attracted to Emma, it is she who asks him to have sex for the first time, after complimenting him on his "really nice penis." They are both in her apartment and as soon as one of Emma's roommates knocks on the door to let her know they should be leaving for work, she turns to Adam and tells him that he has 45 seconds to finish intercourse. They both close each other's mouths so as not to be heard and a sex montage, similar to that in *Friends with Benefits*, ensues after the two protagonists share a brief scene where Emma sets the rules of their future sexual arrangement.

Both films re-introduce the representation of sex in a genre that is supposed to celebrate both the romantic and the sexual union of two individuals. Although most sex scenes in both films are sensual, and beautifully photographed, they initially present sex as another natural need and do not equate intercourse with true love or a committed relationship.

I would argue that the cinematic representation of sex does not only re-introduce sexual expression into the genre but also destabilizes perceived gender attitudes. As was previously noted, rarely are couples in most mainstream romantic comedies seen sharing anything more than a kiss, whether they are married (*Date Night*, 2010, *Couples Retreat*, 2009, *Fool's Gold*, 2008) or not (*The Proposal*, 2009, *Baby Mama*, 2008, *Serendipity*, 2001). What is more, the female characters in both *Friends with Benefits* and *No Strings Attached* are as interested in intercourse as the male characters; thus showing that no-strings sex has stopped being a male prerogative. In *Friends with Benefits*, it is Jamie who confesses that she misses sex and begins the discussion that leads up to her and Dylan becoming lovers as well as friends; in *No Strings Attached*, it is Emma who dictates the rules of her hookups with Adam, who would want to also see her in the daytime.

The fictional female reaction towards hookups in the two films—in other words, their unabashed promotion and acceptance of a freer sexual interaction with men for the initial purpose of satisfying their carnal needs, without having to emotionally invest in a more committed relationship—comes closer to the opinions that actual millennial young women share about contemporary romantico-sexual practices. For instance, Rosin interviewed a number of Yale students, who were in favor of this trend in the college's sexual landscape; in particular, a female student told the journalist that her hookup period during her freshman year was "empowering." Other female collegians, who participated in a study conducted at Indiana University, explained their preference for hookups and simultaneous avoidance of relationships with phrases such as "I just don't see myself being someone who marries young and lives off of some boy's money"; "I want to get secure in a city and in a job ... I'm not in any hurry at all" (Rosin). Although Rosin notes that these studies also reveal that some young women with numerous sexual partners are stigmatized as "sluts," as well as others who do not care for the ephemeral pleasure of this sexual interaction, the overwhelming majority of them would not wish for the disappearance of this choice. Rosin notes that "[t]he most [...] thorough research about the hookup culture shows that over the long run, women benefit greatly from living in a world where they can have sexual adventure without commitment or all that much shame, and where they can enter into temporary relationships that don't get in the way of future success."

Although both *Friends with Benefits* and *No Strings Attached* begin by examining and also accepting a strictly sexual relationship between two young, yet consenting adults, they end up by having their protagonists commit to a loving relationship. One could argue that the more "traditional" ending in a way negates what happened before and the audience is left with the impression that sex should be reserved for a loving, monogamous relationship and/or that hookups can only lead to misunderstandings and even heartache. On the other hand, it could also be argued that both films' young heroines succeed in both sustaining a no-strings sexual relationship without being stigmatized and in moving forward to the "level" of an intimate and probably monogamous relationship with the same two men once they understand they share much more with their respective partners than sex.

Intertextuality

At the same time that *Friends with Benefits* and *No Strings Attached* discover a new territory in the romantic comedy narrative schema, they also refer to a number of intertextual[5] references that deserve attention, as they reveal how older and different texts inform, alter, and lead the fictional—and even sometimes the real?—romantic narrative. Contemporary romantico-sexual narratives cannot but be informed by other popular culture narratives which bombard everyone on a daily basis: from love songs to celebrity news about the hottest new couple; the secret "new" couple; wedding preparations, and of course, the Hollywood romantic comedies themselves. As television critic Maureen Ryan notes, "This is one of the main purposes of great storytelling: Very specific characters and artfully constructed stories help us experience the struggles of others and realize that their concerns, mistakes and insecurities are not all that different from ours." Therefore, the emergence and wide practice of the hookup in the dating world is informed by a variety of news and fictional stories of every type and form, as well as by the lessons passed down by the second and third feminist waves and more particularly, those that have to do with the self-management of the body, freedom of sexual choice and the abandonment of traditional and oppressive gender roles.

Friends with Benefits openly refers to and converses with a number of previous television and film texts, from *Will and Grace* (NBC, 1998–2006) and *Seinfeld* (NBC, 1990–1998) to *The Ugly Truth* (1990), and Nora Ephron's rom coms, proving that "every text is a montage of cited texts, mentioned texts and evoked texts which are arranged in a sort of textual "depth" (Jean Fontanille 129). The "real" world that Jamie and Dylan inhabit is almost always in constant communication with the fictional utopia that Hollywood promotes as far as romantic entanglements are concerned. To begin with, when Jamie begins her narrative journey, breaking up with her boyfriend, she confesses that she needs to stop buying into the Hollywood cliché of true love, and she then accuses the actor Katherine Heigl of being a liar, shouting at a poster of the star's popular 2009 rom com, *The Ugly Truth*. Similarly, when Dylan asks Jamie why women believe that they need to manipulate men, she answers: history, personal experience, and romantic comedies.

Finally, the discussion which leads to the protagonists' having sex without getting involved takes place right after they finish watching a romantic comedy on television. Although both Dylan and Jamie seem to be very comfortable about the genre conventions, they still enjoy the narrative culmination of the couple getting back together, despite acknowledging and voicing the artificiality and utopianism that surround the traditional rom com endings. The number of mainly television and cinematic intertextual references that are interwoven in the narrative fabric of *Friends with Benefits* or accompany the most significant moments of the plot (from the beginning of Jamie and Dylan's hookup adventure to their deciding to become a couple at the end), demonstrate how popular culture narratives permeate new cultural texts as well. It also confirms the overwhelming importance of moving images (TV, film, social media) to millennials, who have grown up consuming an innumerable array of information through images on a daily basis. In addition, the insistence by the characters about the power of the romantic comedy to define their real relationships validates Ryan's argument about how great narrative characters and stories manage to infiltrate reality in different ways. Of course, these references constitute a fictional confirmation of the influence of older texts, since Jamie is a character in a film, which is referencing another fictional "reality," as she explains how women are taught relationship guidelines from romantic comedies. In other words, a romantic comedy (the story of Jamie and Dylan) is constructed within the context of the romantic comedy (the Hollywood genre), aided by the conventions of a third romantic comedy (watched by and commented upon by Jamie and Dylan and starring television comedy stars Jason Segel and Rashida Jones in cameos).

On the other hand, intertextuality in *No Strings Attached* appears in more subtle ways, although there are references to well-known narratives of the past, such as the television show *Beverly Hills, 90210* (Fox, 1990–2000). First, Adam's dad is a famous television actor/icon while Adam is working for a show which resembles the acclaimed Fox musical dramedy *Glee* (Fox, 2009–present), aiming to become a writer. This narrative proximity to Hollywood is used to emphasize that reality is different from fiction—Adam's dad, still adored by the public as an iconic television dad, is in reality a selfish individual who pays more attention to his latest conquest than his own son and decides to change his ways only when his life is in danger—corroborating the assumption that glamour, celebrity and wealth do not necessarily account for a happy family life. More importantly, however, it is the narrative structure of *No Strings Attached* that reveals the film's communication with previous texts. Emma and Adam meet at three different times in their life, some years apart, the same times Harry met Sally in the classic *When Harry Met Sally...* (1989). The difference is that while Harry and Sally decide to become friends during their third chance encounter because they have just broken up with their partners, Emma and Adam choose to hookup in order to avoid the heartache and psychological dependencies a relationship with an expiration date can bring.

Whether explicit or implicit, intertextuality enriches both cinematic narratives discussed above. Not only do the "hidden" texts beneath *Friends with Benefits* and *No Strings Attached* offer another level of enjoyment to the knowledgeable viewer, they also provide new knowledge to the younger viewer who may miss some of the references. In this way, older texts become re-visited or known for the first time, transferring and disseminating valuable cultural information through various narrative levels; thus simultaneously demonstrating that the genre itself is much more than a collection of simplistic comic love stories. These instances of commentary on the repeated formulae of contemporary relationships are also revealing in demonstrating the persistence of human desire, and of the millennials' desire, in particular, for "true love." The majority of intertextual references found in the two films examined in this essay allude to the power of narrative—in our case the narrative of the romantic comedy genre and the myth of true love—in everyday life; in other words, both *Friends with Benefits* and *No Strings Attached* underline the pervasive influence of the fictional televisual and cinematic "true love" narratives *within* the fictional world of the romantic comedy narrative, thus amplifying the power of the myth. The films also prove how intertextuality, especially in the form of "quoting" popular culture texts, is part of the millennial generation's way of communicating and can constitute a humorous yet definite form of argumentation for or against a given issue.

Conclusion

As this conclusion is being written in the summer of 2013, a number of interesting observations can be reached. First, although *Friends with Benefits* and *No Strings Attached* earned around $350 million in admissions, which is considered successful based on their relatively low budgets, they did not manage to persuade the Hollywood industry to invest in similar narratives; that is romantic comedies including a more "racy" representation of sex and focus on millennial characters. The "raunchiness" of these two films seems to have "moved" to other female-centered comedies, such as *Bachelorette* (2012), and *Identity Thief*, and *Heat* (both 2013).[6]

One would think that the liberating and empowering millennial heroines of the two films, combined with the global viewers' acceptance—translated in the mentioned healthy profit—would certainly find Hollywood studios receptive to a number of films with similar female characters. Yet, this did not happen. Female-centered films, irrespective of genre, continue to get made—mostly by male teams—but their numbers are still very small. It would seem that independent, young women who enjoy on-screen sex outside a relationship but who also invest in a committed relationship when they decide to do so, are still characters *non grata* for the male Hollywood executives. Indeed, as research from the Geena Davis Institute on Gender in Media corroborates, based on "11,927 speaking characters" in family films, television and cable reveal (between 2006 and 2012), "females are still stereotyped and sexualized in popular entertainment," "still suffer from an employment imbalance" and "slam into a glass ceiling" (Stacy L. Smith et al.).

Regarding the representation of millennials, the situation is even worse in the romantic comedy genre and despite the abundance and popularity of both female and male millennial stars, such as Zac Efron, Shia LaBeouf, Anne Hathaway, Mila Kunis, etc. Nevertheless, the continuing desire for "the one" still exists and cinematic fictional narratives should adapt to contemporary social mores regarding relationships. Perhaps, it is not yet the time for a rom com reboot. Perhaps, a little more time is needed for these stories to better capture some of the real changes in the world. Perhaps not.

Notes

1. The corpus in question was compiled for my 2013 book-length study on the millennial Hollywood romantic comedy (2000–2010) which demonstrated that, despite a well-known narrative formula, rom coms cannot and should not be discarded *a priori* as unimportant, repetitive stories with no impact on and/or influence by the specific sociopolitical circumstances they were produced within. The mostly negative treatment the genre continues to receive is problematic insofar as most genre films, such as horror, sci-fi, action-adventure, are also structured on pre-existing narrative schemas, yet they are deemed worthy of more positive reviews in the press, as well as in-depth scholarly investigation. Of course, there are those rom coms "which promote neo-conservative messages regarding marriage, sexual relationships, and gender roles," but there are also those "which opt for a more liberal consideration of the above" and open up new avenues for the genre as well as the future of romance in the western world (Kaklamanidou 154).
2. I should note that *Knocked Up* is included in my millennial rom-com list mainly because of its male protagonist, Seth Rogen, who was born in 1982 and therefore belongs to the millennial demographic, and not Katherine Heigl, who was born a little earlier, in 1978. Based on the 1982–1994 birth criterion, I also excluded all the Kate Hudson films as she was born in 1979. In addition, as my 2000–2010 corpus includes exclusively mainstream studio productions, the independent millennial rom com *(500) Days of Summer* (2009) is also excluded.
3. Of course, intertextuality is not solely the prerogative of 1970s romantic comedies as it can be found in earlier decades as well. In the classic screwball comedy *His Girl Friday* (1941), for instance, when threatened by the mayor of New York City, the bossy newspaper editor Walter Burns (Cary Grant) responds with the phrase "Listen, the last man that said that to me was Archie Leach just a week before he cut his throat," referring to his real name—Archibald Leach. Similarly, in the same film, when Walter wants to "diminish" his ex-wife Hildy's (Rosalind Russell), future husband, Bruce, he describes him by saying: "He looks like that fellow in the movies—Ralph Bellamy." Not only is Bruce played by Ralph Bellamy, but the actor had already been associated with supporting roles; moreover, Bellamy was cast in the same role—that of the nice-yet-not-nice-enough "other" man once again opposite Cary Grant, in *The Awful Truth* (1937).
4. It should be noted that both *Friends with Benefits* and *No Strings Attached* received an R rating by the Motion Picture Association of America (MPAA) in 2011; that is a Restricted—Under 17 prohibition to enter the theatre—because of "violent content and brief sexuality," and "for sexual content, language and some drug material," respectively. At the same time, the films that dominated the 2011 box office, such as *Mission: Impossible—Ghost Protocol*, *Transformers: Dark of the Moon*, and included the deaths of tens and even hundreds of characters received a PG13 rating "for sequences of intense action" and "for intense prolonged sequences of sci-fi action violence, mayhem and destruction" respectively. Daniel P. Franklin writes that "[i]n a society where a man's making love to a woman is considered obscene but a man's killing a woman is not, there are some seriously misplaced priorities" (177).
5. As a theoretical term, intertextuality begins with Mikhail Bakhtine's concept of *dialogism*, which was developed in the 1920s in order to underline the ways in which "a living enunciation, that significantly appears in a historic moment and in a determined social milieu cannot but touch thousands of living dialogic fibers, intertwined by the socio-ideological conscience around the object of any enunciation and participate actively in the social dialogue" (100). Dialogism was later translated by Julia Kristeva as *intertextuality* and was defined as "the transposition of one or more system of signs into another, accompanied by a new articulation of the enunciative and denotative position" (Robert Stam, 204).
6. Although the aim of the essay is not to provide specific analyses on genre history, the

following data is interesting and should constitute the subject of another study. Despite the handsome profit—provided by boxofficemojo.com—the romantic comedy genre made in 2011 with 12 major productions (*Bad Teacher, Crazy, Stupid, Love, Friends with Benefits, Larry Crowne, Something Borrowed, Just Go with It, How Do You Know, New Year's Eve, I Don't Know How She Does It, No Strings Attached, Midnight in Paris, What's Your Number?*), which returned more than $1.2 billion worldwide, 2012 marked a steep decline; only five major and star-driven productions (*This Means War, The Five-Year Engagement, What to Expect When You're Expecting*, and *Wanderlust*) were released worldwide, making around $313 million worldwide.

Labor Narratives and *The Devil Wears Prada*

CHRISTOPH BÜETTNER

The intention of this essay is to interpret *The Devil Wears Prada* (2006) as a film about work, to show how it examines the requirements asked of the individual and of young millennials in modern working environments, and to show how it draws on different traditional Hollywood narratives about the workplace. *The Devil Wears Prada* is a very intriguing example, because at first sight, some might not even interpret it as a film about work. I will argue otherwise. The film constitutes one of the biggest recent box office successes of a work driven narrative, grossing nearly $330 million worldwide, making it a significant example for this essay[1] (Hilary Radner 151). Linking the film to current business and social theories about millennials at work, I claim that *The Devil Wears Prada* functions to scrutinize the labile border between work and life, between personality and labor-capacity. My argumentation will be based on a critical position towards neoliberalism and modern developments in the social sphere of work. I will examine three salient aspects of David Frankel's film which allude to this topic: the transformation of the self through work, the conflict of work-life balance and the self-determination narrative.

The Devil Wears Prada has been widely regarded as a fashion-satire (Anke Sterneborg 47), and has pejoratively been called a "chick flick" (Ashley Elaine York 4). However, it has also been described as a "women's version of *Wall Street* [1987]" (Liese Spencer 50), and thus a movie about our modern economy. Critics have pointed to the relatedness of the working environment in the film and daily-life experiences of the film's audience, and their endurance of abusive superiors (Martha P. Nochimson 50). The plot features the twenty-something college graduate Andrea Sachs, played by Anne Hathaway, herself a member of the millennial cohort, who takes on her first job as an assistant to Miranda Priestly (Meryl Streep), chief editor of the fictional *Runway* fashion magazine. At first, Andrea struggles with her new tasks and her new boss, but she soon manages to cope with the stress at work, while becoming alienated from her private life. She eventually quits her job and opts for a position at a political newspaper in New York.

Work on the Screen

While American television has recently created some very popular productions that treat the transition of millennials into the workforce (e.g. *New Girl* [Fox, 2011–present], *Two Broke Girls* [CBS, 2011–present], *Girls* [HBO, 2012–present]),[2] this topic has not been as prominently featured in American popular cinema. This might be due to the fact that millennials have only recently come of age to be in the workplace, and thus their entrance into the workforce is a relatively recent phenomenon. However, it may be related more generally to a dearth of images of labor in cinema. "[F]or the movies the subject of work was [since the early 20th century] rather like 'the dark side of the moon,'" as Peter Stead puts it (243). The reasons lie in institutional and economic constraints, and in a "larger than life" tradition, that has the tendency to undervalue work's "mundanities (routine, repetition)" (Yvonne Tasker 25) as well as "the constraints and asymmetrical power relations of labor" (Martin O'Shaughnessy 60). By contrast, television's multiplicity and economic organization are understood as enabling the creation of lower threshold opportunities to represent the topic of work on screen (Tasker 15).

Nevertheless, Julie Levinson argues for a "genre" of "corporate workplace film" in cinema, with its own iconic and structural characteristics (88). Although one could argue that reflections on this "corporate workplace film" (which can be similarly found with Emma Bell) fail to contextualize their subject within the entirety of Hollywood's movie production (that is only a marginal appearance), the common characteristics Levinson identifies are very revealing about a continuity in the narration about work in American popular cinema. In her view, common narratives about the corporate environment include a young job novice who "initially buys into the corporate *modus operandi* as the path to the top [emphasis in original]" (67), and advances in his (or her[3]) career but eventually comes across a moral dilemma and thus decides to leave the corporation (67–8). The plot of *The Devil Wears Prada* fits this very brief definition of Levinson, showing that it is primarily a film about work. Still, there are some differences. For example, in Levinson's account, the narrative is closed by the withdrawal from the world of work, but in *The Devil Wears Prada* one job is easily traded for another, a fact that I will expand upon later.

While the narrative frame of American workplace films can be understood with Levinson as somewhat continuous, several assertions about historical discontinuities can be found in descriptions about the economic frame of millennials at work. Such assertions include epochal changes in expectations and attitudes of millennials, as well as in the social organization of labor. This essay seeks not only to cinematically historicize *The Devil Wears Prada*, but also to interpret it alongside recent developments of and theories on the configuration of millennials at work in the (post-)modern economy. Therefore, I will give a brief outline of the different and conflicting narratives about millennials at work.

Millennials at Work

Plenty of popular articles, social studies and business guidebooks try to understand how the perceived difference in millennials' personalities can be integrated into existing business structures and how they will transform the economy of the future (see Götz Richter; Eric Greenberg and Karl Weber; Joanne G. Sujansky and Jan Ferri-Reed; and Martin Klaffke, among others). Empirical studies on the subject range from mainly descriptive numbers on employment (Paul Taylor and Scott Keeter) to business-guidelines that attempt to incorporate the millennial's attitudes into corporate policy (PricewaterhouseCoopers). While the notion of the "new Millennial generation" has become some kind of stereotype that seems to superimpose other approaches to social formation (Jennifer G. Deal, David G. Altman, and Steven G. Rogelberg 198; Chip Espinoza 24), definitions as to who belongs to that generation differ. Fittingly, theories and conceptions about millennials at work are heterogeneous and sometimes even contradictory (Deal, Altman, and Rogelberg 191).

Nevertheless, across the different types of publications on millennials at work, one narrative seems to be very popular: the self-determined millennial worker (see Kerstin Bund, Uwe Jean Heuser, and Anne Kunze). In this narrative, millennials are self-confident and skilled enough to emancipate themselves from the principal dominance of the economic system over their lives. PricewaterhouseCoopers goes as far as to predict that "the employee may call the shots in tomorrow's world" (4). The underlying mechanism, explaining their ability to do so, is described as a demographic shortage of skilled workers in the near future (Bund, Heuser, and Kunze; PricewaterhouseCoopers 4) and as an effect of changed values in the upbringing of millennials (Andrea Hershatter and Molly Epstein 219–20; Espinoza 24). One of the most noted characteristics of the "fiercely independent" millennials is their presumed high job mobility (Espinoza 24). If an employer does not fit their demands, they will leave and take on another job opportunity, resulting in a high turnover rate (Sujansky and Ferri-Reed 4; Bund, Heuser, and Kunze). Job mobility seems to become a value for itself, one that millennials are demanding[4] (PricewaterhouseCoopers 5).

Other requirements that millennials supposedly have of their workplace include the opportunity to continually upgrade, or learn new skills, as well as to have a more equal work-life balance than employees in earlier generations have had. "Millennials think 'skills,' not 'career,' because they do not trust companies to keep them employed" (Espinoza 28). Thus, they would expect training and qualification programs from their employers to strengthen their proficiencies, which may be less concrete; work-related skills but rather abstract, personal abilities. Evaluation of those skills should then be implemented into day-to-day work, as well as become the basis for promotions, instead of older criteria, such as longevity (Hershatter and Epstein 218–19; Martin Klaffke and Andreas Parment 13).

Millennials are perceived to embrace a work-life balance more than their preceding generations, wanting fun, jobs, and self-fulfillment all at the same time and having "the confidence and conviction to demand it from their employers" (Hershatter and Epstein 219). Increasingly flexible work schedules and new technological possibilities could aid in realizing this because they free "employees to work at a time and place convenient to them" (Hershatter and Epstein 219; also Sujansky and Ferri-Reed 7). That the boundary between work and private life is simultaneously softened is, in this perspective, a welcomed fact. PricewaterhouseCoopers even finds that most millennials are comfortable with employers having more influence over their personal lives (12).

What is, in this narrative of the self-determined employee, described as a demand, or positive expectation by millennials, is, however, understood in a different light by some theories of modernized economies, stemming from sociological research of industrial and labor organizations. Theories of post-industrialism and post-fordism emphasize a change in the economic framework, transforming the organization and content of work. These approaches reverse the causality in regard to the above mentioned aspects of millennial labor. Although they pose no homogenous theoretical framework either, some of those theories pose a notable contradiction to the self-determination narrative.

In this perspective, changed labor-relations can be retraced to a deep economic transformation. Catalyzed by information technology, employment rates and economic value shift towards an increasingly non-material economy (Christiane Reinecke et al. 5–7; Gertraude Mikl-Horke 205–6). As the uniformed, mass production loses importance in favor of a "flexible specialization"[5] (Bernadette Loacker 34), the organization of labor undergoes a "de-standardization"[6] (Ulrich Beck 220), as predicted by Beck in 1986. High turnover rates and flexible contracts supersede lifelong job relations (Beck 227). In this narrative though, this is no intrinsic demand of the millennial generation, but rather the flexibility is the result of an external development. Increases of part-time jobs, limited contracts, and labor leasing are understood as proof of these theories (Eva Senghaas-Knobloch 28–29).

At the micro level, for the individual millennial worker, the diagnosis of a tendency towards self-entrepreneurship is another popular narrative. This perspective emphasizes that the "institutional cushion between individual and market [is being dismantled]"[7] (Dieter Sauer 557), meaning that employees are asked to think in managerial terms, and to act according to their companies' interest. G. Günter Voß and Hans J. Pongratz state this internal economization of labor in their influential model of self-entrepreneurship as an element of rationalization. While enterprises used to buy raw labor they treated with control-mechanisms to obtain a desired result, modern employees take measures of self-regulation to do the same (138–41). Millennials must therefore become managers of their own capital resources in order to play a more active role on the job-market. This means not only the managing of one's resume, but of one's private field as well. Spare-time, for instance, has to be efficiently and strategically organized. Furthermore, private activities and contacts may be aligned to their economic usability: sports to indicate mental strength and teamwork-capacities, or friends to build a potential career network (Heiner Minssen 112; Kerstin Jürgens 496).

At the same time, the border between private and professional life that began to become established only since the onset of industrialization in the early 19th century, begins to blur again. The human factor has largely been regarded as a disturbance of the scaling of labor as an input factor in classical labor economics. Thus, labor-capacity and personality, as well as professional and private life, became more or less separated, resulting in a classical form of dependent employment (Jürgens 486–87). Recently, some sociologists stated a new "demand for subjectivity"[8] (Minssen 118), meaning that individual personalities become a resource for economic exploitation. Therefore, the evolved boundary becomes blurred again, when personal traits are no longer hindrances for the control of labor processes, but valuable economic assets. (Minssen 118–22) This historic ambivalence is still present in many current post-fordist models of labor organization (Frank Kleemann and G. Günter Voß 432–33).

As I briefly showed, conceptions about millennials at work differ greatly and can even be said to offer contradictory explanations of the same phenomena. Empirically accessible circumstances, such as high turnover rates or the blurring of work and life, are subject to different interpretations alongside specific narratives. Moreover, some of these assertions, especially the more positive ones from the business economics perspectives, mostly apply to educated middle-class and white-collar workers only. Traditionally, these were also the workplace milieus depicted in Hollywood cinema, where working class heroes predominately had their role in "success myth" narratives, ascending to middle-class (Stead 241). In *The Devil Wears Prada* the focus on middle-class white collar work is reproduced in the main character's social standing and education, as well as in the service-sector workplace that is *Runway*.

Self-Transformations

In *The Devil Wears Prada*, the world of fashion functions as an intensive exemplar for the treatment of the self-transformation through work. The film opens with an ordinary workday; different women get up in the morning, put on their clothes, and are seen on the way to work. This brief montage lays out the potential conflict of the whole movie in alternating shots of the main heroine, Andrea, getting ready for her first day, and other women who are investing a great deal of effort in their outer appearance. The difference between Andrea and the other women is marked by fashion styles, neighborhoods, flat interiors, and means of transportation: While Andrea takes her clothes out of an Ikea drawer, another woman takes hers out of a walk-in closet; while the view from Andrea's bedroom is a brick wall, another bedroom shown is large, open and brightly lit; while Andrea takes the subway, all the other women take taxis; etc. Interestingly, these factors signify disparities in socio-economic status rather than merely different styles of fashion, which strengthens my argument that *The Devil Wears Prada* is less a movie about fashion than about economic mobility.

Andrea is introduced as an idealistic, intelligent (she has a prestigious bachelors degree from Northwestern University) young woman, interested in social issues (she did a college article series on the janitors' union). Her counterpart and superior, Miranda, is, by contrast, experienced, arrogant, and, at times, scheming and plotting. While Andrea initially states: "I don't see the point in changing everything about myself, just because I have this job," in order to become successful at her work, she has to perform a convergence towards becoming like Miranda. Both are often and even early on paralleled: visually, e.g. in similar shots of their entrance to the office via elevator, or their clothing style which becomes increasingly similar (in their last dialogue scene they are nearly wearing the same); as well as narratively, e.g. in their personal struggles that comes with professional success. It is in the moment of their greatest convergence—when Miranda tells Andrea: "I see a great deal of myself in you"—that Andrea makes her final decision to return to her former self and quits.

The difference implied in Andrea's transformation is most visually obvious in her styles of clothing, hair, and make-up. After Andrea is rebuked by Miranda about her "cerulean" sweater, and is told that it signifies that she "take[s] herself too seriously to care," in the next scene, she is shown putting on her Northwestern-University hooded sweatshirt, which functions both as a cozy armor against the outer world and as a return to her educational values. Another rebuke later, Andrea undergoes, through the help of Nigel (Stanley Tucci) in "Miranda's holy of holies" (Nochimson 49), an outer transformation to high fashion. Until she undergoes this transformation, she is not able to be viewed as doing anything right at work or get credit for it. When Miranda eventually chooses Andrea to accompany her to Paris for the fashion collections, Andrea is the farthest in her professional progress—which is matched by a dramatic difference in the way she looks. She now wears excessive make-up, a trendy hairstyle, while her fashionable clothes underline her femininity and sexuality. Her transformation marks her success in a double way. It shows her convergence towards the fashion world, and thus the climbing of the career ladder, but it also alludes to a more general code of success, since "[w]ork is the primary measure of self-worth, in the contemporary American mind, and the material goods [fancy dresses and accessories] that are signifiers of success are the just rewards for one's labor" (Levinson 65).

In her transformation to high-fashion, Andrea performs what Tasker identified in regard to *Working Girl* as "cross-class dressing" (21). The only difference is that Andrea does not "dress up" from working-class (as *Working Girl*'s protagonist), but from middle- to upper-class, wearing expensive designer-clothes and accessories. Cross-class dressing can reveal the function of external signs, constituting appearance and habitus, and their importance for social affiliation (Tasker 21–2). Andrea can thus only be accepted at the top of work and society after her transformation. However, while classical forms of cross-class dressing at work included a visual convergence of women towards masculinity (shorter haircuts, business jackets, shoulder-pads, etc.), in *The Devil Wears Prada*, Andrea's transformation strongly emphasizes her femininity.[9]

Andrea's transformation is not restricted to clothes and accessories. For a great deal of the narrative, Miranda repeatedly calls her "Emily"—the name of her first assistant (Emily Blunt). This "mistake" refers not only to Miranda's "ignorance," but to Andrea's exchangeability. As Andrea further rises at work, Miranda begins using the correct name, validating her performance and appearance at the same time. This conflict between exchangeability and (re-)personalization resembles the above mentioned theoretical ambivalence about the personality as a labor-resource.

Her transformation also includes several other "stages," such as fleecing her colleague, reducing her weight, and even changing her vocabulary—in terms of Mikhail Bakhtin modifying her speech genres (60). The importance of language for the world of work is examined by *The Devil Wears Prada* in a couple of comedic scenes. One instance can be found in the second dialogue between Andrea and Miranda. In this scene, Miranda, performs part of what Sarah Kozloff, in her examination of screwball-dialogue, calls "blathering" (183), namely "not letting one's conversational partner get a word in edgewise, using vague vocabulary and referents, and jumping from one topic to the next" (183). Miranda utters the following lines in less than fifteen seconds:

> Please bore someone else with your questions. And make sure we have Pier 59 at 8 a.m. tomorrow and remind Jocelyn I need to see a few of those satchels that Marc is doing in the Pony. And then tell Simone I'll take Jackie if Maggie isn't available. Did DeMarchelier confirm?

Streep manages not to drop any words or syllables, but speaks so rapidly, that neither Andrea nor the viewer is initially able to comprehend what she is talking about. Inconsiderately using expressions and names unfamiliar to those not engaged in fashion refers to both the importance of the existence of a common language system for communication at work and its extreme specificity. It also refers to relations of power connected to the use of language, as there is a considerable asymmetry between both women, which Miranda reinforces by her utterance.

These connections can be found in another example, the "runthrough"-scene: here, Miranda refuses all suggestions (about clothes for a photo shooting) made by her staff, demonstrating her authority, until she herself picks a tulle dress from a rack of clothes. Nigel immediately agrees with Miranda on the dress, thereby reversing his former opinion, while the film presents a reaction shot of Andrea—who has not undergone her transformation yet—showing a disagreeing facial expression. Then a staff member presents two, almost identical to the untrained eye, turquoise belts, stating: "It's a tough call, they're so different." The obvious absurdity of this statement here serves as a strong comic effect. Concurrently, Andrea reacts with a gentle laugh, causing a series of reactions (presented in corresponding shots), in which everybody in the room suddenly stares at her. This amplifies the comic effect, because it indicates a serious faux pas where Andrea seems to be stating the obvious. These two examples of the blathering by Miranda, combined with the silliness of the almost identical belts being considered to be radically different, highlights the ways in which Miranda establishes dominance through the language and aesthetics of the workplace.

    Later however, Andrea is shown easily administering the fashion vocabulary herself, even when meeting with her friends. In another scene, Andrea is talking to her friend on the phone, explaining that she actually dislikes her tasks at her job, when she suddenly comes across Nigel and a chic dress. The encounter then causes her to hang up on her friend and attend to the dress. This demonstrates that Andrea's transformation is not restricted exclusively to the sphere of work. Her interests seem to change, and she largely remains in her modes of speech and appearance even when within her private environment—despite assuring her friends that she still is "the same Andy."

    The equation of a far reaching personal makeover and career success, in combination with the final sense that Andrea rejects that identity, (in terms of "becoming Miranda") evoke a differentiated set of readings. Exploring the personal changes one has to undergo in order to become successful in one's career is not a new phenomenon in film. In her book on 1980s movies, Elizabeth Traube calls this figure "corporate shape-changing" (102). Taking recourse to Robert Jackall, Traube argues that "[w]hat matters is how closely one can transform oneself to meet the organizational ideal, and this requires relentless self-scrutiny and a capacity for self-rationalization" (103). Nonetheless, her model still asserts a separation of the real personality from the "public face" (Traube 103). This separation becomes blurred not only in *The Devil Wears Prada*, but its blurring becomes a central requirement of the modern, neoliberal worker (Minssen 118–22). Hence, the self-transformation, as depicted in the film, has a very topical meaning for millennials at work.[10]

    The question remains whether Andrea's quitting of her job could function as a rejection of the totalizing logic of neoliberal labor organization. Bell argues against this: "Even if the central character ultimately decides to leave the organization, such as in [...] *The Devil Wears Prada* (2006), it is only after they have proven their ability to become a successful organizational member" (113). With regard to the suggested trajectory of interpretation,[11] one could argue that Andrea has proven her ability to adapt to the requirements of the modern economy. I will emphasize this point later on, when I analyze the importance of self-determination in Frankel's film.

Work-Life-Balance

Over the course of her transformation, Andrea radically distances herself from her friends. This alienation constitutes a central conflict in *The Devil Wears Prada*, and alludes to another considerable aspect of the film: the balance of work and life. The film plot consists of an alternation of longer sequences showing Andrea's progress at work and shorter scenes of her in her private environment. Hence, boyfriend and friends function mainly to heighten the potential fall for Andrea. The relationship with her boyfriend Nate (Adrian Grenier) suffers increasingly as Andrea succeeds at work, to the point when they temporarily split up. Nate admonishes her that Miranda and her work, "that's the relationship you're in."

Private and professional environments are also staged differently, emphasizing this opposition. While the office of *Runway* is kept bright, with fairly cold lighting, Andrea's flat, and the restaurants where she meets her friends, are lit in a warmer light and color palette and the backgrounds are kept darker, resulting in a cozier atmosphere. That Andrea keeps meeting her private acquaintances in restaurants—the reconciliation meeting with Nate takes place at "Mayrose comfortable food"—and that her boyfriend is a cook, matches the semantic structure of the *Runway* world in which abdication of food is equated with work. Thus, when Andrea is given only a fifteen minute break during her workday, she is not only denied recreation time, but also time to eat properly. In the lunch-break scene, consequently, Miranda cancels the break altogether, and Nigel throws Andrea's lunch away. Nigel and Miranda, semantically linked to the world of work, thereby reduce the space for Andrea's personal (and bodily) needs to zero. The fact that work becomes more important than bodily needs is expressed also in other comic situations. Andrea's colleague, Emily, tells her to "man the desk at all times," even if she would "slice her hand open." What seems exaggerated at that point is perceived to be taken extremely seriously by Emily, who does not even dare to go to the toilet when she has to urinate.

Andrea not only has to work extra hours, at night or early in the morning, but her work also takes over her spare-time. A central motif employed in the film is the cellular telephone and its relation to overtime. Already in her first scene, Miranda's arrival is heralded by a text message, which throws the entire personnel into panic—a foreboding to what Andrea will have to endure. Over the course of the film, Miranda executes power over Andrea via the phone during working hours, but also when Andrea meets with friends or family. She even answers her phone while splitting up with her boyfriend. Thus, Miranda is equated with the electronic device that has become a technological cipher for modernized economies and serves as the prerequisite for the blending of private and professional life. Consequently, Andrea executes her decision to return to her private life by throwing her cell-phone, and thus symbolically, Miranda and the *Runway*-job, into a fountain.

As for the work-life balance, the film seems to avoid a positive stance. Andrea shows no sign of a "confidence and conviction to demand" a positive balance (Hershatter and Epstein 219). Flexible work schedules and new technological possibilities here force her "to work at a time and place convenient to" Miranda (Hershatter and Epstein 219). Of course the conflict between work and life is by itself neither an innovation of the millennial age, nor of the millennial age cinema. But in the modern economy, as in *The Devil Wears Prada*, it goes far beyond a dispute over the time one can devote to one or the other sphere. Work breaks into the most private moments (a breakup for example), it consumes one's own self (as shown above), and even starts to control bodily needs. Correspondingly, the negotiation between increasingly blurring fields of work- and spare-time resembles the negotiation between labor-capacity and personality, and, as I briefly showed above, constitutes a central question in the discussion of millennial labor.

Self-Determination

It seems, at first, that Andrea is rather subjected to Miranda's will and power. Numerous critics have used military-based metaphors to describe the work relations at *Runway* (see Katja Nicodemus; Verena Lueken; Fritz Göttler, among others), stating, Miranda "goes [...] to work, like a general to the battlefield"[12] (Nicodemus). I, however, argue that *The Devil Wears Prada* reiterates the narrative of self-determination.

In the first of the two job-interview scenes of the film, Andrea manages to get the job at *Runway* despite being "not skinny or glamorous" (Andrea). She does so by speaking up to Miranda, who first utters a dismissive opinion, and shows disinterest by skimming through a newspaper, and not paying attention to the potential employee. Andrea's direct approach towards her future superior is supplemented by her emphasis on the traditional values of a work-ethic: "I'm smart, I'll learn fast and I will work very hard." By that, she is able to raise the interest of Miranda despite her initial indifference. Cinematically, this moment is stressed by a slight camera-tracking movement towards Miranda's face as she looks up from her paper and steadily gazes at Andrea—who remains off-screen. Later, Andrea's work-ethic is explicitly called into question by Miranda and Nigel over the impossible task of organizing a flight during a hurricane: Miranda condescendingly remarks Andrea's "big speech about your so called work-ethic," and Nigel tells Andrea that she does not "really want" the job and that she "only deigns" to work at *Runway*. While at first upset and broken-hearted about her situation at work, Andrea quickly comes to the conclusion: "okay, so I'm screwing it up," and thinks of a way to comply with the requirements at work. She then actively begs Nigel for her outer transformation, thereby demonstrating her own initiative and her will to "learn fast" and "work very hard."

The Devil Wears Prada consistently works with recurring elements, which are slightly modified and eventually placed in a prominent role. One of those elements is the perpetual plea of Andrea: "I didn't have a choice." This is made plausible by the constant humiliations she has to endure. In a central scene, Miranda tells Andrea: "If you don't go [to Paris], I'll assume you're not serious about your future at *Runway*. Or any other publication. The decision's yours." In Andrea's logic, this utterance works as a threat, because it implies that Miranda has the power to hinder any career, even outside *Runway*. It is also a provocation of Andrea's work ethic ("you're not serious about your future"). Nonetheless, later on, the utterance shines in a more ambivalent light, because of the choices Andrea is able to make. Before she actively chooses to deviate from Miranda by throwing the ringing phone into the Parisian fountain, Andrea is again lectured by her superior:

> ANDREA: I couldn't do what you did to Nigel, Miranda. I couldn't do something like that.
> MIRANDA: Mmmh. You already did. To Emily.
> ANDREA: That's not what I... No that was, that was different. I didn't have a choice.
> MIRANDA: No, no. You chose. You chose to get ahead. [...]

This emphasis on the possibility of choice at the climax of the film is especially striking because the film, up until that point, led Andrea—and the viewer, as the film is closely focalized with the protagonist—to believe that the trip to Paris was absolutely necessary to keep her job.

Subsequently, Andrea is able to find another job with *The New York Mirror*, a reputable publication that is shown to be the opposite of *Runway*: the editorial office is untidy, and the building's façade is historical, in contrast to the glass and steel architecture of the *Runway* building. The transition there is presented as rather unproblematic. Thus, the choice Andrea is making narrows down to giving up her ideals for a highly glamorous job, or leading a normal, comfortable life, employed in a prestigious New York paper. Frictional difficulties or unemployment threats play no role in *The Devil Wears Prada*. In this perspective, perverted, life-consuming working environments are problems of the social upper-class (note that e.g. the "Fontain des Fleuves," where Andrea "sinks her job" is at the premier address in Paris) that Andrea could enter, but self-determinately chooses not to. The film therein reiterates a typical American success narrative in which the individual can socially progress through hard work and dedication, but in which the upper-class, "all those who amass wealth, without toil, and who consume it conspicuously" remain highly suspect (Traube 100–1). Andrea moves from her morally intact middle-class position towards the upper-class, but is then purified in the face of its moral corruptness. At the same time, the upper-class, and its representative Miranda, can function to dislocate "[t]he structural dynamics that may lead to inequality or immorality [...] onto the figure of the evil boss" (Levinson 68), which is a conventional Hollywood mechanism. Traditionally, the ills were not portrayed as lying in the capitalist system itself, but in corrupted individuals abusing it (Harry M. Benshoff, and Sean Griffin 172–4).

In this way, *The Devil Wears Prada* stands as a cinematic recurrence of an individualistic ideal, which is closely bound to the self-determination narrative in the reflection of millennial labor. This is not only implied in the claim of proactive choice the film so strongly emphasizes, but has its symbolic equivalent in the world of fashion. As the organization man became a prominent figure in popular sociological research and film in the 1950s, it superseded the individual entrepreneur, an adventurer on the free market, as the core figure of American economic success. Conformity rather than individual venture became the key to climbing the career ladder (Levinson 75–6). In *The Devil Wears Prada*, this configuration changes significantly. Of course, Andrea still has to conform to corporate values to progress, but the crucial factor for her success is her individual difference, namely being smarter and working harder than the other fashion girls. Where Emily could be characterized as a classical organization woman, who is just submissive to corporate values, Andrea partly retains her own will and personality—which reiterates my point about the ambivalence between oppressing and retaining one's personality as a labor resource. Moreover, the organization man had been a standardized mass product, analog to the products the companies produced or sold; their personality reduced to a mere number, which was reflected in their standardized uniform of the "grey flannel suit" (Bell 95–6). Andrea, however, has to adjust her clothing as well, but her "uniform" is different in the sense that the trendy outfits worn by *Runway* employees constitute a visual difference despite their basic conformity to the rules and demands of the fashion industry. The world of fashion, which is the world of work in *The Devil Wears Prada*, correspondingly can be read as the sphere of postulated ultimate individualism, despite fundamental equity. It can therefore stand as a complete metaphor for our modern neoliberal sphere of work (or capitalism).

Concluding Considerations

The Devil Wears Prada clearly sets out to explore the modern world of work, and the challenges it holds for millennials starting their work life. However, the slice of society it depicts is a restrictive one. Andrea is clearly established as a white middle-class girl who attended a well-known university and who is now facing special difficulties in what relates to modern urban white-collar working environments. Nonetheless, such a restricted interpretation can be short-sighted. Levinson finds that "corporate milieus as advertising, insurance, or finance are simply class signifiers: a sort of cultural code for the white-collar professional world" (69). Additionally, middle-class America on film has traditionally been a signifier for larger scales of society than would be adequate from a social science perspective, since many Americans associate themselves with that milieu, even if they fall short of, or exceed the corresponding economic level (Benshoff and Griffin 159). Within that context, American cinema, in its emphasis on middle-class narratives, is not only reinforcing this identification, but it can utilize the middle-class as an exemplar for larger social phenomena. Nevertheless, *The Devil Wears Prada*, especially in its depiction of the frictionless transition from one job to another, excludes aspects about the working class, the working poor, or even lower socio-economic levels, and reinforces an individualistic middle-class ideology of hard work, ignoring possible structural constraints existing in capitalism.

In this conformance with traditional images in American cinema, and in the emphasis on the possibility of self-determination, the film can be seen as highly affirmative of the ideal of the middle-class millennial worker, as described by the above mentioned positivistic narratives. Still, *The Devil Wears*

Prada does explore the dilemmas of completely blending life-spheres and blurring former boundaries in modernized economies. As I tried to show, these amalgamations are understood to be symptomatic for a (post-)modern, or neoliberal society, and thus possess a stronger referent in films about the millennial generation. In this regard, *The Devil Wears Prada* can be read as critical of the effects that neoliberal capitalism has had on our lives. What seems to be a contradiction in reading the film resembles the principal theoretical insecurities and contradictions about millennial labor that I briefly summarized above. It also can be attributed to what Tasker calls the "fundamental ambivalence of cultural products" (17), meaning the principal possibility of complex and contradictory meaning implied in the reading of culturally produced texts, such as films. Or, as Doyle Greene puts it: "Read symptomatically, seemingly affirmative films can open textual spaces to be read as subversive and ostensibly oppositional films open textual spaces to be read as affirming dominant ideology" (8).

Notes

1. More relatively successful examples include *Horrible Bosses* (2011) with approximately $210 million worldwide, and *The Pursuit of Happiness* (2006) with approximately $307 million worldwide (figures from BoxOfficeMojo.com). Other "work" films, such as *Entry Level* (2007), or *Outside Sales* (2006) could only garner some festival appearances and DVD releases.
2. Interestingly, all of these shows focus on female protagonists, as does *The Devil Wears Prada*. In a film and cultural studies perspective, this can raise a variety of questions concerning gender and the workplace, especially since older workplace narratives used to feature male protagonists almost exclusively (exceptions include *Norma Rae* [1979] and *Working Girl* [1988]). *The Devil Wears Prada* becomes furthermore a very fertile site for a gender related analysis, not only because of its fashion subject. However, due to restrictions in length and complexity, and to follow a clear line of interpretation, I will focus less on the gender aspects of the film and I will only briefly hint on the correlation between the increase in female work on screen with a post-fordist, or neoliberal, need for women's work.
3. In Levinson's description the gender of the novice is male.
4. Of course this description is a highly idealized vision of job mobility that presupposes the existence of open positions for young people. However, e.g., in Europe the average unemployment rate in the first quarter of 2013 was above 20 percent, in Greece and Spain even above 50 percent (Eurostat).
5. Original: "Flexible Spezialisierung." All translations from German belong to the author.
6. Original: "Entstandardisierung."
7. Original: "Die bisherigen institutionellen Puffer zwischen Individuum und Markt [werden abgebaut]."
8. Original: "Subjektivitätsbedarf."
9. There is an underlying sexualization of Andrea at work in the film, since she strengthens her erotic appeal to both her boyfriend and her later lover by her outer transformation. This

fits Tasker's argument, that "Hollywood representation is characterised by an insistent equation between working women, women's work and some form of sexual(ised) performance," meaning that economic success is somehow "bought" with sexual availability (3).

10. Nevertheless, this is no absolute novelty, since some concepts of the organization man included similar thoughts (Bell 95–6).

11. I focus less on the representation of the organization itself, which has been a major trajectory of the American scholarly tradition, but more on the preconditions of the individual millennial's role in the neoliberal or modern economy.

12. Original: "Geht [...] zur Arbeit wie ein General aufs Schlachtfeld."

Works Cited

Ablow, Keith. "We Are Raising a Generation of Deluded Narcissists." *Fox News*. 8 January 2013. Web. 16 July 2013.

Akande, Zainab. "'Me Me Me Generation: Top 5 'Time' Magazine Cover Parodies." Policymic.com. 14 May 2013. Web. 15 May 2013.

Alexander, Bryan. "*The Blair Witch Project*: Expulsion from Adulthood and Versions of the American Gothic." *Nothing That Is: Millennial Cinema and the* Blair Witch *Controversies*. Eds. Sarah L. Higley and Jeffrey Weinstock. Detroit: Wayne State University Press, 2004. 145–61.

Alsop, Ron. *The Trophy Kids Grow Up: How the Millennial Generation Is Shaking Up the Workplace*. San Francisco: Jossey Bass, 2008.

Alston, Joshua. "Bloody, Gross ... Empowering?" TheDailyBeast.com. 7 Jun. 2007. Web. 8 Mar. 2013.

Altman, Rick. *Film/Genre*. London: BFI, 2006.

Andreeva, Nellie. "CBS Nabs Michael Patrick King/Whitney Cummings Multi-Camera Comedy [Web log post]." Deadline.com. Deadline Hollywood. 10 Dec. 2010. Web. 20 Mar. 2013.

"Are Gen Y Women Poised to Take Over Comedy?" *Ypulse*. April 2013. 7 May 2013.

Associated Press. "Moviegoers Shrug Over Scream 4." *Pittsburgh Post-Gazette*, April 18, 2011.

Auerbach, Nina. *Our Vampires, Ourselves*. Chicago: University of Chicago Press, 1995.

Austin, Erica Weintraub, and Bruce E. Pinkleton. "Positive and Negative Effects of Political Disaffection on the Less Experienced Voter." *Journal of Broadcasting & Electronic Media* 39.2 (1995): 215.

Baker, Katie J.M. "Finally, Someone Says It: Hookup Culture Is Good for Women." 24 Aug. 2012. *Jezebel*. Web. 9 Mar. 2013.

Bakhtin, Mikhail. *Esthétique et théorie du roman*. Paris: Gallimard, 1978.

_____. *Rabelais and His World*. Cambridge, MA: MIT Press, 1968.

Barnes, Brooks. "ABC Family Spins Gold in Dramas." *New York Times*. 7 March 2011. B1.

Barthes, Roland. *Mythologies and Lesson*. Transl. Kaiti Xatzidimou and Ioulietta Ralli. Athens: Rappa, 1957, 1979 (in Greek).

Bauerlein, Mark. *The Dumbest Generation: How the Digital Age Stupefies Young Americans and Jeopardizes Our Future (Or, Don't Trust Anyone Under 30)*. New York: Tarcher, 2009.

Becher, Jonathan. "A Multitude of Myths About Millennials." *Forbes*. 15 Oct. 2012. Web. 7 July 2013.

Beck, Ulrich. *Risikogesellschaft. Auf dem Weg in eine andere Moderne*. Frankfurt am Main: Suhrkamp, 1986.

Bell, Emma. *Reading Management and Organization in Film*. Basingstoke: Palgrave, 2008.

Bennett, William J. "Hookup Culture Debases Women." CNN. 4 Apr. 2012. Web. 5 May 2013.

Benshoff, Harry M., and Sean Griffin. *America on Film: Representing Race, Class, Gender, and Sexuality at the Movies*. Malden, MA: Blackwell, 2004.

Black, Dan. "Defending Gen Y: Why Millennials Mean Business." *Huffington Post*. 19 Dec. 2012. Web. 9 May 2013.

Blatterer, Harry. "Contemporary Adulthood: Reconceptualizing an Uncontested Category." *Current Sociology.* 55 (2007): 771–92.

Bogle, Kathleen A. *Hooking Up: Sex, Dating, and Relationships on Campus*, New York: New York University Press, 2008.

Borsellino, Mary. "Damon Salvatore: Vampire Hunter." *A Visitor's Guide to Mystic Falls.* Ed. Red and Vee of Vampires-Diaries.net. Dallas: BenBella Books, 2010. 129–142.

Borstelmann, Thomas. *The 1970s: A New Global History from Civil Rights to Economic Inequality.* Princeton, NJ: Princeton University Press, 2012.

Braxton, Greg. "Q: Which of These Is Out of Place? 'Mr. Bill,' 'The 700 Club,' 'Pee-Wee's Playhouse': A: None..." *Los Angeles Times.* 15 Aug. 2013. F1.

Brennan, Sarah Rees. "Women Who Love Vampires Who Eat Women: Gender Dynamics and Interspecies Dating in Mystic Falls." *A Visitor's Guide to Mystic Falls.* Ed. Red and Vee of Vampires-Diaries.net. Dallas: BenBella Books, 2010. 1–20.

"Bronies." *Know Your Meme.* N.p.: n. pag. 30 May 2013.

Brooks, David. "If It Feels Right..." *New York Times.* 12 Sept. 2011. Web. 18 Apr. 2013.

Bund, Kerstin, Uwe Jean Heuser, and Anne Kunze. "Wollen die auch arbeiten?" *Die Zeit.* 7 Mar. 2013. n.pag. Web. 17 Apr. 2013.

Butler, Judith. "Merely Cultural." *New Left Review* 227 (1998): 33–44. *EBSCOhost.* Web. 10 April 2013.

Capsuto, Steven. *Alternate Channels: The Uncensored Story of Gay and Lesbian Images on Television: 1930s to the Present.* New York: Ballantine, 2000.

Carter, Bill. "In the Tastes of Young Men, Humor Is Most Prized, a Survey Finds." *New York Times.* 19 Feb. 2012. Web. 22 May 2013.

Chau, Joanna. "Millennials Are More 'Generation Me' Than 'Generation We,' Study Finds. " *Chronicle of Higher Education* 15 March 2012. Web. 4, June 2013.

CIRCLE: The Center for Information and Research on Civic Learning and Engagement. "*Updated Estimate: Youth Turnout Was 50 Percent in 2012; Youth Turnout in Battleground States 58 Percent.*" 2012.

Clark-Flory, Tracy. "Mockery: Women's New Weapon." *Salon.com.* 18 Mar. 2012. Web. 22 May 2013.

Clarke, John, Stuart Hall, Tony Jefferson, and Brian Roberts. "Subcultures, Cultures, and Class. *Resistance Through Rituals: Youth Subcultures in Post-War Britain.* Ed. Stuart Hall and Tony Jefferson. Abingdon, Oxon: Routledge, 2006. 3–60.

Clover, Carol J. *Men Women and Chain Saws: Gender in the Modern Horror Film.* Princeton, NJ: Princeton UP, 1992.

Collins, Jim, Hilary Radner and Ava Preacher Collins. *Film Theory Goes to the Movies.* New York: Routledge, 1993.

Cook, Chanon. "Consumer Insights: Comedy Natives." Blog. Viacom. 6 Dec. 2012. Web. 4 June 2013.

Costea, Bogdan, Norman Crump and John Holm. "Dionysus at Work? The Ethos of Play and the Ethos of Management." *Culture and Organization.* 11 (2005): 139–51.

Coupland, Douglas. *Generation X: Tales for an Accelerated Culture.* New York: St. Martin's, 1991.

Craig, Pamela, and Martin Fradley. "Teenage Traumata: Youth, Affective Politics, and the Contemporary American Horror Film." *American Horror Film: The Genre at the Turn of the Millennium.* Ed. Steffen Hantke. Jackson: University Press of Mississippi, 2010. 77–97. *ebrary.* 10 May 2012.

Craig, Stephen C., Richard G. Niemi, and Glenn E. Silver. "Political Efficacy and Trust: A Report on the NES Pilot Study Items." *Political Behavior* 12.3 (1990): 289–314.

Craig, Stephen C., Stephen Earl Bennett, eds. *After the Boom: The Politics of Generation X.* Boston: Rowman and Littlefield, 1997.

Crawford, Kate. "Adult Responsibility in Insecure Times: The Post-Crash World Necessitates a Redefinition of Adulthood." *Soundings.* 41 (2009): 45–55.

———. *Adult Themes: Rewriting the Rules of Adulthood.* Basingstoke: Pan Macmillan, 2006.

Curtin, Michael. "On Edge: Culture Industries in the Neo-Network Era." *Making and Selling Culture*. Ed. Richard Ohmann. Hanover, NH: Wesleyan University Press, 1996. 181–202.

D'Addario, Daniel. "Has the Onion Gotten Too Mean?" Salon.com. 9 May 2013. Web. 9 June 2013.

Davé, Shilpa S. *Indian Accents: Brown Voice and Racial Performance in American Television and Film*. Urbana: University of Illinois Press, 2013.

Davis, Blair, and Kial Natale. "'The Pound of Flesh Which I Demand': American Horror Cinema, Gore, and the Box Office, 1998–2007." *American Horror Film: The Genre at the Turn of the Millennium*. Ed. Steffen Hantke. Jackson: University Press of Mississippi, 2010. 35–57. *ebrary*. 10 May 2012.

Deal, Jennifer G., David G. Altman, and Steven G. Rogelberg. "Millennials at Work: What We Know and What We Need to Do (If Anything)." *Journal of Business Psychology* 25.2 (2010): 191–199. *Springer Link*. Web. 17 Apr. 2013.

Dempsey, John. "ABC Family Unlocks 'Secret' of a Teen Hit." *Variety*. 18–24 August. 2008. 16.

_____. "Alphabet Spells Out 'Family' Resemblance." *Variety*. 7 Oct 2002. 17.

_____. "Frog Leaps for Syndication Revenues." *Variety*. 27 Sept 27–Oct 3 2004. 24.

Deresiewicz, William. "Generation Sell." NYTimes.com. 12 Nov. 2011. Web. 2 May 2013.

Diamond, Lisa M. "The Development of Sexual Orientation Among Adolescent and Young Adult Women." *Developmental Psychology* 34.5 (1998): 1085–1095. EBSCOhost. Web. 22 March 2013.

Dika, Vera. "The Stalker Film, 1978–1981." In *American Horrors: Essays on the Modern American Horror Film*. Eds. Gregory A. Waller. Urbana: University of Illinois Press, 1987. 86–101.

Donnelly, Ashley M. "The New American Hero: Dexter, Serial Killer for the Masses." *Journal of Popular Culture*. 45.1 (2012): 15–26.

Doty, Alexander. *Making Things Perfectly Queer: Interpreting Mass Culture*. Minneapolis: University of Minnesota Press, 1993.

Dunleavy, Trisha. "Hybridity in TV Sitcom: The Case of Comedy Verité." *FlowTV*. 11 Dec. 2008. Web. 15 Jan. 2013.

Dyer, Richard. *Gays and Film*. New York: Zoetrope. 1984.

Ebert, Roger. "*Funny Games*." RogerEbert.com. 13 Mar. 2008. Web. 3 Mar. 2013.

_____. "*The Texas Chainsaw Massacre.*" RogerEbert.com. 17 Oct. 2003. Web. 3 Mar. 2013.

Edelstein, David. "Now Playing at Your Local Multiplex: Torture Porn." NYMag.com. N.d. 2 May 2013.

Em and Lo. "'Twilight,' Take Me Away!" *New York Magazine*. 15 Nov. 2009. Web. 30 May 2013.

Espinoza, Chip. "Millennial Integration: Challenges Millennials Face in the Workplace and What They Can Do About Them." *Dissertation,* Antioch University, 2012. *Ohiolink*. Web. 17 Apr. 2013.

Eurostat. "Harmonisierte Arbeitslosenquote nach Geschlecht—Alter 15–24." *epp.eurostat.ec.europa.eu*. Eurostat, n.d. 24 Jul. 2013.

Fairbanks, Amanda M. "Post-9/11 Generation: Millennials Reflect on Decade Since Terrorist Attacks." *The Huffington Post*. 9 Sept. 2011. Web. 1 April 2013.

Falconer, Rachel. *The Crossover Novel: Contemporary Children's Fiction and Its Adult Readership*. New York: Routledge, 2009.

Feasey, Rebecca. "Anxiety, Helplessness and 'Adultescence': Examining the Appeal of Teen Drama for the Young Adult Audience." *European Journal of Cultural Studies*. 12 (2009): 431–46.

Fielder, Robyn L., Kate B. Carey, and Michael P. Carey, "Are Hookups Replacing Romantic Relationships? A Longitudinal Study of First-Year Female College Students." *Journal of Adolescent Health* 52(5): 657–59.

Fischer-Baum, Reuben. "Women Didn't Abandon Rom-Coms; Rom-Coms Abandoned Women." *Jezebel*. 20 May 2013. Web. 1 June 2013.

"5 Millennial Truths: We Have More Close Friends." *Our Values*. 2013. Web. 15 April 2013.

Flint, Joe. "Thomopoulos Aims Family Channel at Mainstream." *Variety*. 10–16 July, 1995. 24.

Flores, Michelle. "Racist and Postfeminism in *The Mindy Project*." *Gender/Sex/Media*. 28 Mar. 2013. Web. 29 May 2013.

Fogel, Matthew. "*Grey's Anatomy* Goes Colorblind." *New York Times*. 8 May 2005. Web. 14 May 2013.

Fontanille, Jacques, *Sémiotique et littérature: Essais de méthode*, Paris: Puf, 1999.

Franklin, Daniel P. *Politics and Film*. Lanham: Rowman and Littlefield, 2006.

Gabler, Neal. "Perspective: Millennials Seem to Have Little Use for Old Movies." *Los Angeles Times*. 14 July 2012. Web. 7 Jan. 2012.

Gee, James Paul. *An Introduction to Discourse Analysis: Theory and Method*. 3d ed. New York: Routledge, 2011.

Gelder, Ken. *New Vampire Cinema*. London: Palgrave Macmillan/British Film Institute, 2012.

Genette, Gérard. "Introduction to the Paratext." *New Literary History*, 1991, 22: 261–272.

German, Myna. "The Millennial Student and Technology: Insatiable Quest or Part of a Reliable Pattern of History." *Faculty Resource Network*, New York Univeristy. 2006. Web. 12 May 2013.

"Getting to Know the Millennials" *Advertising Age*. 9 July 2007. A1–A6.

Gilbert, Matthew. "In with the Out Crowd." *The Boston Globe*. 16 October 2011. Web. 28 April 2013.

Gitlin, Marty. *The Baby Boomer Encyclopedia*. Santa Barbara, CA: Greenwood, 2011.

Gitlin, Todd. *Media Unlimited, Revised Edition: How the Torrent of Images and Sounds Overwhelms Our Lives*. New York: Picador, 2007.

_____. *The Whole World Is Watching: The Media in the Making and the Unmaking of the New Left*. Berkeley: University of California Press, 1980.

GLAAD. "Where Are We in TV Report: 2010–2011 Season." 2011. Web. 17 May 2013.

_____. "Where Are We in TV Report: 2011–2012 Season." 2012. Web. 17 May 2013.

_____. "Where Are We in TV Report: 2012–2013 Season." 2013. Web. 17 May 2013.

Goldstein, Richard. *The Attack Queers: Liberal Society and the Gay Right*. New York: Verso. 2002.

Gonzalez, Sandra. "First Details on the 'Pretty Little Liars' Spin-off, 'Ravenswood.'" *Entertainment Weekly*. 24 May 2013. 23.

Göttler, Fritz. "Guck' mal wer da mobbt!" *Süddeutsche Zeitung*. 17 May 2010. Web. 17 Apr. 2013.

Grabianowski, Ed. "How Generation Me Works." HowStuffWorks.com, May 23, 2011. Web. May 22, 2013.

Grant, Elizabeth Charlotte. "Make 'Em Laugh: Sitcom Humor for Millennials." PopMatters.com. 28 Nov. 2012. Web. 20 May 2013.

Gray, Herman. *Cultural Moves: African Americans and the Politics of Representation*. Los Angeles: University of California Press, 2005.

_____. *Watching Race: Television and the Struggle for Blackness*. Minneapolis: University of Minnesota Press, 2004.

Gray, Mary L. "Negotiating Identities/Queering Desires: Coming Out Online and the Remediation of the Coming-Out Story." *Journal of Computer-Mediated Communication* 14.4 (2009): 1162–1189. Web. 20 April 2013.

Greenberg, Eric, and Karl Webber. *Generation We: How Millennial Youth Are Taking Over America and Changing Our World Forever*. Emeryville: Patsatusan, 2008.

Greene, Doyle. *The American Worker on Film: A Critical History, 1909–1999*. Jefferson, NC: McFarland, 2010.

Grewal, Inderpal. "Transnational America: Race, Gender and Citizenship after 9/11." *Social Identities: Journal for the Study of Race, Nation and Culture* 9.4 (2003): 535–61. Web. 13 Dec. 2012.

Griffith, Kristin and Michelle Hebl. "The Disclosure Dilemma for Gay Men and Lesbians: 'Coming Out' at Work." *Journal of Applied Psychology* 87.6 (2002): 1191–1199. *EBSCOhost*. Web. 5 August 2013.

Grosman, Lev. "Grow Up? Not So Fast." *Time Magazine*. 16 Jan. 2005: n. pag. Web. 10 June 2013.

Gross, Larry. *Up from Invisibility*. New York: Columbia University Press, 2001.

Hall, Stuart, and Tony Jefferson, eds. *Resistance through Rituals: Youth Subcultures in Post-War Britain*. 2d ed. New York: Routledge, 2006.

Halpin, John, and Karl Agne. "The Political Ideology of the Millennial Generation: A National Study of Political Values and Beliefs Among 18- to 29-Year-Olds." Center for American Progress May 2009. PDF.

Halse, Mici L., and Brenda J. Mallinson. "Investigating Popular Internet Applications as Supporting e-learning Technologies for Teaching and Learning with Generation Y." *International Journal of Education and Development Using Information and Communication Technology (IJEDICT)* Vol. 5, Issue 5 (2009): 58–71.

Hantke, Steffen. "They Don't Make 'Em Like They Used To: On the Rhetoric of Crisis and the Current State of American Cinema." *American Horror Film: The Genre at the Turn of the Millennium*. Ed. Steffen Hantke. Jackson: University Press of Mississippi, 2010. vii–xxxii. *ebrary*. Web. 10 May 2012.

Hartley, John. "Situation Comedy, Part 1." *The Television Genre Book*. Ed. Glen Creeber. London: British Film Institute, 2001. 65–67.

Haverty, Mike. "Bridesmaids' and the Science of Female Comedy." *Heave Media*. 31 May 2011. Web. 4 June 2013.

Hayward, Keith. "Pantomime Justice: A Cultural Criminological Analysis of 'Life Stage Dissolution.'" *Crime Media Culture*. 8: (2012): 213–29.

Heffner, Alexander. "Could Jon Stewart's Satire Engage Young Voters for Obama." *Tampa Bay Times*, 4 May 2012. Web. 4 June 2013.

Herbenic, Debby. "Can Hookups Be More Fun?" Salon.com. 12 September 2012. Web. 9 Mar. 2013.

Hershatter, Andrea, and Molly Epstein. "Millennials and the World of Work: An Organization and Management Perspective." *Journal of Business Psychology* 25.2 (2010): 211–223. *Springer Link*. Web. 17 Apr. 2013.

Hills, Rachel. "Adult Themes: Rewriting the Rules of Adulthood." *The Age Book Reviews*. 24 Nov. 2006: n. pag. Web. 21 June 2013.

Hoffman, Adam "Hookup Culture Not as Prevalent as Believed, Study Shows— Brown Daily Herald." *Brown Daily Herald*. Web. 9 Mar. 2013.

Holtzman, Linda. *Media Messages: What Film, Television, and Popular Music Teach Us About Race, Class, Gender, and Sexual Orientation*. New York: M.E. Sharpe, 2000.

Holz Ivory, Adrienne, Rhonda Gibson, and James D. Ivory. "Gendered Relationships on Television: Portrayals of Same-Sex and Heterosexual Couples." *Mass Communication and Society* 12.2 (2009): 170–192.

"Horror Isn't Just for Halloween: Students' Favorite Movie Genres and Sweet Treats." VisibilityPR.com. 25 Oct. 2011. Web. 15 Apr. 2013.

Howe, Neil, and Reena Nadler. "Millennials Rising." *Leadership for Student Activities*, 2008, 36 (8): 17–21.

Howe, Neil, and William Strauss. *Millennials Rising: The Next Great Generation*. New York: Vintage, 2000.

Humphries, Reynold. "A (Post)Modern House of Pain: *FearDotCom* and the Prehistory of the Post–9/11 Torture Film." *American Horror Film: The Genre at the Turn of the Millennium*. Ed. Steffen Hantke. Jackson: University Press of Mississippi, 2010. *Ebrary*. 58–74. *ebrary*. Web. 10 May 2012.

Huntley, Rebecca. *The World According to Y: Inside the New Adult Generation*. Sydney: Allen and Unwin, 2006.

Jameson, Fredric. *Postmodernism or, the Cultural Logic of Late Capitalism*. Durham: Duke Univeristy Press, 1991.

Jeffers McDonald, Tamar. *Romantic Comedy: Boy Meets Girls Meets Genre*. London: Wallflower, 2007.

Johnson, Corey W., and Rudy Dunlap. "'They Were Not Drag Queens, They Were Playboy Models and Bodybuilders': Media, Masculinities and Gay Sexual Identity." *Annals of Leisure Research* 14.2–3 (2011): 209–223.

Johnson, Kevin C. "Craven Promises New Twist for Horror Film *Scream 4*." *McClatchy—Tribune Business News*, n. pag., 10 Apr. 2011.

Jones, Darryl. *Horror: A Thematic History in Fiction and Film*. London: Arnold, 2002.

"Joss Whedon Talks Cabin in the Woods." TrueFilm.com. 16 Feb. 2012. Web. 20 Apr. 2013.

Jürgens, Kerstin. "Subjekt und Arbeitskraft: Arbeit und Leben." *Handbuch Arbeitssoziologie*. Ed. Böhle, Fritz, G. Günter Voß, and Günther Wachtler. Wiesbaden: VS Verlag für Sozialwissenschaften, 2010. 438–510.

Kaklamanidou, Betty. *Genre, Gender and the Effects of Neoliberalism: The New Millennium Hollywood Rom Com*. London: Routledge, 2013.

Kaling, Mindy. *Is Everyone Hanging Out Without Me? (And Other Concerns)*. New York: Three Rivers, 2011.

Kaslow, Sally. *Slouching Towards Adulthood: Observations from the Not-So-Empty Nest*. New York: Viking, 2012.

Kaufman, Amy. "Box Office: 'Thor' Thunders to the Top Again, Hammering 'Bridesmaids' and 'Priest' [Updated]." *LA Times: Business*. 15 May 2011. Web. 1 June 2013.

Kelly, Christopher. "Cutting-Edge Horror Movies Mirror Generation Y Anxieties." thestaronline.com. 31 Mar. 2006. Web. 19 Feb. 2013.

Kendall, Lori. "The Nerd Within: Mass Media and the Negotiation of Identity Among Computer-Using Men." *Journal of Men's Studies*. 3 (1999): 353–67.

Kerner, Ian. "Why You Should Talk About Sex Before Marriage." CNN. 24 January 2013. Web. 16 Mar. 2013.

Kirby, David. "The Boys in the Writers' Room." *New York Times*. 17 June 2001. Web. 18 August 2013.

Kirchoff, Lindsey. "Why Millennials Watch Children's Movies." *How to Market to Me: The Guide to Getting the Millennial Market*. 7 Apr. 2012. Web. 22 May 2013.

Klaffke, Martin, ed. *Personalmanagement von Millennials: Konzepte, Instrumente und Best-Practice-Ansätze*. Wiesbaden: Gabler, 2011.

Klaffke, Martin, and Andreas Parment. "Herausforderungen und Handlungsansätze für das Personalmanagement von Millennials." *Personalmanagement von Millennials: Konzepte, Instrumente und Best-Practice-Ansätze*. Ed. Martin Klaffke. Wiesbaden: Gabler, 2011. 3–22.

Kleemann, Frank, and G. Günter Voß. "Subjekt und Arbeitskraft: Arbeit und Subjekt." *Handbuch Arbeitssoziologie*. Ed. Böhle, Fritz, G. Günter Voß, and Günther Wachtler. Wiesbaden: VS Verlag für Sozialwissenschaften, 2010. 415–450.

Klein, Christina. "The *American* Horror Film? Globalization and Transnational U.S.-Asian Genres." *American Horror Film: The Genre at the Turn of the Millennium*. Ed. Steffen Hantke. Jackson: University Press of Mississippi, 2010. 5–14. ebrary. Web. 10 May 2012.

Kozloff, Sarah. *Overhearing Film Dialogue*. Berkeley: University of California Press, 2000.

Krattenmaker, Tom. "Millennials Aren't Amoral and Adrift." *USA Today*. 11 Mar. 2012. Web. 22 Apr. 2013.

Lane, Carson. "Viewpoints: Young and Immoral? Not So Fast." *Reporting Texas*. 15 Dec. 2011. Web. 14 July 2013.

Lee, Christina. *Screening Generation X: The Politics and Popular Memory of Youth in Contemporary Media*. Farnham: Ashgate, 2010.

Lepore, Meredith. "The Decline of Romantic Comedies in 11 Slides." *The Jane Dough*. 24 May 2013. Web. 2 June 2013.

Levinson, Julie. *The American Success Myth on Film*. London: Palgrave Macmillan, 2012.

Liesse, Julie. "Millennial Appeal." *Advertising Age*. 9 July 2007: A2-A4.

Lipsitz, George. "The Meaning of Memory: Family, Class and Ethnicity in Early Network Television Programs." *Cultural Anthropology* 1.4 (1986): 355–87.

Loacker, Bernadette. *Kreativ Prekär. Künstlerische Arbeit und Subjektivität im Postfordismus.* Bielefeld: Transcript, 2010.

Lotz, Amanda D. *The Television will be Revolutionized.* New York: New York University Press, 2007.

Lueken, Verena. "In der Hölle der Modewelt: 'Der Teufel trägt Prada'." *Frankfurter Allgemeine Zeitung* 11 Oct. 2006: 35.

Maira, Sunaina Marr. "Henna and Hip-Hop: The Politics of Cultural Production and the Work of Cultural Studies." *Journal of Asian American Studies* 3.3 (2000): 329–69. Web. 1 May 2013.

Malone, Noreen. "The Kids Are Actually Sort of Alright." Nymagazine.com. New York Magazine. 16 Oct. 2011. Web. 19 Mar. 2013.

Mangels, Andy. "Lesbian Sex = Death?" *Advocate* 869 (2002): 1–3. EBSCOhost. Web. 20 June 2013.

Marano, Hara Estroff. *A Nation of Wimps: The High Cost of Invasive Parenting.* New York: Crown Archetype, 2008.

Marchie, Melanie. "Girl Power: Teens Hit the Cosmetics Scene." *Household and Personal Products Industry*. September 2001. 64.

Martin, Denise. "New Tween Scene." *Variety.* 16–22 Oct. 2006. 24–25.

Marwick, Alice, and Danah Boyd. "Teens Text More Than Adults, but They're Still Just Teens." *The Daily Beast*, 20 May 2012. Pew Internet, Pew Research Center. Web. 21 May 2013.

Matchar, Emily. "How Those Spoiled Millennials Will Make the Workplace Better for Everyone." WashingtonPost.com. 16 Aug. 2012. Web. 3 May 2013.

Maxwell, Brandon. "Olivia Pope and the Scandal of Representation." *The Feminist Wire.* 7 Feb. 2013. Web. 14 May 2013.

McNamara, Mary. "Television Review: '2 Broke Girls.'" *Los Angeles Times.* 19 Sept. 2011. Web. 20 Mar. 2013.

McRobbie, Angela. "Postfeminism and Popular Culture: *Bridget Jones* and the New Gender Regime." *Interrogating Postfeminism: Gender and the Politics of Popular Culture.* Eds. Diane Negra and Yvonne Tasker. Durham: Duke University Press, 2007. 1–13.

Meister, Jeanne C., and Karie Willyerd. "Mentoring Millennials." *Harvard Business Review.* May 2010. Web. 6 April 2013.

Melamed, Jodi. "The Spirit of Neoliberalism: From Racial Liberalism to Neoliberal Multiculturalism." *Social Text* 26.4 (89) (2006): 1–24. Web. 1 Dec. 2013.

Mellencamp, Patricia. "Situation Comedy, Feminism, and Freud: Discourses of Gracie and Lucy." *Feminist Television Criticism: A Reader.* Eds. Charlotte Brundson, Julie D'Acci, and Lynn Spigel. Oxford: Clarendon, 1997. 60–73.

Mikl-Horke, Gertraude. *Industrie und Arbeitssoziologie.* München, Wien: Oldenbourg, 2007.

"Millennials: Confident. Connected. Open to Change." Pew Research Social and Demographic Trends. 24 Feb. 2010. Web. 1 July 2013.

Mills, Brett. "Comedy Verite: Contemporary Sitcom Form." *Screen* 45.1 (2004): 63–78. Web. 15 Nov. 2013.

Minssen, Heiner. *Arbeit in der modernen Gesellschaft. Eine Einführung.* Wiesbaden: VS Verlag für Sozialwissenschaften, 2012.

Mittell, Jason. "A Cultural Approach to Television Genre Theory." *Cinema Journal* 40.3 (2001): 3–24. EBSCOhost. Web. 28 May 2013.

Mittman, Asa Simon. "Introduction: The Impact of Monsters and Monster Studies." *The Ashgate Companion to Monsters and the Monstrous.* Ed. Asa Simon Mittman and Peter J. Dendle. Farnham: Ashgate, 2012. 1–15.

Mizejewski, Linda. "Queen Latifah, Unruly Women, and the Bodies of Romantic Comedy." *Genders* 46 (2007). Web. 8 May 2013.

Moore, Tracey. "It's Not Too Late to Save the Rom-Com from Itself." *Jezebel.* 24 Feb. 2013. Web. 2 June 2013.

"MTV Howls Over *Teen Wolf*, Renewing the Show for a Third Season and Doubling the Episode Order to 24." MTV Press. 12 July 2012. Web. 18 July 2013.

Munoz, Lorenza. "The Female Fear Factor: Young Women Are Flocking to, and Revolutionizing, Horror Films." *Los Angeles Times*.com. 8 Nov. 2003. Web. 15 Apr. 2013.

Nazarian, Vera. "You're My Obsession." *A Visitor's Guide to Mystic Falls*. Ed. Red and Vee of Vampires-Diaries.net. Dallas: BenBella Books, 2010. 85–101.

Netzley, Sara B. "Visibility That Demystifies: Gays, Gender, and Sex on Television." *Journal of Homosexuality* 57.8 (2010): 968–986.

Newman, Michael Z., and Elana Levine. *Legitimating Television: Media Convergence and Cultural Status*. New York: Routledge, 2012.

Nicodemus, Katja. "Angst vor der eigenen Courage." *Die Zeit*. 16 Oct. 2006. Web. 17 Apr. 2013.

"NNAAC Joins Muslim, Sikh, and South Asian American Partners to Urge Unity and Restraint." National Network for Arab American Communities. 19 Apr. 2013. Web. 16 May 2013.

Nochimson, Martha P. "The Devil Wears Prada." *Cineaste* 32.1 (2006): 48–50.

Oh, David C., and Omotayo O. Banjo. "Outsourcing Postracialism: Voicing Neoliberal Multiculturalism in *Outsourced*." *Communication Theory* 22.4 (2012): 449–70. Web. 31 Jan. 2013.

O'Hehir, Andrew. "I'll Tell You What's Funny." Salon.com. 2 Mar. 2013. Web. 22 May 2013.

Orloff, Ann. "Gender in the Welfare State." *Annual Review of Sociology* 22 (1996): 51–78.

Osgerby, Bill. "'So Who's Got Time for Adults!' Femininity, Consumption and the Development of Teen TV—From Gidget to Buffy." *Teen TV: Genre, Consumption, Identity*. Eds. Glyn Davis and Kay Dickinson. London: BFI, 2004. 71–86.

O'Shaughnessy, Martin. "Filming Work and the Work of Film." *L'Esprit Créateur* 51.3 (2011): 59–73. ProjectMUSE. Web. 17 Apr. 2013.

Owram, Doug. *Born at the Right Time: A History of the Baby-Boom Generation*. Toronto: Toronto University Press, 1996.

Padva, Gilad. "Media and Popular Culture Representations of LGBT Bullying." *Journal of Gay and Lesbian Social Services* 19.3 (2008). 105–118. Print

Pappademas, Alex. "*The Cabin in the Woods* Portmortem: This Is Not the Slasher Flick You're Looking For." Grantland.com. 17 Apr. 2012. Web. 15 Apr. 2013.

Pardee, Thomas. "Media-Savvy Gen Y Finds Smart and Funny Is 'New Rock 'n' Roll.'" *Advertising Age*. 11 Oct. 2010. Web 22 May 2013.

Paskin, Willa. "'Inside Amy Schumer: A Female-centric Take on Bro-Comedy." Salon.com. 13 Apr. 2013. Web. 2 June 2013.

Paul, Pamela. "Nouveau Niche." *American Demographics*. July 2003. 6+.

Petersen, Anne Helen. "*Revenge* as Postfeminist Dystopia." *Celebrity Gossip, Academic Style*. 14 Feb. 2012. Web. 16 May 2013.

Pew Research Center. "Millennials: Confident, Connected. Open to Change. *Pew Social & Demographic Trends*. 24 Feb. 2010. Web. 14 Feb. 2013.

Phillips, Kendall R. *Projected Fears, Horror Films and American Culture*. Westport: Praeger, 2005.

Picart, Carol Joan (Kay). Rev. of *The Biology of Horror: Gothic Literature and Film*, by Jack Morgan. *Journal of Criminal Justice and Popular Culture* 11.1 (2004): 35–57. Web. 20 May 2012.

Pinedo, Isabel Christina. "Postmodern Elements of the Contemporary Horror Film." In *The Horror Film*, edited by Steven Prince. New Brunswick: Rutgers UP, 2004. 85–117.

Portman, Jamie. "The Debate over *Scream 4*; Revolting Slasher Film or Classical Theatre for a Modern Age? The Argument Continues." *The Ottawa Citizen*, April 14, 2011.

Prashad, Vijay. *The Karma of Brown Folk*. Minneapolis: University of Minnesota Press, 2001.

PriceWaterhouseCoopers. "Millennials at Work—Perspectives from a New Generation." *Managing Tomorrow's People*. Price WaterhouseCoopers, 2008. Web. 17 Apr. 2013.

Radish, Christina. "Creator/Showrunner Amy Sherman-Palladino Talks BUNHEADS, Casting the Highly Specific Characters, Knowing Her Endgame, Writing Movies and More." *Collider*. 4 Feb. 2013. Web. 20 May 2013.

Radner, Hilary. *Neo-Feminist Cinema: Girly Films, Chick Flicks and Consumer Culture*. London: Routledge, 2011.

Rainer, Thom S., and Jess W. Rainer. *The Millennials: Connecting to America's Largest Generation*. Nashville, TN: B&H, 2011.

Rainer, Tom. "The Parental Factor." TomRainer.com, 21 Aug. 2012. 4 June 2013.

Rainey, James. "Changed Minds, Not Young Voters, Boost Same-Sex Marriage Support." LATimes.com. Los Angeles Times, 25 Oct. 2012. Web. 19 Mar. 2013.

Raley, Amber B., and Jennifer L. Lucas. "Stereotype of Success? Prime-Time Television's Portrayal of Gay, Lesbian, and Bisexual Characters." *Journal of Homosexuality*, 51.2 (2006). 19–38.

Reeve, Elspeth. "Every Every Every Generation Has Literally Been the Me Me Me Generation." TheAtlanticWire.com. 9 May 2013. Web. 10 May 2013.

Reinecke, Christiane, et al. "Wissen und soziale Ordnung. Eine Kritik der Wissensgesellschaft." *Schriftenreihe des Sonderforschungsbereichs 640, Working Papers* 1 (2010): 4–30. Web. 17 Apr. 2013.

Resnick, Evan. "Defining Engagement." *Journal of International Affairs* 54.2 (2001): 551–567.

Richter, Götz, ed. *Generationen gemeinsam im Betrieb. Individuelle Flexibilität durch anspruchsvolle Regulierungen*. Bielefeld: Bertelsmann, 2009.

Rideout, Victoria J., Ulla G. Foehr, and Donald F. Roberts. "Generation M^2: Media in the Lives of 8- to 18-Year-Olds." *Henry J. Kaiser Family Foundation* (2010). ERIC. Web. 20 April 2013.

Rockoff, Adam. *Going to Pieces: The Rise and Fall of the Slasher Film, 1978–1986*. Jefferson, NC: McFarland, 2002.

Rosen, Christine. "Virtual Friendship and the New Narcissism." *The New Atlantis: A Journal of Technology and Society* 17 (Summer 2007): 15–31. TheNewAtlantis.com. Web. 5 May 2013.

Rosenberg, Alyssa. "Michael Patrick King Defends '2 Broke Girls' Stereotypes: 'I Don't Find It Offensive, Any of This.'" Web log post. 11 Jan. 2012. Web. 19 Mar. 2013.

_____. "Romantic Comedies Aren't What They Used to Be. Then Again, Neither Is Love." *Slate*. 22 Feb. 2013. Web. 2 June 2013.

Rowe, Gene, and Lynn J. Frewer. "A Typology of Public Engagement Mechanism." *Science, Technology, and Human Values* 30.2 (2005): 251–290.

Rowe, Kathleen. "Roseanne: Unruly Woman as Domestic Goddess." *Screen* 31.4 (1990): 408–19.

Ryan, Maureen. "Why 'Girls' Season 1 Was Terrific and Why It's a Hit with Guys Too." *The Huffington Post*. 17 June 2012. Web. 4 Mar. 2013.

"SAALT Expresses Condolences for Boston Marathon Bombing Victims." South Asian Americans Leading Together. 17 Apr. 2013. Web. 16 May 2013.

Sandberg, Bryn Elise. "In Defense of Seth MacFarlane." *Millennial Influx*. 1 Mar. 2013. Web. 22 May 2013.

Sarr, Ramou. "We Just Want the Chance to Be as Vapid as Everyone Else: Why We Need *The Mindy Project*." *Hello Giggles*. 4 Dec. 2012. Web. 1 May 2013.

Sauer, Dieter. "Vermarktlichung und Vernetzung der Unternehmens- und Betriebsorganisation." *Handbuch Arbeitssoziologie*. Ed. Böhle, Fritz, G. Günter Voß, and Günther Wachtler. Wiesbaden: VS Verlag für Sozialwissenschaften, 2010. 545–568.

Savin-Williams, Ritch C. *"And Then I Became Gay": Young Men's Stories*. New York: Routledge, 1998.

_____. "An Exploratory Study of Pubertal Maturation Timing and Self-Esteem Among Gay and Bisexual Male Youths." *Developmental Psychology* 31.1 (1995): 56–64. EBSCOhost. Web. 23 March 2013.

_____. *The New Gay Teenager*. Cambridge, MA: Harvard University Press, 2005.

Schneider, Michael. "Part of the Family." *Variety*. 25 Feb.–2 Mar. 2008. 16.

Sederer, Lloyd L. "The Enemy Is Apathy." *Psychiatric Times* 29.9 (2012): 1–4.

Seidman, Robert. "Monday Broadcast Final Ratings." *TvByTheNumbers.com*. 20 Sept. 2011. Web. 19 Mar. 2013.

Semigran, Aly. "'2 Broke Girls': Promising Series Nailed Twentysomething Poverty. NYC, Not So Much." *Pop Watch.com*. 20 Sept. 2011. Web. 19 Mar. 2013.

Senghaas-Knobloch, Eva. "Arbeitskraft ist mehr als eine Ware. Arbeiten in der postfordistischen Dienstleistungsgesellschaft." *Aus Politik und Zeitgeschichte* 61.15 (2011): 24–31.

Shary, Timothy. *Teen Movies: American Youth on Screen*. New York: Wallflower, 2011.

Shugart, Helene A. "Reinventing Privilege: The New (Gay) Man in Contemporary Popular Media." *Critical Studies in Media Communication* 20.1 (2003): 67–91.

Silverstein, Melissa, "The Glass Ceiling: Why Doesn't Hollywood Trust Women?" CNN.com, Web. 1 July 2013.

Smith, Stacy L., et. al. "Gender Roles and Occupations: A Look at Character Attributes and Job-Related Aspirations in Film and Television." Annenberg School for Communication and Journalism. University of Southern California. Web. 28 June 2013.

Spangler, Lynn C. *Television Women from Lucy to "Friends": Fifty Years of Sitcoms and Feminism*. Westport, CT: Praeger, 2003.

Spencer, Liese. "The Devil Wears Prada." *Sight and Sound* 10 (2006): 50–52.

Spigel, Lynn. "Entertainment Wars: Television after 9/11." *American Quarterly* 56.2 (2004): 235–70. Web. 15 Nov. 2013.

Stam, Robert, Robert Burgoyne and Sandy Flitterman-Lewis. *New Vocabularies in Film Semiotics*. London: Routledge, 1992.

Stanley, Alessandra. "New Crop of Sitcom Women Can Dish It Like the Big Boys." *New York Times*. 19 Sept. 2011. Web. 20 Mar. 2013.

———. "A Teenage Pregnancy, Packaged as a Prime-Time Cautionary Tale." *New York Times*. 1 July 2008. E1.

Stead, Peter. *Film and the Working Class: The Feature Film in British and American Society*. London, New York: Routledge, 1989.

Stein, Joel. "The New Greatest Generation: Why Millennials Will Save Us All." *Time* 20 May 2013: 26–32, 34.

Sterneborg, Anke. "Der Teufel trägt Prada." *epd-film* 23.10 (2006): 47.

Stevens, Dana. "Bridesmaids": The Raunchy Women's Comedy We've Been Waiting For." Slate.com. 12 May 2011. Web. 4 June 2013.

Stransky, Tanner. "Pretty Little Phenom." *Entertainment Weekly*. 1 Mar. 2013. 26–33.

Strauss, William, and Neil Howe. *Generations: The History of America's Future, 1584–2069*. 1991. New York: Perennial, 1992.

Sujansky, Joanne G., and Jan Ferri-Reed. *Keeping the Millennials: Why Companies Are Losing Billions in Turnover to This Generation—and What to Do About It*. Hoboken, NJ: Wiley, 2009.

Sweeney, Richard. *Millennial Behaviors and Demographics*. 2006. Web. 10 July 2013.

Syder, Andrew. "Knowing the Rules: Postmodernism and the Horror Film." *Special Issue of Spectator* 22: 2 (Fall 2002): 78–88.

T., Sarah. "Weight, Weight, Don't Tell Me: Body Image in 'The Mindy Project.'" *Girls Like Giants*. 10 Sept. 2012. Web. 15 Jan. 2013.

Taft, Jessica K. "Girl Power Politics: Pop-Culture Barriers and Organizational Resistance." *All About the Girl*. Ed. Anita Harris. New York: Routledge 2004. 69–78.

Tasker, Yvonne. *Working Girls: Gender and Sexuality in Popular Cinema*. London: Routledge, 1998.

Taylor, Paul, and Scott Ketter. *Millennials: A Portrait of Generation Next*. Washington, DC: Pew Research, 2010. Web. 15 March 2013.

"Technology and Social Networks." Pew Institute. 16 June 2011. Web. 30 May 2013.

Terkel, Amanda. "White Out: Media Heap Suspicion on Brown People in Boston

Marathon Bombing." *Huffington Post.* 18 Apr. 2013. Web. 1 May 2013.

Thistle, Susan. *From Marriage to the Market: The Transformation of Women's Lives and Work.* Berkeley: University of California Press, 2006.

Thompson, Ethan. "Comedy Verité? The Observational Documentary Meets the Televisual Sitcom." *The Velvet Light Trap.* 60 (2007): 63–72. Web. 15 Nov. 2013.

Thompson, Kristin, and David Bordwell. "Return to Paranormalcy." *DavidBordwell.net.* 13 Nov. 2012. Web. 20 May 2012.

Traister, Rebecca. "Early Signs of a "Bridesmaids" Bump." Salon.com. 27 Sept. 2011. Web. 2013.

Traube, Elizabeth G. *Dreaming Identities: Class, Gender, and Generation in 1980s Hollywood Movies.* Boulder, CO: Westview, 1992.

Tropiano, Stephen. *The Prime Time Closet: A History of Gays and Lesbians on TV.* New York: Applause Theatre and Cinema, 2002.

Tuchman, Gaye. *Making News: A Study in the Construction of Reality.* New York: Free, 1978.

Twenge, Jean M. *Generation Me: Why Today's Young Americans Are More Confident, Assertive, Entitled—and More Miserable Than Ever Before.* New York: Free Press, 2006.

———. "Millennials: The Greatest Generation or the Most Narcissistic." *The Atlantic.com.* 2 May 2012. Web. 7 Jan. 2013.

———, and W. Keith Campbell. *The Narcissism Epidemic: Living in the Age of Entitlement.* 2009. New York: Atria, 2013.

———, ———, and Elise C. Freeman. "Generational Differences in Young Adults' Life Goals, Concern for Others, and Civic Orientation, 1966–2009." *Journal of Personality and Social Psychology* Vol. 102, No. 5, (2012): 1045–1062.

"2012 Theatrical Market Statistics." *MPAA.org.* Web. 20 May 2012.

Utah Jack Squint. "Preening Monsters of Inconsequence." Rev. of *The World According to Y: Inside the New Adult Generation,* by Rebecca Huntley. Amazon.com. 18 June 2007. Web. 4 May 2013.

Vaccaro, Annemarie. "Intergenerational Perceptions, Similarities and Differences: A Comparative Analysis of Lesbian, Gay, and Bisexual Millennial Youth with Generation X and Baby Boomers." *Journal of LGBT Youth* 6.2 (2009): 113–134.

VanDerWerff, Todd. "2 Broke Girls Co-Creator Defends Show's Racial Humor in Worst Possible Terms." Avclub.com, A.V. Club. Web. 11 Jan. 2012.

Van Dyk, Deirdre. "Parlez-Vous Twixter?" *Time.* 24 Jan. 2005: n. pag. Web. 10 June 2013.

Verba, Sidney, and Norman H. Nie. *Participation in America: Political Democracy and Societal Equality.* New York: Harper and Row, 1972.

Vesey, A., and K. Lambert. "'I Can Have It All': Liz Lemon Negotiates Power, One Sandwich at a Time." *FlowTV.* 24 July 2008. Web. 8 May 2013.

Vidali, Debra Spitulnik. "Millennial Encounters with Mainstream Television News: Excess, Void, and Points of Engagement." *Linguistic Anthropology* 20.2 (2010): 372–388.

Visweswaran, Kamala. "Diaspora by Design: Flexible Citizenship and South Asians in U.S. Racial Formations." *Diaspora: A Journal of Transnational Studies.* 6.1 (1997): 5–23. Web. 1 May 2013.

Voß, G. Günter and Hans J. Pongratz. "Der Arbeitskraftunternehmer. Eine neue Grundform der Ware Arbeitskraft?" *Kölner Zeitschrift für Soziologie und Sozialpsychologie* 50.1 (1998): 131–158.

Walkerdine, Valerie. *Schoolgirl Fictions.* London: Verso, 1990.

Walters, Suzanna D. *All the Rage: The Story of Gay Visibility in America.* New York: Columbia University Press, 2001.

Wampole, Christy. "How to Live Without Irony." *New York Times.* 17 Nov. 2012. Web. 15 May 2013.

Wee, Valerie. "The *Scream* Trilogy, 'Hyperpostmodernism,' and the Late-Nineties Teen Slasher Film." *Journal of Film and Video.* 57.3 (2005): 44–61.

Weiner, Andrew. "The 'Found Footage' Theory." *Huffington Post.* 1 Mar. 2013. Web. 20 May 2012.

Williams, Michael Paul. "Today's Young Adults Can't Afford to Skip Voting." TimesDispatch.com, *Richmond Times-Dispatch*. 11 May 2012.

Williams, Ray B. "Is the 'Me Generation' Less Empathetic?" *Wired for Success: How to Fulfill Your Potential*. PsychologyToday.com. 6 June 2010. Web. 5 May 2013.

Winograd, Morley, and Michael D. Hais. *Millennial Momentum: How a New Generation Is Remaking America*. New Brunswick, NJ: Rutgers University Press, 2011.

Wong, Curtis M. "'Glee' Suicide Storyline Leads to Spike in Web Traffic, Phone Calls for LGBT Youth Group." *Huffington Post*. 28 Feb. 2012. Web. 25 May 2013.

Woodruffe, Charles. "Generation Y." *Training Journal*, July 2009, 31–35.

Wray-Lake, Laura, and Daniel Hart. "Growing Social Inequalities in Youth Civic Engagement? Evidence from the National Election Study." *Political Science and Politics* 45.3 (2012): 456–461.

Wyatt, Edward. "The Big Surprise of 'Big Bang': The Bigger Audience." *New York Times*. 4 Oct. 2009: n. pag. Web. 10 June 2013.

York, Ashley Elaine. "From Chick Flicks to Millennial Blockbusters: Spinning Female-Driven Narratives into Franchises." *The Journal of Popular Culture* 43.1 (2010): 3–25. *ProQuest*. Web. 17 Apr. 2013.

Zapatka, Jennifer Ann. *Understanding Second-Wave Millennial College Students through a Generational Lens*. Diss., University of South Carolina, 2009.

About the Contributors

Bernice **Alston** is a doctoral candidate and research assistant in higher education leadership at Morgan State University. Her research interests include student engagement, student-faculty interaction and retention within post-secondary institutions.

Christoph **Büettner**, a video-journalist and producer, has taught in the Department of Media Studies at the University of Bonn. His research focuses on socio-political concepts and film and German cinema.

Margo **Collins** is a visiting assistant professor of English at DeVry University, and her research focuses on the study of gothic literature and popular culture. She co-edits the journal *Supernatural Studies* and is a fiction author.

Betty **Kaklamanidou** is a visiting research fellow at the University of East London and lecturer of film history and theory at Aristotle University of Thessaloniki, Greece. She is the author of *Genre, Gender and the Effects of Neoliberalism: The New Millennium Hollywood Rom Com*, the co-editor of *The 21st Century Superhero: Essays on Gender, Genre and Globalization in Film* (McFarland) and author of two Greek books on film adaptation and the Hollywood romantic comedy.

Caryn **Murphy** is an associate professor of communication at the University of Wisconsin Oshkosh. She has published on gender, youth and television in the *Historical Journal of Film, Radio and Television*, *MP*, *Networking Knowledge*, and several edited volumes.

Alison N. **Novak** is a Ph.D. candidate at Drexel University in the Department of Culture and Communication. Her research explores the millennial generation's political engagement and relationship with political news sources. She also writes on the millennial generation for the *Huffington Post*.

Sotiris **Petridis** is a Ph.D. candidate in film studies at Aristotle University of Thessaloniki, Greece, researching the impact of societal sociopolitical circumstances on the slasher film subgenre. He teaches film theory and history at the Institutes of Vocational Training in Thessaloniki.

Karen J. **Renner** is a lecturer at Northern Arizona University, where she teaches classes in American literature and popular culture. She is editor of *The "Evil Child" in Literature, Film, and Popular Culture*.

Sean **Robinson** is an associate professor of higher education at Morgan State University in Baltimore. His research centers on the identity formation of underserved and underrepresented individuals within both K-12 and higher education settings.

Janice **Shaw** is a lecturer of critical and creative writing, film and media studies and children's literature at the University of New England, Australia. Her publications include articles on the Australian writers Frank Moorhouse and Beverley Farmer in the journals *Antipodes, Clues* and *Body, Space, Technology.*

Janani **Subramanian** is an assistant professor of film studies at Indiana University–Purdue University Indianapolis. Her research includes race and representation in science fiction and horror and representations of identity across popular culture. She is working on a book manuscript about race, fantasy and representation in speculative media.

Margaret **Tally** is chair of the Policy Studies Programs and professor of social policy in the School for Graduate Studies at the State University of New York, Empire State College. She is author of *Television Culture and Women's Lives* and has written on the marketing of teens in Hollywood and on changing gender roles as portrayed in television series from the 1960s to the 1990s.

Index

ABC 5, 44, 62, 66, 72, 77
ABC Family 1, 8, 9, 15, 16, 17, 18, 19, 20, 21, 22, 23, 24, 25, 26, 28, 29, 30, 32, 37, 38
Ablow, Keith 103
Accola, Candice 95
activism 16, 26
Adler, Max 35
adulthood 5, 9, 10, 25, 51, 78, 79, 80, 81, 82, 83, 86, 91, 92, 104, 123, 129, 143
adultification 93
Advertising Age 22, 23, 144
Age of Conan 87
Agne, Karl 77
Akande, Zainab 122
Alexander, Bryan 123
Alloy Entertainment 21
Alsop, Ron 115
Alston, Joshua 9, 124
Altman, David G. 171
Altman, Rick 159
Ambudkar, Utkarsh 76
The Amityville Horror 123
Anderson, Wes 146
Andreeva, Nellie 51
Annie Hall 157
Ansari, Aziz 141
apathy 9, 47, 48, 49, 50, 52, 53, 55, 56, 57, 58, 59, 60, 61
Apollo 18, 124
April Fool's Day 123
Arnett, Jeffrey 5
Arquette, David 129
Arrested Development 68
Auerbach, Nina 94, 96
Avengers 117
The Awful Truth 167

baby boom 128
baby boomers 3, 33, 130, 143, 144

Baby Mama 162
The Bachelor 19
Bachelorette 166
Bad Teacher 168
Baker, Katie J.M. 157
Bakhtine, Mikhail 167, 176
Banjo, Omotayo 67
Baranski, Christine 81
Barnes, Brooks 19, 20
Barthes, Roland 156
Bauerlein, Mark 111
Becher, Becher 96
Beck, Urlich 173
Behrs, Beth 50, 70
Bell, Emma 170, 177, 182, 184
Bell, Kristen 133, 139
Bellamy, Ralph 167
Bellisario, Troian 38
Ben and Kate 5
Bennett, William J. 95, 160
Benshoff, Harry M. 181, 182
Benson, Ashley 38
Beverly Hills 90210 34, 165
The Big Bang Theory 10, 62, 66, 67, 78, 79, 80, 81, 82, 83, 84, 85, 86, 87, 89, 90, 91
Bissett, Josie 37
Black Christmas 123, 138
The Blair Witch Project 116
Blatterer, Harry 79, 80, 81, 92
Blunt, Emily 176
Blyth, Mark 4
Bogle, Kathleen A. 157, 158
Bordwell, David 123
Borsellino, Mary 106
Borstelmann, Thomas 158
Bowie, John Ross 85
Boyd, Danah 98
Braxton, Greg 18
The Break-Up 155
Brennan, Sarah Rees 100, 105

Bridesmaids 12, 149, 150, 151, 152, 153, 156
Bridget Jones's Diary 74
Bringing Down the House 73
Brooks, David 19, 103, 104
Buffy the Vampire Slayer 44, 100, 108
Bullock, Sandra 72
Bund, Kerstin 171, 172
Bunheads 21, 26
Burns and Allen 67
business 17, 53, 54, 55, 56, 57, 58, 59, 60, 106, 115, 142, 169, 171, 174, 176
Butler, Judith 39

The Cabin in the Woods 11, 12, 112, 116, 117, 122, 125
Campbell, Keith W. 112, 130
Campbell, Neve 128
Canning, Sara 100
capital 90, 115, 130, 173
capitalism 3, 13, 65, 67, 77, 127, 182, 183
Capsuto, Steven 39
career 4, 46, 47, 49, 54, 63, 76, 79, 83, 87, 144, 170, 172, 173, 175, 177, 180, 181
Carey, Kate B. 157
Carey, Michael P. 157
Carrell, Steve 69, 145
Carrie 90, 124
Carter, Bill 142
CBN 18
CBS 1, 5, 9, 16, 17, 20, 44, 47, 50, 62, 66, 67, 68, 70, 78, 140, 170
Chando, Alexandra 27
Charmed 78, 83
Chau, Joanna 143
chick flick 150, 169
Children of the Corn 123
Chronicle 124
citizenship 64, 65, 66
Clarke, John 47
Clooney, George 160
Clover, Carol 125, 127, 128, 134, 138
Cloverfield 124
CNN 160
Colbert, Stephen 141
The Colbert Report 141
Colfer, Chris 35
Collins, Jim 7
Comaroff, Jean 3, 4
Comaroff, John L. 3, 4
Come Out and Play 123
comedy 9, 12, 13, 23, 27, 35, 63, 67, 68, 69, 70, 71, 73, 77, 79, 91, 92, 141, 142, 143, 145, 146, 147, 148, 149, 150, 153, 165, 167
Comedy Central 12, 141, 142, 153
community 24, 27, 32, 33, 41, 42, 44, 45, 84, 95, 99, 101, 102, 103, 108, 130, 136, 137, 139
Confessions of a Shopaholic 6
Connolly, Kristen 119
consumerism 25, 78, 79, 82, 90
Cook, Chanon 141, 142, 143
Coolidge, Jennifer 51
The Cosby Show 68
Costea, Bogdan 84, 86
Coupland, Douglas 128
Couples Retreat 162
Cox, Courteney 129
Craig, Pamela 124
Craig, Stephen 48
Craven, Wes 130, 131, 132, 133
Crawford, Kate 82, 83
Crazy, Stupid, Love 168
The Crossover Novel 92
Crump, Norman 84
Culkin, Rory 130
cultural studies 7, 31, 183
Cummings, Whitney 50, 70, 71, 140
Cuoco, Kaley 79
Curtin, Jane 1
Curtis, Jamie Lee 136
The CW 16, 20, 21, 28, 32, 34, 44, 94, 95

D'Addario, Daniel 147
The Daily Show with Jon Stewart 141
Dancing Fools 30
Dark Water 123
Date Night 162
Davé, Shilpa 64, 74, 75
Davis, Blair 115
Davis, Geena 166
Davis, Matthew 99, 124
Dawn of the Dead 123
Dawson's Creek 44, 94
Dempsey, John 19, 21
Dennings, Kat 50, 70, 71
Deresiewicz, William 115
Deschanel, Zooey 70, 71, 140, 149
The Devil Inside 124
The Devil Wears Prada 6, 13, 169, 170, 171, 174, 176, 177, 179, 180, 181, 182, 183
The Devil's Rejects 124
Dewey, Tommy 75
dialogism 167

Diamond, Lisa 42
diaspora 77
Dika, Vera 126
disengagement 9, 49, 50, 52, 53, 55, 56, 58, 59, 60, 61
The Disney Channel 18
Dobrev, Nina 95
documentary 68, 145
Donnelly, Ashley M. 124
Donovan, Trevor 34, 95
Don't Trust the B——in Apt. 23 5
Doty, Alexander 32
dramedy 72, 165
Dunham, Lena 70, 71, 140, 145
Dunlap, Rudy 31
Dunleavy, Trisha 68
Durand, Chris 136
Dyer, Richard 34

Ebert, Roger 111
Edelstein, David 115, 124
Efron, Zac 166
8 Simple Rules for Dating My Teenage Daughter 19
Ellen 44, 92
employment 78, 79, 80, 83, 86, 87, 88, 89, 91, 166, 171, 173
engagement 9, 22, 23, 24, 27, 46, 47, 48, 49, 50, 52, 53, 54, 55, 56, 57, 58, 59, 60, 61, 64, 115, 130
entitlement 112, 115, 135
Entry Level 183
environmentalism 16
Ephron, Nora 164
Epstein, Molly 172, 179
Espinoza, Chip 171, 172
Evil Dead 124, 125
Ewell, Kayla 105

Facebook 8, 85, 100, 116, 132, 133, 135, 154
Failure to Launch 159
Fairbanks, Amanda M. 77
Falconer, Rachel 86, 92
The Family Channel 18
Family Guy 148
femininity 25, 26, 73, 175, 176
feminism 16, 22, 29, 63, 139, 141
Ferrara, America 72
Ferri-Reed, Jan 171, 172
Fey, Tina 77, 141
Field, Sally 15

Fielder, Robyn L. 157
Final Destination 124
Final Girl 121, 125, 128, 132, 134, 136, 137, 138
Fisher-Baum, Reuben 151
(500) Days of Summer 167
The Five-Year Engagement 168
Flint, Joe 18
Flores, Michelle 77
Foehr, Ulla 31
The Fog 123
Fogel, Matthew 63
Fontanille, Jean 164
Fool's Gold 162
Forgetting Sarah Marshall 156
found footage 113, 114, 116, 123, 124
Fox 5, 17, 18, 29, 32, 34, 35, 44, 62, 66, 68, 140, 148, 165, 170
Fradley, Martin 124
Franklin, Daniel P. 167
Frasier 45
free market 181
Freeman, Elise C. 130
Frewer, Lynn J. 50
Friday the 13th 109, 123, 132, 138
Friends 78, 85
Friends with Benefits 6, 12, 156, 158, 159, 161, 162, 163, 164, 165, 166, 167, 168
Funny Games 111, 124
FX 22, 147

Gabler, Neal 111, 115
Galecki, Johnny 79
The Gay & Lesbian Alliance Against Defamation 43, 44
Gee, James Paul 52
Gelder, Ken 94, 108
Generation Me 7, 10, 11, 126, 129, 130, 134, 135, 136, 143
Generation We 7, 10, 112, 129, 134, 143
Generation Xers, Gen Xers 1, 2, 7, 11, 13, 32, 33, 90, 110, 113, 127, 128, 129, 130, 131, 132, 136, 137, 138, 139, 143
Generation Y 62, 63, 64, 66, 70, 78, 79, 80, 81, 85, 87, 89, 90, 94, 95, 126, 129
Genette, Gérard 101
Gere, Richard 73
German, Myna 114
Gibson, Mel 124
Gibson, Rhonda 41
Gidget 15, 16, 29

Giffords, Gabrielle 48
Gilbert, Matthew 39
Giles, Tanya 142
Gilmore Girls 19, 21, 29
Girl Power 25
Girls 5, 12, 13, 70, 73, 140, 170
Gitlin, Marty 13
Gitlin, Todd 4, 145
GLAAD *see* The Gay & Lesbian Alliance Against Defamation
Glee 29, 32, 35, 37, 42, 165
Going the Distance 159
The Goldbergs 67
Goldstein, Richard 40
Gonzalez, Sandra 21
The Good Wife 66
The Goodbye Girl 157
Gossip Girl 21, 95
Grabianowski, Ed 129, 135
The Graduate 157
Graham, Kat 95
Grammer, Kelsey 45
Grant, Cary 167
Grant, Elizabeth Charlotte 146
Grave Encounters 124
Gray, Herman 25, 41, 68
Great Depression 6
Greek 23
Greenberg, Eric 112, 171
Greene, Doyle 183
Grenier, Adrian 178
Grewal, Inderpal 65, 66
Grey's Anatomy 62, 63
Griffin, Sean 181, 182
Gross, Larry 43
Grossman, Lev 81, 92
The Grudge 123

Hais, Michael D. 65, 112
Hale, Lucy 38
Hall, Stanley G. 5
Hall Pass 156
Halloween 109, 123, 126, 132, 138, 139
Halloween H20: 20 Years Later 136
Halloween: Resurrection 136
Halpin, John 77
Hampton, Brenda 20, 27
The Hangover 12, 149, 153
The Hangover Part III 153
Hantke, Steffen 112, 113
Happy Endings 5
Harelik, Mark 88

Hart, Daniel 50
Hartley, John 80
Hatch, Jessica 107
Hathaway, Anne 166, 169
Haverty, Mike 149, 150
Hayward, Keith 82, 93
HBO 5, 22, 50, 70, 78, 95, 139, 140, 170
Heat 166
Heffner, Alexander 141
Heigl, Katherine 156, 160, 164, 167
Helberg, Simon 79
Hellraiser 125
Hemsworth, Chris 117, 120
Herbenic, Debby 157
Heuser, Uwe Jean 171, 172
Hill, Jonah 141
Hills, Rachel 34, 80
The Hills Have Eyes 124
His Girl Friday 167
Hitch 155, 159
The Hitcher 123
Hoffman, Adam 160
Hollywood 17, 65, 73, 113, 114, 132, 133, 138, 139, 141, 147, 148, 149, 153, 154, 155, 160, 163, 164, 165, 166, 167, 169, 170, 174, 181, 184
Holm, Anders 75
Holt, Claire 106
Holtzman, Linda 39
homosexuality 41, 42, 43
The Honeymooners 67
hookup 157, 158, 160, 161, 162, 163, 164, 165
Horrible Bosses 183
horror 11, 12, 95, 110, 111, 112, 113, 114, 115, 116, 117, 118, 119, 120, 121, 122, 123, 124, 125, 127, 131, 132, 133, 138, 139, 167
Hostel 113, 115, 124
How Do You Know 168
How I Met Your Mother 5
How to Lose a Guy in 10 Days 159
Howe, Neil 29, 45, 96, 112, 114
Hudson, Kate 167
Huge 21, 26
humor 8, 12, 51, 67, 69, 71, 75, 76, 84, 91, 140, 141, 142, 144, 145, 146, 147, 148, 149, 150, 152, 153, 154
Humphries, Reynold 115
The Hunger Games 82
Huntley, Rebecca 81, 124
Hutchison, Anna 120
Hyde-Pierce, David 45

I Don't Know How She Does It 168
I Know What You Did Last Summer 109, 114
I Love Lucy 67
I Spit on Your Grave 124
identity 5, 9, 10, 13, 17, 18, 19, 22, 25, 26, 27, 28, 29, 31, 32, 33, 34, 35, 36, 37, 38, 39, 40, 41, 42, 52, 59, 62, 63, 64, 66, 68, 69, 70, 75, 76, 77, 81, 84, 87, 89, 91, 97, 103, 128, 177
Identity Thief 166
Independent Film Channel 145
Indiana Jones 90
infantilization 93
Inside Amy Schumer 153
intertextuality 156, 165, 167
intimacy 6, 31, 33, 37, 160, 161
It's Always Sunny in Philadelphia 147
It's Complicated 156
Ivory, James 41

Jaffe, Marielle 134
Jameson, Fredric 132
Jane by Design 26
Janollari, David 108
Jeffers-MacDonald, Tamar 156
Jefferson, Tony 47
Jenkins, Richard 118
Jones, Rashida 74, 126, 165
Joost, Henry 123
Juergens, Kate 21
Just Go with It 168
Just Like Heaven 6

Kacho, Samantha 105
Kaling, Mindy 10, 62, 63, 64, 65, 66, 68, 69, 70, 71, 72, 76, 77, 140, 149, 151
Kaslow, Sally 47
Kate & Allie 1, 13
Kaufman, Amy 149
Kaur, Valarie 104
Keeter, Scott 171
Kelly, Chistopher 115
Kendall, Lori 84, 87, 92
Kennedy, Jamie 128
Kerner, Ian 161
Ketter, Scott 32
kidult 82, 91, 92
Kinney, Taylor 105
Kirby, David 40, 45, 132
Kite, Jonathan 51
Klaffke, Martin 171, 172

Kleemann, Frank 174
Klein, Christina 114
Knight and Day 155
Knocked Up 6, 152, 156, 167
Knudsen, Eric 131
Kozloff, Sarah 176
Kranz, Fran 121
Krattenmaker, Tom 104
Kristeva, Julia 167
Kunis, Mila 159, 166
Kunze, Anne 171, 172
Kutcher, Ashton 159
Kyle XY 23

LaBeouf, Shia 166
labor 169, 170, 171, 172, 173, 174, 175, 176, 177, 179, 181, 183
Lane, Carson 97, 103, 104
Lanter, Matt 35
Larry Crowne 168
The Last Exorcism 124
The Last House on the Left 124
Lawson, Bianca 38
Leap Year 159
Leclerc, Katie 24
Lee, Christina 13
Lepore, Meredith 151
Let Me In 123
Levine, Elana 26
Levinson, Julie 170, 171, 175, 181, 182, 183
LGBTQ 9, 31, 32, 33, 34, 39, 40, 41, 42, 43, 44, 45
Life with Luigi 67
Life with Luigi and Mama 67
Lincoln Heights 23
Lionsgate 117
Lipsitz, George 67
Loacker, Bernadette 173
Lord of the Rings 69
Lost 62
love 12, 16, 24, 31, 36, 37, 41, 46, 50, 62, 71, 72, 73, 75, 76, 82, 93, 95, 97, 101, 102, 107, 111, 150, 151, 152, 155, 159, 160, 161, 162, 163, 164, 165, 167
Love and Other Drugs 156
Lucas, Jennifer L. 33
Lueken, Verena 179
The Lying Game 21, 24, 26, 27

MacFarlane, Seth 148
Madman 146
Make It or Break It 26

Malcolm in the Middle 68
Mallinson, Brenda J. 129
Malone, Noreen 46, 61
Mangels, Andy 39
Marano, Hara Estroff 111
Marano, Vanessa 24
Marchie, Melanie 25
Martin, Denise 28
Marwick, Alice 98
masculinity 84, 176
Matchar, Emily 124
Maxwell, Brandon 77
McCarthy, Melissa 150
McDonnell, Mary 130
McNamara, Mary 51
McQueen, Steve R. 95
McRobbie, Angela 74
Meister, Jeanne C. 96
Melamed, Jodi 67
Mellencamp, Patricia 67
Meriweather, Liz 70
Meron, Neil 148
Messina, Chris 73
Metcalf, Laurie 81
Meyer, Stephenie 100
Meyers, Josh 73
MGM 117
Midnight in Paris 168
Mikl-Horke, Gertraude 173
Mills, Brett 68
The Mindy Project 5, 12, 62, 63, 70, 140, 153
Minssen, Heiner 173, 174, 177
Mission: Impossible—Ghost Protocol 167
Mitchell, Shay 24, 38
Mittell, Jason 32
Mizejewski, Linda 73
Monteith, Cory 36
Moore, Tracy 151
morality 95, 103, 104, 105, 106, 107, 108, 124
Morris, Heather 36
Motion Picture Association of America 167
Moy, Matthew 51
MPAA *see* Motion Picture Association of America
MTV 5, 108, 141, 142, 153
multiculturalism 29, 63, 65, 67, 68, 71, 77
Munoz, Lorenza 124
Murdoch, Rupert 18
My Big Fat Greek Wedding 155
My Bloody Valentine 123

Nadler, Reena 96
Nagoski, Emily 161
narcissism 112, 130
NASA 79
Natale, Kial 115, 124
National Network for Arab American Communities 76
Nayyar, Kunal 66, 79
Nazarian, Vera 104
NBC 16, 17, 44, 45, 50, 62, 65, 66, 67, 70, 78, 140, 145, 149, 164
neoliberalism 169
Net Generation 4, 129
Netzley, Sara B. 42, 43
New Girl 5, 51, 62, 70, 73, 140, 170
New in Town 159
New Nightmare 127
New Year's Eve 168
Newman, Michael Z. 26
News Corp 18
N'Gom, Abdoulaye 74
Nickelodeon 18
Nicodemus, Katja 179
Nies, Norman H. 48
A Nightmare on Elm Street 109, 124, 132, 138
9/11 10, 63, 64, 65, 66, 76, 77, 124, 129, 146
The Nine Lives of Chloe King 21, 26
90210 32, 34, 40, 41
NNAAC *see* National Network for Arab American Communities
No Strings Attached 6, 12, 156, 157, 158, 159, 160, 161, 162, 163, 165, 166, 167, 168
Nochimson, Martha P. 169
Norma Rae 183
Notting Hill 71
Novak, B.J. 9, 69

Obama, Barack 4, 65, 141
The Office 62, 63, 64, 66, 68, 69, 70, 76, 145, 146
Oh, David 62, 67, 147
O'Hehir, Andrew 148
O'Malley, Mike 36
The Omen 123
One Tree Hill 95
The Onion 146, 147
The Orphanage 123
O'Shaughnessy, Martin 170
Outside Sales 183

Outsourced 67
Owram, Doug 13

Padva, Gilad 31, 33
Palladino, Sherman 21
Panettiere, Hayden 132
Pappademas, Alex 125
Paquin, Anna 133, 139
Paranormal Activity 116, 117, 123
paratext 101, 102
Pardee, Thomas 143, 144
Parker, Sarah Jessica 90
Parks and Recreation 62, 66, 145
Parment, Andreas 172
parody 132
Parsons, Jim 79
Partners 5
Paskin, Willa 153
The Passion of the Christ 124
pastiche 132
Peeples, Nia 38
Peter Pan syndrome 83
Petersen, Anne Helen 77
Phillips, Kendall R. 128
Pieterse, Sasha 38
Pinedo, Isabel 127
Pinkleton, Bruce E. 47, 48, 49, 52, 59, 60, 61
Pitch Perfect 153
Poehler, Amy 141
Pongratz, Hans J. 173
Portlandia 145
Portman, Natalie 131, 159
postfeminism 63, 77
Powell, Colin 65
Prashad, Vijay 64, 75
Precious 74, 75
Pretty Little Liars 21, 23, 26, 27, 32, 38, 41
Prom Night 123
The Proposal 155, 162
Pulse 123
Purdy, Jolene 16
The Pursuit of Happiness 183

Quarantine 123, 124
Queen Latifah 73
queer 31
racism 25, 114
Radish, Christina 21
Radner, Hilary 169
Raiders of the Lost Ark 90
Rainer, Thom S. 124, 143

Rainey, James 46
Raisa, Francia 37
Raising Hope 5
Raley, Amber B. 33
Ravenswood 21
redemption 106
Redford, Blair 24
Reeve, Elspeth 113
Reinecke, Christiane 173
Relativity Media 149
Resnick, Evan 47, 48, 49, 52, 53, 54, 59, 61
Revenge 66, 77
Rhimes, Shonda 63
Riabko, Kyle 34
Rice, Condoleeza 65
Rideout, Victoria 31
The Ring 114, 118
Ringu 114, 118
Rivera, Naya 35
Roberts, Donald 31
Roberts, Emma 130
Roberts, Julia 71, 73
Rockoff, Adam 127
Rocky 88
Roerig, Zach 95
Rogelberg, Steven G., 171
Rogen, Seth 156, 167
romantic comedy 13, 65, 66, 70, 71, 72, 73, 75, 151, 152, 155, 156, 158, 160, 161, 163, 164, 165, 166, 167, 168
Rosen, Christine 124
Rosenberg, Alyssa 51, 151
Rosin, Hanna 157, 160, 162, 163
Roth, Eric 113
Rowe, Kathleen 50, 73
Rue, Sara 88
Rules of Engagement 5
Russell, Rosalind 167
Ryan, Maureen 163

SAALT *see* South Asian Americans Leading Together
Saban Entertainment 18
Sabrina, the Teenage Witch 19
Saint James, Susan 1
Sandberg, Bryn Elise 148
Sandin, Will 126
Sarr, Ramou 77
satire 141, 169
Saturday Night Live 149
Sauer, Dieter 173
Savin-Williams, Ritch 42

Saw 124, 147
Scandal 62, 63
Schulman, Ariel 123
Schumer, Amy 153
Scream 11, 12, 112, 114, 118, 126, 127, 128, 129, 130, 131, 132, 133, 136, 137, 138, 139
Scream 2 128, 129, 139
Scream 3 128, 129, 139
Scream 4 11, 12, 126, 128, 129, 130, 131, 132, 133, 134, 135, 136, 137, 138, 139
The Secret Life of the American Teenager 20, 26, 32, 37
Sederer, Lloyd L. 47, 48, 49, 52, 57, 59, 60, 61
Segel, Jason 165
Seidman, Robert 51
Seinfeld 66, 164
Semigran, Aly 51
Senghaas-Knobloch, Eva 173
Serendipity 162
The 700 Club 18
7th Heaven 19, 20, 27, 29
sex 13, 24, 31, 33, 37, 41, 73, 119, 127, 141, 150, 151, 152, 155, 156, 157, 158, 159, 160, 161, 162, 163, 164, 166
Sex and the City 50, 78, 85, 90
sexuality 9, 31, 33, 34, 35, 36, 37, 38, 39, 40, 41, 42, 43, 45, 73, 150, 156, 167, 175
Shary, Timothy 5
Shaw, Lindsey 10, 15
Shugart, Helene A. 40
Shutter 123
Silent generation 32
Silent House 123
Silverstein, Melissa 153
Sister, Sister 19
Skype 85
slasher 11, 108, 114, 118, 126, 127, 128, 129, 132, 133, 136, 137, 138, 139
Sleepless in Seattle 156
Smallville 19, 21, 29
Smash 66
Smith, L.J. 94
Smith, Stacy L. 166
Somerhalder, Ian 95
Something Borrowed 168
South Asian Americans Leading Together (SAALT) 76
Spangler, Lynn C. 13
Spencer, Liese 169
Spigel, Lynn 65, 70
Stam, Robert 167

Stanley, Alessandra 5, 27, 51
Star Trek 89, 91
Stead, Peter 170
Steger, Michael 35
Stein, Joel 113, 122, 124
Steinberg, Eric 38
stereotype 9, 10, 11, 40, 81, 87, 92, 128, 129, 142, 152, 171
Sterneborg, Anke 169
Stevens, Dana 150
The Strangers 124, 125
Stransky, Tanner 23
Strauss, William 29, 45, 112, 114
Streep, Meryl 169, 176
Stroup, Jessica 35
subculture 79, 82, 84, 91, 93
subgenre 124, 126, 127, 128, 132, 134, 137, 138, 151
subjectivity 70, 71, 74, 173
Sujansky, Joanne G. 171, 172
Sweeney, Anne 20, 28
Sweeney, Richard 96
Switched at Birth 24, 26, 27, 28
Syder, Andrew 127

Taft, Jessica K. 25
A Tale of Two Sisters 123
Tasker, Yvonne 170, 175, 183, 184
Taylor, Paul 171
Teen Wolf 108
Telfer, Paul 107
10 Things I Hate About You 15, 16, 17, 22, 26
Terkel, Amanda 77
The Texas Chainsaw Massacre 111, 114, 138
textual analysis 31, 34
30 Rock 145
This Means War 168
Thistle, Susan 158
Thompson, Ethan 68, 69
Thompson, Kristin 123
Timberlake, Justin 159
Time Warner 18
Tortorella, Nico 131
torture porn 113, 114, 115, 116, 117, 124
Tosh-O 142
Traister, Rebecca 149
Transformers: Dark of the Moon 167
Traube, Elizabeth 177, 181
Trevino, Michael 95
The Trevor Project 45
Troll Hunter 123

Index

Tropiano, Stephen 39
True Blood 95, 139
Tucci, Stanley 175
Tuchman, Gaye 145
Tumblr 122
Twenge, Jean 45, 112, 124, 129, 130
24 66
Twilight 82, 94, 100, 107
Twitter 23, 24, 64, 76, 85, 132, 135
2 Broke Girls 5, 9, 12, 13, 47, 49, 50, 51, 52, 58, 59, 60, 61, 70, 140, 170

Ugly Betty 72
The Ugly Truth 155, 160, 164
Ulrich, Skeet 131
Underemployed 5
underemployment 144
unemployment 144, 181, 183
The Uninvited 123
Universal Pictures 149
UPN 139
Urban Legend 114

Vacancy 124
Vaccaro, Annemarie 33, 34
The Vampire Diaries 10, 11, 21, 94, 95, 96, 100, 101, 104, 106, 107, 108
Van Dyk, Deirdre 81, 92
Variety 19, 21
Verba, Sidney 48
Veronica Mars 139
Viacom 141
Vidali, Debra S. 47, 49, 52, 56, 59, 60, 61
The Vineyard 30
violence 41, 108, 115, 116, 124, 148, 167
Visweswaran, Kamala 76

Walkerdine, Valerie 83
Wall Street 169
Walsh, Maiara 105
Walt Disney Company 19
Walters, Suzanna D. 39, 41, 42, 43
Wampole, Christy 72
Wanderlust 168
Warner Bros. 20, 29
Washington, Kerry 63
the WB 16, 17, 18, 19, 20, 21, 23, 27, 28, 29, 44, 78, 94, 100
Weber, Karl 171
Wee, Valerie 71

Weiner, Andrew 124
Weintraub Austin, Erica 47
Wesley, Paul 95
The West Wing 65
What to Expect When You're Expecting 168
What Women Want 155
What's Up Doc? 156
What's Your Number? 156, 168
Whedon, Joss 117, 118, 121, 125
When a Stranger Calls 123
When Harry Met Sally{ellip} 71, 160, 165
White, Brian 121
Whitford, Bradley 118
Whitney 50, 51, 140
Whose Line Is It Anyway? 19
Wiig, Kristen 141, 149
Wildfire 23, 26
Wilds, Tristan 35
Will and Grace 44, 164
Williams, Jesse 120
Williams, Todd 105
Williamson, Kevin 94, 127, 139
Willyerd, Karie 96
Wilson, Rainn 69
Wilson, Rebel 153
Winograd, Morley 65, 112
Wolf Creek 124
Wong, Curtis 42
Woodley, Shailene 27
Woodruffe, Charles 129
work 2, 5, 6, 7, 8, 10, 13, 33, 37, 47, 49, 50, 53, 54, 55, 59, 63, 70, 74, 76, 79, 80, 84, 86, 88, 91, 95, 116, 118, 121, 131, 135, 145, 147, 152, 156, 160, 162, 169, 170, 171, 172, 174, 175, 176, 177, 178, 179, 180, 181, 182, 183, 184
Workaholics 142, 147
Working Girl 175, 183
World of Warcraft 87
Wray-Lake, Laura 50
Wrong Turn 124
Wuthering Heights 96
Wyatt, Edward 92

York, Ashley Elaine 169
You've Got Mail 71
Zack and Miri Make a Porno 156

Zadan, Craig 148
Zapatka, Jennifer 45

www.ingramcontent.com/pod-product-compliance
Ingram Content Group UK Ltd.
Pitfield, Milton Keynes, MK11 3LW, UK
UKHW042003140426
5217IPUK00015B/951